Making the GRADE

Everything Your Kindergartner Needs to Know

by
Daniel A. Van Beek

BARRON'S

About the Author

Daniel A. Van Beek has educated children of all ages in many different environments for several years. Involved in the educational publishing industry for more than five years, he has developed literacy and mathematics textbooks for several grades, from kindergarten through middle school. Daniel holds a B.A. in communication studies and a B.A. in history from the University of Michigan.

All inquiries should be addressed to:
Barron's Educational Series, Inc.
250 Wireless Boulevard
Hauppauge, New York 11788
http://www.barronseduc.com

Library of Congress Catalog Card No. 2003052483

International Standard Book No. 0-7641-2475-7

Library of Congress Cataloging-in-Publication Data
Van Beek, Daniel A.
    Making the grade : everything your kindergartner needs to know / Daniel A. Van Beek.
        p. cm
    Includes bibliographical references and index.
    ISBN 0-7641-2475-7 (alk. paper)
    1. Kindergarten—Curricula—United States. 2. Home and school—United States. I. Title.

  LB1180.V36 2004
  372.21'8—dc21   2003052483

Printed in China
9 8 7 6 5 4 3 2 1

Table of Contents

PROMOTING LITERACY

MATH

How to Use This Book

Welcome to the *Making the Grade* series! These seven books offer tools and strategies for hands-on, active learning at the kindergarten through sixth-grade levels. Each book presents real-world, engaging learning experiences in the core areas of language arts, math, science, and social studies at age-appropriate levels.

Who should use this book?

Whether you're a stay-at-home or working parent with children in school, a homeschooler who's guiding your children's education, or a teacher who's looking for additional ideas to supplement classroom learning experiences, this book is for you.

- If you have children in school, *Making the Grade* can be used in conjunction with your child's curriculum because it offers real-world, hands-on activities that exercise the concepts and topics he or she is being taught in school.

- If you're a homeschooler who's guiding your children's education, this series presents you with easy-to-access, engaging ways to interact with your child.

- If you're a teacher, this book also can be a source for additional activities.

This book is your passport to a whole new world, one that gives you enough support to be a successful educator while encouraging independent learning with one child or shared learning among your children.

What is *Making the Grade*?

We're glad you asked! First, we'd like to tell you what it's not. It's not a textbook series. Rather, each book in the series delivers age-appropriate content in language arts, math, science, and social studies in an open-ended, flexible manner that incorporates the "real" world. You can use this book as a supplement to your core learning instruction or use it to get a jump start on the fundamentals.

Each subject section presents lessons comprised of both "teaching" pages and "student" pages. And each book in the *Making the Grade* series is perforated for flexible learning so that both you and your child can tear out the pages that you're working on and use one book together.

How do the lessons work?

The teaching and student pages work together. The lesson instruction and teaching ideas for each specific lesson appear first. Activities that offer opportunities for your child to practice the specific skills and review the concepts being taught follow. Creativity and imagination abound! Throughout each lesson, hands-on activities are incorporated using concepts that are meaningful and relevant to kids' daily lives. The activities account for all kinds of learners—that is, visual, auditory, or kinesthetic learning. For more information on learning styles, see the Glossary on page 353.

Objective and Background

Each lesson opens with an objective that tells you exactly what the lesson is about. The background of the lesson follows, giving you the rationale behind the importance of the material being addressed. Each lesson is broken down for you so that you and your student can see how the skills and concepts taught are useful in everyday situations.

Materials and Vocabulary

Have you ever done a project and found out you're missing something when you got to the end? A list of materials is given up front so you'll know what you need before you begin. The lessons take into account that you have access to your local library, a computer and the Internet, writing instruments, a calculator, and a notebook and loose paper, so you won't find these listed. The materials are household items when possible so that even the most technical of science experiments can be done easily. The *Making the Grade* series paves the way for your learning experience whether you and your student are sitting side by side on the couch or in a classroom, at the library, or even on vacation!

Following the materials list, vocabulary words may be given offering clear, easy-to-understand definitions.

Let's Begin

Let's Begin is just that, "Let's Begin!" The instructional portion of the lesson opens with easy, user-friendly, numbered steps that guide you through the teaching of a particular lesson. Here you'll find opportunities to interact with your student and engage in discussions about what he or she is learning. There also are opportunities for your student to practice his or her critical-thinking skills to make the learning experience richer.

In the margins are interesting facts about what you're studying, time-savers, or helpful ideas.

Ways to Extend the Lesson

Every lesson concludes with ways to extend the lesson—teaching tips, such as hints, suggestions, or ideas, for you to use in teaching the lesson or a section of the lesson. Each lesson also ends with an opportunity for you to "check in" and assess how well your student has mastered the skill or grasped the concepts being taught in the lesson. The For Further Reading section lists books that you can use as additional references and support in teaching the lesson. It also offers your student more opportunities to practice a skill or a chance to look deeper into the content.

Student Learning Pages

Student Learning Pages immediately follow the teaching pages in each lesson. These pages offer fun opportunities to practice the skills and concepts being taught. And there are places where your student gets to choose what to do next and take ownership of his or her learning. Since reading may be a new skill for your student, be patient as he or she reads the directions and activities on these pages. Be prepared to read them aloud as your student follows along.

Visual Aids

Throughout the book you'll see references to the Venn Diagram, T Chart, Web, Sequence Chain, and Writing Lines found in the back of the book. Many lessons incorporate these graphic organizers, or visual methods of organizing information, into the learning. If one is used in a lesson, it will be listed in the materials so that prior to the lesson you or your student can make a photocopy of it from the back of the book or you can have your student copy it into his or her notebook. See the Glossary for more information on graphic organizers.

What if my student is just learning how to read?

Many children begin reading at this age, so be sure to guide your student in a noncritical and nonjudgmental manner as he or she navigates through unfamiliar territory. Let your student guide you as to his or her pace and comfort level for learning how to read.

What about field trips or learning outside the classroom?

One very unique feature of the *Making the Grade* series is the In Your Community activities at the end of each subject section. These activities describe ways to explore your community, taking advantage of your local or regional culture, industry, and environment while incorporating the skills learned in the lessons. For example, you can have your student help out at a farmer's market or with a local environmental group. These unique activities can supplement your ability to provide support for subjects. The activities give your student life experiences upon which he or she can build and expand the canvas upon which he or she learns.

These pages are identified in the Table of Contents so that you can read them first as a way to frame your student's learning.

How do I know if my student is learning the necessary skills?

Although each lesson offers an opportunity for on-the-spot assessment, a formalized assessment section is located in the back of this book. You'll find a combination of multiple-choice and open-ended questions testing your student on the skills, concepts, and topics covered.

Also, at the end of every subject section is a We Have Learned checklist. This checklist provides a way for you and your student to summarize what you've accomplished. It lists specific concepts, and there is additional space for you and your student to write in other topics you've covered.

Does this book come with answers?

Yes. Answers are provided in the back of the book for both the lessons and assessment.

What if this book uses a homeschooling or educational term I'm not familiar with?

In addition to the vocabulary words listed in the lessons, a two-page Glossary is provided in the back of the book. Occasionally terms will surface that may need further explanation in order for the learning experience to flourish. In the Glossary, you'll find terms explained simply to help you give your student a rewarding learning experience free from confusion.

Will this book help me find resources within the schools for homeschoolers?

In Communicating Between Home and School, there are suggestions for how to take advantage of the opportunities and resources offered by your local schools and how these benefits can enhance your homeschooling learning experiences.

I'm new to homeschooling. How can I find out about state regulations, curriculum, and other resources?

In For Homeschoolers at the beginning of the book, you'll find information about national and state legislation, resources for curriculum and materials, and other references. Also included is a comprehensive list of online resources for everything from homeschooling organizations to military homeschooling to homeschooling supplies.

How can I use this book if my student attends a public or private school?

Making the Grade fits into any child's educational experience—whether he or she is being taught at home or in a traditional school setting. Some kindergartners may be adjusting to being in a school setting for the first time, so be encouraged to work together with your student to choose activities—you may wish to only take advantage of certain lessons, exercises, or components. Let your student guide you!

For Homeschoolers

Teaching children at home isn't a new phenomenon. But it's gaining in popularity as caregivers decide to take a more active role in the education of their children. More people are learning what homeschoolers have already known, that children who are homeschooled regularly succeed in college, the workplace, and society.

Whether you're new to homeschooling or have been educating your children at home for quite some time, you may be in need of additional homeschooling resources. This book hopes to minimize your search for resources by offering information on state regulations, homeschooling approaches and curriculum, and other resources to keep you on the path toward a rewarding learning experience.

Regulations

There never has been a federal law prohibiting parents from homeschooling their children. A homeschooler isn't required to have a teaching degree, nor is he or she required to teach children in a specific location. Each state has its own compulsory attendance laws for educational programs as well as its own set of regulations, educational requirements, and guidelines for those who homeschool.

No matter what level of regulation your state has, there are ways to operate your homeschool with success. Here are a few tips as you negotiate the homeschooling waters:

- Be aware of your district's and state's requirements.
- Don't let these laws, rules, and regulations deter you. The National Home Education Network (NHEN) may be able to help. Go to the association's Web site at *http://www.nhen.org*. For even more information on your state's laws and related references, see Homeschooling Online Resources that follow. They can help you find information on your specific state and may be able to direct you to local homeschooling groups.
- Veteran homeschoolers in your area can be a source of practical knowledge about the laws. Consult a variety of homeschoolers for a clear perspective, as each family has an educational philosophy and approach that best suits it.

Homeschooling Military Families

Moving from location to location frequently can be exhausting for families with one or more parent in the military. If you have school-age children, it can be even more complicated. Schools across states and U.S. schools in other countries often don't follow the same curriculum, and states often can have varying curriculum requirements for each grade.

The Department of Defense Dependent Schools (DoDDS) is responsible for the military educational system. There are three options for military families in which they can educate their children:

1. attend school with other military children
2. if in a foreign country, attend the local school in which the native language is spoken, although this option may require approval
3. homeschool

Homeschooling can provide consistency for families that have to relocate often. The move itself, along with the new culture your family will be exposed to, is a learning experience that can be incorporated into the curriculum. Note that military families that homeschool must abide by the laws of the area in which they reside, which may be different from where they claim residency for tax purposes. If your relocation takes your family abroad, one downside is the lack of curriculum resources available on short notice. Nonetheless, military homeschoolers may be able to use resources offered at base schools.

Approaches and Curriculum

If you're reading this book you've probably already heard of many different approaches to and methods of homeschooling, which some homeschoolers sometimes refer to as *unschooling* (see the Glossary for more information). Unschooling is not synonymous with homeschooling; it's a philosophy and style of education followed by some homeschoolers. It's important that you choose one approach or method that works best for you—or a mixture of them to fit the needs of different children. There's no right or wrong way to homeschool!

The curriculum and materials that are used vary from person to person, but there are organizations that offer books, support, and materials to homeschoolers. Many homeschoolers find that a combination of methods works best. That's why *Making the Grade* was created!

Support Groups and Organizations

Homeschooling has become more popular, and the United States boasts a number of nationally recognized homeschooling organizations. Also, nearly every state has its own homeschooling organization to provide information on regulations in addition to other support. Many religious and ethnic affiliations also have their own homeschooling organizations too, in addition to counties and other groups.

Homeschooling Online Resources

These are just some of the online resources available for homeschoolers. You also can check your phone book for local organizations and resources.

National Organizations

Alliance for Parental Involvement in Education
http://www.croton.com/allpie/

Alternative Education Resource Organization (AERO)
http://www.edrev.org/links.htm

American Homeschool Association (AHA)
http://www.americanhomeschoolassociation.org/

Home School Foundation
http://www.homeschoolfoundation.org

National Coalition of Alternative Community Schools
http://www.ncacs.org/

National Home Education Network (NHEN)
http://www.nhen.org/

National Home Education Research Institute (NHERI)
http://www.nheri.org

National Homeschooling Association (NHA)
http://www.n-h-a.org

Homeschooling and the Law

Advocates for the Rights of Homeschoolers (ARH)
http://www.geocities.com/arhfriends/

American Bar Association
http://www.abanet.org

Children with Special Needs

Children with Disabilities
http://www.childrenwithdisabilities.ncjrs.org/

Institutes for the Achievement of Human Potential (IAHP)
http://www.iahp.org/

National Challenged Homeschoolers Associated Network (NATHHAN)
http://www.nathhan.com/

Military Homeschooling

Department of Defense Dependent Schools/Education Activity (DoDDS)
http://www.odedodea.edu/

Books, Supplies, Curriculum

Federal Resources for Educational Excellence
http://www.ed.gov/free/

Home Schooling Homework
http://www.dailyhomework.org/

Home School Products
http://www.homeschooldiscount.com/

Homeschooler's Curriculum Swap
http://theswap.com/

HomeSchoolingSupply.com
http://www.homeschoolingsupply.com/

General Homeschooling Resources

A to Z Home's Cool
http://www.gomilpitas.com/

Family Unschoolers Network
http://www.unschooling.org

Home Education Magazine
http://www.home-ed-magazine.com/

Home School Legal Defense Association (HSLDA)
http://www.hslda.org

Homeschool Central
http://www.homeschoolcentral.com

Homeschool Internet Yellow Pages
http://www.homeschoolyellowpages.com/

Homeschool World
http://www.home-school.com/

Homeschool.com
http://www.homeschool.com/

HSAdvisor.com
http://www.hsadvisor.com/

Unschooling.com
http://www.unschooling.com/

Waldorf Without Walls
http://www.waldorfwithoutwalls.com/

Communicating Between Home and School

For homeschoolers, often there is limited contact with the schools beyond that which is required by the state. Yet a quick glance at your local schools' resources may reveal opportunities that can aid you in creating extracurricular activities that follow your interests and supplement your child's total learning experience.

Special Needs

If you have a child with special needs, such as dyslexia or ADHD (attention deficit hyperactivity disorder), taking advantage of the programs and services your public school provides can expand your support system and give you some relief in working with your child. In many instances, the easy access and little or no cost of these services makes this a viable option for homeschoolers.

Depending on your child's diagnosed needs, some school districts may offer full services and programs, while some may only provide consultations. Some school districts' special education departments have established parent support networks that you may be able to participate in as a homeschooler. States and school districts vary in terms of what homeschoolers are allowed to participate in, so check with your local school administrator and then check your state's regulations to verify your eligibility.

Two organizations, the Home School Legal Defense Association (HSLDA) and the National Challenged Homeschoolers Association Network (NATHHAN), offer a wide range of information and assistance on services and programs available for special needs children. Check them out on the Internet at *http://www.hslda.org* and *http://www.nathhan.com.* Your local homeschooling group—especially veteran homeschoolers—will have practical information you can use.

Additionally, some homeschooling parents combine the resources of a school with those offered by a private organization to maximize support.

Gifted Children

If your child is considered gifted, your local public school may have programs available for students who require additional intellectual attention. Check with your local school administrator and your state's regulations first. In addition to providing information on special needs children, HSLDA and NATHHAN offer resources for parents of gifted children.

Don't be afraid to check out the colleges in your area, too. Many times colleges, especially community colleges, offer classes or onetime workshops that might be of interest to your child. Check with your local schools to see how you can take advantage of these opportunities.

Extracurricular Activities

Opportunities abound for homeschoolers to get involved with extracurricular activities. Clubs and interest groups allow children and parents to interact and share ideas with other homeschoolers. Extracurricular activities not only enrich the learning experience, they can also provide opportunities for friendship.

You might want to meet regularly for planned activities focusing on a particular subject matter, such as math instruction, science workshops, or pottery classes. You could meet at someone's home or perhaps at a community or religious center. Another enriching idea is to form a theme group or club based on a group's interests. You could gather together as a quilting group, a nature club, a chess club, a play group, and more—let your interests guide you. Or you could just get together to simply share ideas or plan group activities, such as a craft project, a book discussion, or the creation of a newsletter. Parents and children can work together to plan activities and events or to create their own sporting teams, such as golf, water polo, and fencing, to name a few.

If you can't find a meeting on a particular subject area or theme in your region, don't hesitate to form one in your community. One way to begin might be to check out the Homeschool Social Register at *http://www.homeschoolmedia.net*. Here you can find other homeschoolers in your area and homeschoolers who share your educational philosophy and interests.

Other extracurricular activities, such as 4-H, Girl Scouts, Boy Scouts, religious youth groups, arts and crafts, athletics, music, and language or debate clubs, may be offered in your community. They can provide additional opportunities for your homeschooler to interact with his or her peers and have a valuable learning experience at the same time. Extracurricular activities offered at local schools also may prove worthwhile to investigate.

Returning to School

If you plan on having your child return to school, taking advantage of the programs and opportunities offered can help ease the transition back into the classroom. Your child will already experience a sense of familiarity with his or her surroundings and peers, which can help smooth the transition to a different structure of learning.

Meet Your Kindergartner

You may find that your kindergartner is all smiles. Agreeable, compliant, and confident, your child has reached a special age of inner balance. On the outside a kindergartner's growing physical and intellectual abilities make him or her able to do more, while on the inside your child's heart still belongs to you. But stay on your toes, because most kindergarten children make a shift toward independence at a certain point and the agreeableness begins to wane.

Of course, not all five to six and a half year olds are the same. Each kindergartner will develop at his or her own rate according to differences in personality, genetics, environment, and a host of other factors. Nonetheless, some common developmental characteristics among age groups do exist. Understanding the behavioral tendencies associated with your child's growth stage can save you from undue concern and can enhance your own intuitive guidance of how to support and nurture your child as he or she matures.

Enjoy Compliance

The good-natured, positive disposition of a kindergartner can seem too good to be true. So eager to be good and meet your expectations, your kindergartner may seem nearly perfect. Many children at this age show a general acceptance of the world and are eager to comply and be praised. Your child may be particularly proud of acting more like a grown-up and even comment on his or her own progress in behavior, saying such things as "Now that I'm older I can help set the dinner table." Although your kindergartner's disposition may be positive overall, it will probably lean more toward the serious than the silly.

Promote Confidence

A kindergartner can show strong confidence and comfort in his or her abilities. The awareness that he or she excels at one or two particular skills can easily offset a lack of accomplishment with others. Although your confident kindergartner may feel insecure in certain situations, he or she is levelheaded about acknowledging them. A kindergartner often instinctively knows what he or she needs to feel more secure and is able to ask for it. It might be something as simple as receiving a bit of extra attention before bed or holding your hand in the doctor's office. You may see your kindergartner seesaw between independent risk taking and the need to be coddled and comforted, or flip from bossy to babyish behavior. Be warned that the otherwise prudent kindergartner may overstep his or her limits around fire. Take extra precautions with children at this age to keep them away from matches and other sources of flame.

This is a good time for your child to develop a strong sense of self. Kindergartners are beginning to receive a reality check on their fantasy worldview. Your child may be realizing that just because he or she wants to be a ballerina doesn't mean it will happen. Give your child encouragement to work at the things he or she desires. Take time to point out the progress he or she has already made since being a toddler. Share your own stories of effort and accomplishment with a skill or goal. Of course, keep all tasks and expectations at an age-appropriate level and provide your child with as much assistance as needed. Be prepared, however, for the day when your five and a half or six year old begins a more shaky stage of development.

Recognize Love of Home and Security

Most kindergartners are not interested in adventure. Your child's attention will more likely be focused on the present moment than on worries about the future or memories from the past. Similarly, he or she appreciates tangible things, such as his or her bedroom, toys, house, and family. A kindergarten child's sense of fun is generally more contained and quiet. Your child finds great comfort in his or her inner feeling of security and safety, which contributes to the positive outlook. A kindergartner enjoys asking and receiving permission to do things and the feeling of being able to act according to your wishes. At this time your child's world revolves around you, the parent or main caregiver. You are still the central focus of his or her universe.

Not only does your kindergartner feel securely confident in himself or herself, but your child also feels confident in you. In general, your kindergartner thinks you're great. Kindergartners can be especially adoring of their primary caregiving parent. If you say he or she is good, your assurance will override the scolding or criticism of another adult. Kindergartners enjoy having a place in the family and love the special treatment they may receive from grandparents, although they may quantify it only in material terms, such as receiving treats and gifts.

Encourage Intellectual Opening

Intellectually your kindergartner is eager to engage and interact. He or she likes to organize and sort things and to solve simple puzzles. Many kindergartners can name the days of the week, know what day it is, and associate events with particular days. A kindergartner is also aware of his or her age. Although generally more in tune with time in relation to the calendar than the clock, most kindergartners know what their bedtime is and understand the concept of an event commencing when the hands of the clock reach a certain place. Counting by ones and progressing to numbers up to 20 is normal kindergarten number knowledge.

Children at this age are at a good developmental stage to be prompted to think about why things happen. In his or her stability and levelheadedness, a kindergartner can consider cause and effect and answer questions such as "Why do you think your brother got angry while you were playing?" or "Why do you think your friend felt sad?" Encouraging your child to push his or her level of awareness now will help him or her in relationships and in understanding consequences later on.

Combine Learning and Playing

For a kindergartner, learning and playing remain wonderfully intertwined. Kindergartners love to play and now have enough motor control and agility to play more independently. Physical activity is important, especially playground activities such as swinging, jumping, and the like. Kindergartners are developing proficiency using the tools of hands-on learning, such as cutting with scissors, pasting, finger painting, painting with brushes, and using pencils. Your child may also be enamored with building toys and with building in general. Many children at this age enjoy creating large structures. Indoor forts made from blankets or couch cushions are very popular. Your kindergartner enjoys the secure and cozy feeling of a close, comfortable space.

Talking, singing, and chanting are key learning mechanisms at this age. In fact, your kindergartner may be something of a chatterbox, talking nonstop. Kindergartners tend to be ready and uninhibited storytellers. Encourage and prompt your kindergartner to make up stories spontaneously. This promotes his or her intellectual development and furthers your understanding of what's going on inside your child's mind and the state of his or her emotions. Your kindergartner may still mix up his or her fantasies with the facts, and made-up stories may be unrealistically fantastic or exaggerated. Try to realize that this is the way your child's perceptions work at this time and be mindful not to correct or override his or her version of a story.

Tactile, creative activities, such as puppetry, working with clay, and dancing, tend to be favorites with kindergartners and will promote your child's development intellectually, emotionally, and physically. Games with other children tend to have a role-playing nature, especially role-playing games based on known story characters such as superheroes. Playing "house" and "store" are also common kindergarten games.

Understand Shift in Worldview

You may want to make a special effort to enjoy the bright, stable temperament of your kindergartner while you can. Like all growth stages, it won't last forever. As he or she matures, your kindergartner's belief that you are infallible will change. Your child is beginning to understand human limitations. The change can be sudden or more gradual. Either way, "yes" begins to fade and "no" is spoken more often as your kindergartner realizes that you aren't really in control of his or her life.

Through this process, your child is moving into seat number one in his or her universe. This can be a daunting reality check and profound change in worldview. Although your child's consciousness isn't developed enough to identify what is happening, you will comprehend his or her moodiness and periodic disobedience as signals of the inner pressure to move away from you emotionally and establish a more independent way of being. Contrary language, defiance, aggression, sulking, wasting time, and avoidance are all normal behaviors as your child works through this stage.

Although it may be disconcerting to see a happy child turn sulky, be assured that these changes are signs that your child is maturing. At regular points in a child's development there are times of balance followed by a breakdown of his or her internal order. This is simply preparation for the creation and reordering of the next, more advanced version of your child's self.

As this change occurs, one important way to support your kindergartner is by maintaining reliable morning and evening routines. Even if the daytime hours with your kindergartner are often unpredictable or seem out of control, a consistent schedule before bed and upon waking will have a profound, stabilizing effect on your child. This is especially true if you are mindful to include calm, quiet time when special affection can be shared, such as spending a few minutes before bed tucking in your child's blankets just right and sharing a hug or a story.

Be Flexible with Literacy Training

Kindergarten is a time when most children are beginning fundamental learning with the alphabet, writing, and letter sounds. Generally, kindergartners love to be read to and are attracted to looking through books and experimenting with interpreting the meanings of words. Many kindergartners recognize their own written name and possibly other short words if they are written in large letters. Others will be able to print their own first name and possibly the first letter of their last name.

Your kindergartner may show an interest in learning to read but may just as likely not be eager to delve into the world of words at this time. A secure and happy kindergartner may at first show signs of moving forward in letter recognition and writing, only to withdraw when he or she enters the emotionally stormy period of this age. Don't push or force your child to read early if it doesn't come naturally. Be assured that your child will learn to read eventually—and will read better and with more enjoyment if he or she isn't forced. Five and a half to six and a half year olds are known to write letters backward and to have trouble ordering letters in words. This is a reflection of the inner disorder they are experiencing. Don't fear. Give your kindergartner a break from literacy training if he or she needs it. As your child approaches seven, he or she will most likely be ready to take the literary world by storm.

Promoting Literacy

Promoting Literacy

Key Topics

Alphabet *A* to *Z*

Beginning Sounds

Middle Sounds

Ending Sounds

Writing Words

Short-Vowel Sounds

Rhyming Words

Opposites and Descriptive Words

Fiction and Poetry

Making the Grade: Everything Your Kindergartner Needs to Know

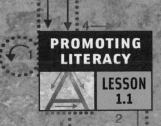

Discovering the Alphabet
A to *M*

The letters of the alphabet are the ingredients of the English language.

OBJECTIVE	BACKGROUND	MATERIALS
To teach your student how to write and sequence the letters *a* to *m*	The letters of an alphabet make up the most basic part of a language. The English alphabet includes 26 letters, which produce more than 40 sounds. In this lesson, your student will learn to place letters in alphabetical order. He or she will also practice writing uppercase and lowercase letters.	■ Student Learning Pages 1.A–1.D ■ 1 set alphabet strips (optional) ■ several sheets construction paper ■ 1 pair scissors ■ markers or crayons ■ 1 copy Writing Lines, page 357 (optional)

VOCABULARY

ALPHABET the letters we use to make words
UPPERCASE LETTERS capital letters
LOWERCASE LETTERS small letters, not capitals

Let's Begin

1 **INTRODUCE** Prepare for the lesson by displaying a complete set of alphabet strips. If you don't have these, make your own. Cut sheets of construction paper in half vertically to make strips. Turn the strips horizontally and write the letters of the alphabet on them in sequential order. Write each uppercase letter first followed by the matching lowercase letter, placing space between each letter. Each letter pair should be on its own strip. Hang the strips on a wall to display the entire alphabet in order. Next, begin the lesson by telling your student that the strips show the letters of the **alphabet.** Define *alphabet* as "the letters we use to make words." Invite your student to repeat after you. Say, *The alphabet shows all the letters we use to make words.*

2 **CONNECT** Tell your student that the letters of the alphabet have an order. Explain that the alphabet song tells the order of the letters. Then begin singing the alphabet song for your student. Ask him or her to repeat the song after you as you point to each letter on the alphabet strips.

3 **PRACTICE** Distribute Student Learning Page 1.A to your student. Help him or her read the directions. Guide your student as he or she sequences the letters in the first basket. Then have your student complete the rest of the page on his or her own.

4 **CLASSIFY** Explain to your student that there are two types of letters in the alphabet—**uppercase letters** and **lowercase letters.** Point out uppercase and lowercase letters on the alphabet strips. Select various uppercase and lowercase letters and write each one on a separate piece of construction paper. Show your student each letter and ask, *Is this an uppercase letter or a lowercase letter?*

5 **WRITE** Give Student Learning Page 1.B to your student. Invite him or her to practice writing uppercase and lowercase letters from *a* to *m*. Guide his or her hand for the first few letters. Model how to follow the arrows to make the lines and curves of each letter. Have your student trace the letters on the page before writing them. Offer praise and encouragement as your student works through the page. You may also use a copy of the Writing Lines found on page 357 to have your student practice writing various letters from *a* to *m*.

6 **IDENTIFY** Distribute Student Learning Page 1.C to your student. Ask him or her to use the first letter of the picture label to find and color the hidden letter. Then have your student write the uppercase and lowercase letter for the letter he or she colored.

7 **ENHANCE** Read out loud the activities on Student Learning Page 1.D. Then allow time for your student to complete an activity he or she chooses.

8 **CHALLENGE** Model for your student how to keep a journal to express his or her thoughts and ideas. Encourage him or her to write or draw in it regularly. Suggest that your student practice writing letters in his or her journal.

TAKE A BREAK

Engage your student's interest in the lesson by making alphabet cookies. Form or cut the cookie dough into shapes of letters. You can also use homemade modeling dough or fingerpaint to make letters.

FOR FURTHER READING

Chicka Chicka Boom Boom, by John Archambault and Lois Ehlert, ill. (Aladdin Library, 2000).

Kathy Ross Crafts Letter Shapes (*Learning Is Fun*), by Kathy Ross and Jan Barger, ill. (Millbrook Press Trade, 2002).

Branching Out

TEACHING TIP

Keep a master copy of Student Learning Page 1.B. Make extra copies of the page to allow your student more opportunities to practice writing letters. If your student writes bigger letters, make larger copies on 11-by-17-inch paper.

CHECKING IN

To assess your student's understanding of the lesson, take down the alphabet strips for the letters *a* to *m*. Mix up the strips and have your student put them in order.

Clean Up the Letter Mess!

Look at the letters in the baskets.
Write them in order on each shelf.

PROMOTING LITERACY

1.A

1.

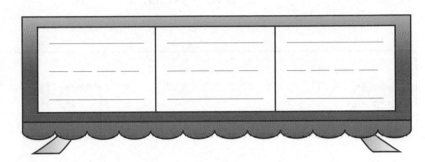

2.

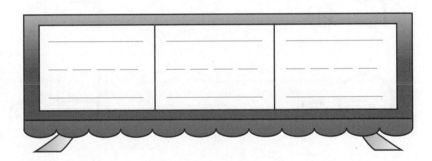

3.

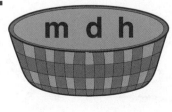

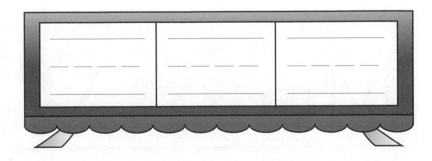

Student Learning Page 1.A: Clean Up the Letter Mess!   **5**

Write Uppercase and Lowercase Letters

Trace and then write the letters on the lines.

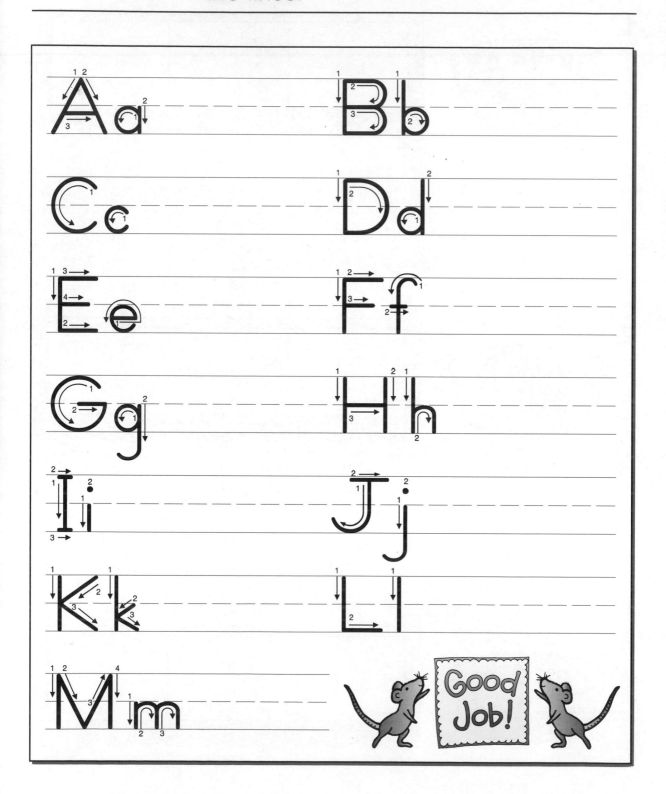

Hunt for Letters

Color the letter hidden in each picture.
Then write the letter in uppercase and
in lowercase.

Guitar

uppercase ‐ ‐ ‐ ‐

lowercase ‐ ‐ ‐ ‐

monkey

uppercase ‐ ‐ ‐ ‐

lowercase ‐ ‐ ‐ ‐

ice cream cone

uppercase ‐ ‐ ‐ ‐

lowercase ‐ ‐ ‐ ‐

Horse

uppercase ‐ ‐ ‐ ‐

lowercase ‐ ‐ ‐ ‐

What's Next? You Decide!

Teacher: *Read aloud the directions and activities. Then have your student choose which activity to do next.*

Now it's your turn to choose what to do next in the lesson. Read the activities and decide which one you want to do—you may want to try them both!

Put Together a Letter Puzzle

MATERIALS

❏ 6 index cards

❏ markers or crayons

❏ 1 pair scissors

STEPS

❏ Choose six different letters from *a* to *m*.

❏ Write each letter on one index card.

❏ Write some of the letters as uppercase letters and some as lowercase letters.

❏ Make each letter large enough to fill the index card.

❏ Cut each index card in half.

❏ Mix up the 12 pieces of letters.

❏ Now try to put each letter back together!

Decorate a Letter

MATERIALS

❏ 1 posterboard

❏ markers or crayons

❏ glue

❏ assorted buttons or beads

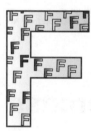

STEPS

Decorate your favorite letter from *a* to *m*!

❏ Choose one letter from *a* to *m*.

❏ Write the letter on the posterboard.

❏ Make the letter large and thick.

❏ Glue buttons or beads to the letter.

❏ Be sure to stay inside the lines of the letter!

❏ Show your fun letter to your family and friends.

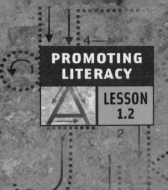

Understanding the Alphabet *N* to *Z*

Mastering the alphabet opens doors to reading and writing adventures.

OBJECTIVE	BACKGROUND	MATERIALS
To teach your student how to write and sequence the letters *n* to *z*	As your student progresses to learning the entire alphabet, he or she will be prepared to gain fluency in reading and writing. In this lesson, your student will learn to place the letters *n* to *z* in alphabetical order. He or she will also practice writing uppercase and lowercase letters.	■ Student Learning Pages 2.A–2.D ■ 1 set alphabet strips (optional) ■ construction paper ■ 1 pair scissors ■ 26 index cards ■ 1 shoebox ■ 1 copy Writing Lines, page 357 (optional) ■ markers or crayons

Let's Begin

1 **INTRODUCE** Display a complete set of alphabet strips. If you don't have these, make your own. (See Lesson 1.1, Step 1, for instructions.) Hang the strips on a wall to display the entire alphabet in order. Then begin the lesson. As a review, invite your student to tell you what the alphabet shows. [the letters we use to make words]

2 **CONNECT** Remind your student that he or she has learned the letters of the alphabet from *a* to *m*. Then tell him or her that in this lesson he or she will learn the letters of the alphabet from *n* to *z*. Invite your student to begin singing the alphabet song. Then join him or her beginning with the letter *n*. (If your student doesn't remember the entire song, sing all of it with him or her.) As you sing with your student, point to each letter from *n* to *z* on the alphabet strips.

3 **SEQUENCE** Ask your student what he or she remembers about the letters of the alphabet. [they have an order] Draw your student's attention to the alphabet strips. Point out that the letters *n* to *z* come after the letters *a* to *m*. Then write each uppercase letter from *N* to *Z* on a separate index card. Place all the index cards in a shoebox and mix them up. Invite your student to choose two index cards. Ask him or her which of the two letters comes first in the alphabet. Have your student repeat

this exercise with other letters. Then challenge him or her to select more letters and sequence as many as he or she can.

4 **EXTEND** Ask, *What's the very first letter of the alphabet?* [a] Ask, *What's the very last letter of the alphabet?* [z] Next, distribute Student Learning Page 2.A. Tell your student that the train cars show letters that come right after one another in the alphabet. Help your student write each missing letter after he or she identifies it.

5 **CLASSIFY** Review upper- and lowercase letters. Then write each lowercase letter from *n* to *z* on a separate index card. Place the index cards in the shoebox with the uppercase letters from Step 3 and mix them up. Select a number of index cards. Show each letter to your student and say, *Reach your hands to the sky if the letter is uppercase! Bend your knees if the letter is lowercase!* Next, find the uppercase and lowercase cards for three letters. Mix up the cards. Have your student match the uppercase letter with its corresponding lowercase letter.

6 **WRITE** Distribute a copy of Student Learning Page 2.B to your student. Invite him or her to practice tracing and writing uppercase and lowercase letters from *n* to *z*. You may also use a copy of the Writing Lines found on page 357 to have your student practice his or her writing.

7 **DISTINGUISH** Give Student Learning Page 2.C to your student. Ask him or her to write each uppercase and lowercase letter in the correct building. Then tell him or her to color the windows in the two buildings that show the same letters. Have your student use a different color marker or crayon for each letter pair.

8 **CONCLUDE** Read out loud the activities on Student Learning Page 2.D to your student. Allow time for him or her to do an activity of his or her choice.

DID YOU KNOW?

The world's alphabets developed from a syllabic system of writing. In this type of writing, symbols are combined to form words that sound like the names of the symbols. For example, a picture of the sea and a picture of the sun placed together might stand for the word *season.*

Branching Out

TEACHING TIP

Show your student a children's dictionary. Point out that the words are listed in alphabetical order. For example, the word *apple*, which begins with *a*, is listed toward the front of the dictionary, while the word *zoo*, which begins with *z*, is listed toward the back.

CHECKING IN

Show your student several headlines from a newspaper or magazine. Point to various letters and have him or her say whether each one is an uppercase or a lowercase letter.

FOR FURTHER READING

A-B-C-D-E-F-G: I Love the Alphabet and It Loves Me, by Lynn Kirpa and Joan Yeziorski, ill. (iUniverse.com, 2000).

A Gull's Story: A Tale of Learning About Life, the Shore, and the ABC's, by Frank Finale and Margie Moore, ill. (Jersey Shore Publications, 2002).

Ride the Alphabet Train

The letters on the train are in order.
Write each letter that is missing.

1. q r ___ t

2. L M N ___

3. ___ g h i

4. W ___ Y Z

Write Uppercase and Lowercase Letters

Trace and then write the letters on the lines.

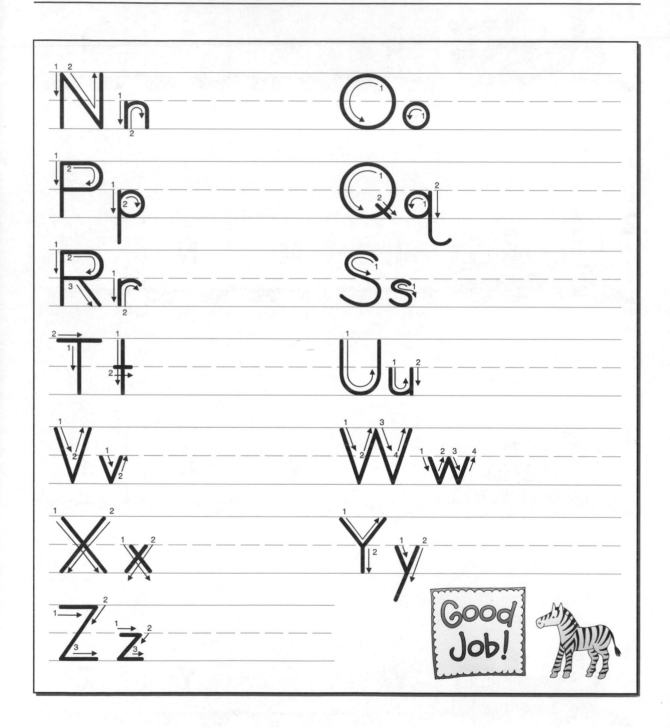

Good Job!

Fill Up the Buildings

Write the uppercase letters in the big building. Write the lowercase letters in the small building.

b Q R g Y B r F q G

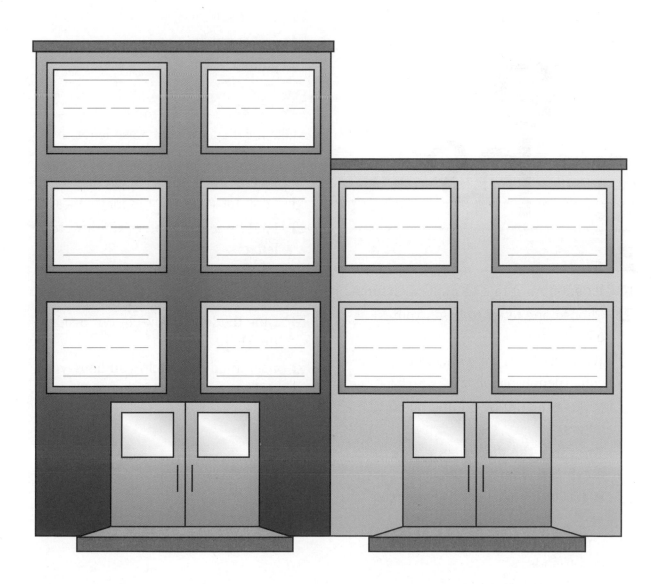

What's Next? You Decide!

Teacher: Read aloud the directions and activities. Then have your student choose which activity to do next.

Now it's your turn to choose what to do next in the lesson. Read the activities and decide which one you want to do—you may want to try them both!

Make a Letter Picture

 MATERIALS

❑ 1 sheet construction paper
❑ markers or crayons

 STEPS

Use letters from *a* to *z* to make a picture.

❑ Choose one letter to begin your picture with.
❑ Write the letter on a sheet of construction paper.
❑ Make a picture by adding other letters.
❑ You can write the letters upside down and sideways, too!
❑ What does your letter picture look like?
❑ Show the picture to your family and friends.
❑ Can they guess what your picture shows?

Create a Collage

 MATERIALS

❑ several old magazines
❑ 1 pair scissors
❑ 1 posterboard
❑ glue

STEPS

Make a collage of uppercase letters and lowercase letters.

❑ Ask an adult for some old magazines.
❑ Look for letters in the magazines.
❑ Find uppercase letters and lowercase letters.
❑ Cut out the letters that you like.
❑ Draw a shape on the posterboard.
❑ Glue the letters you cut out inside the shape.
❑ Ask an adult to help you hang your collage where people can see it.

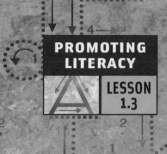

Recognizing the Initial Consonants *b, d, f, m, r, s,* and *t*

Connecting sounds to the letters of the alphabet is like unlocking the code to the mystery of language.

OBJECTIVE	BACKGROUND	MATERIALS
To teach your student to identify initial consonants and sounds and to recognize high-frequency words	When your student learns to associate sounds with the letters of the alphabet, he or she will discover that these letters aren't just a series of lines and curves—they are the keys to learning how to read and write. In this lesson, your student will learn to recognize and pronounce the initial consonants *b, d, f, m, r, s,* and *t*. He or she will also learn frequently used words in reading and writing.	■ Student Learning Pages 3.A–3.B ■ construction paper ■ markers or crayons ■ 1 set picture cards (optional) ■ 1 calendar

VOCABULARY

CONSONANTS the letters in the alphabet that aren't vowels
VOWELS the letters *a, e, i, o,* and *u*
SOUND something a person can hear

Let's Begin

1 INTRODUCE Begin the lesson by reminding your student that he or she has learned to name and write all the letters of the alphabet. Tell him or her that in this lesson he or she will learn about some letters that are **consonants.** Explain that the letters of the alphabet are either **vowels** or consonants. Slowly say the words *vowels* and *consonants* and invite your student to repeat the words after you. Point out that the letters *a, e, i, o,* and *u* are vowels. All of the other letters are consonants. Ask, *Can you name two letters in the alphabet that are consonants?*

2 EXPLAIN Tell your student that every letter has a **sound.** Explain that a sound is something a person can hear. Point out that when we talk, we make sounds. Then sing the first few letters of the alphabet song and clap once for each letter. Invite your student to join you. Encourage your student to listen to the sounds you both make as you sing the letters.

ENRICH THE EXPERIENCE

It's not as important right now that your student pronounces the words *vowels* and *consonants* perfectly. The point of introducing these new words here is to provide a foundation on which to build in future lessons.

3 **CONNECT** Remind your student that we can put letters together to make words. This means that when we say a word, we are saying the different sounds of the letters in the word. Then point to this book. Tell your student that the word *book* starts with the letter *b*. Write *book* in big letters on a piece of construction paper. Sound out each letter while emphasizing the *b*: /b/ /b/ /b/ /o͞o/ /k/, *book*. Invite your student to say *book* after you.

4 **COMPARE** Write the words *boy* and *boat* on separate pieces of construction paper. Slowly read each word out loud while stressing the /b/ sound. Ask, *What's the first letter in both words?* [b] Then think of some common sight words that begin with *b* as well as some words that begin with other consonants, such as *bowl, boy, foot, bee, cow, sock, bear,* and so on. Say the words out loud. Ask your student to clap when he or she hears a word that begins with the consonant *b*. Have your student hold both hands out to the sides if he or she hears a word that doesn't begin with *b*.

5 **IDENTIFY** Show your student the photos. Ask your student to tell you what each picture shows. [a dog, a duck] Ask him or her if both words begin with the same sound. [yes] Ask, *Which sound do you hear at the beginning of each word?* [/d/] Tell your student that the consonant *d* makes this sound. Say each word while emphasizing the *d*: /d/ /ŏ/ /g/, *dog*; /d/ /d/ /d/ /ŭ/ /k/, *duck*. Have your student repeat after you. Then point out other things that begin with this sound. Invite your student to say these sight words, or high-frequency words, after you: *door, desk, dish, doll, dirt,* and *deer*. You may also use picture cards if you have them. Display several different pictures. Then have your student point to pictures that show things beginning with *d*.

6 **CONTINUE** Point to your foot. Ask, *Which part of my body am I pointing to?* [foot] Have your student tell you which sound he or she hears at the beginning of *foot*. [/f/] Then point to your nose. Ask, *Which part of my body am I pointing to?* [nose] Ask, *Does the word* nose *begin with the same sound as the word* foot? [no] Next, point to your finger. Ask, *Which part of my body am I pointing to?* [finger] Ask, *Does the word* finger *begin with the same sound as the word* foot? [yes] Tell your student that the consonant /f/ makes the first sound in the words *foot* and *finger*. Sound out the letters in *foot* and invite your student to repeat after you: /f/ /f/ /f/ /ŭ/ /t/. Then say these sight words out loud: *frog, cake, for, bug,* and *fun*. Ask your student to stomp his or her foot when he or she hears a word that begins with the /f/ sound. As you work through these phonics lessons, remember to incorporate commonly used sight words, which can boost your student's reading abilities.

7 **DISTINGUISH** Slowly say this sentence to your student out loud: *A moose named Molly marched to the market for milk.* Challenge your student to tell you the beginning sound he or she hears the most in the words in the sentence. [/m/] If your student is struggling, say the word *moose* to prompt his or her response. Tell your student that the consonant *m* makes the /m/ sound in words. Then playfully march around the room as your student marches behind you. As you march, say the sentence again and have your student join you. Be sure to emphasize the initial /m/ sound.

8 **DRAW** Invite your student to draw a rainbow on a sheet of construction paper. Have him or her use red, orange, yellow, green, blue, and purple markers or crayons for each ray of the rainbow. When he or she has finished, ask, *What does your picture show?* [a rainbow] Stretch out the /r/ sound as you say the word: /r/ /r/ /r/ . . . *rainbow*. Point out that the consonant *r* makes the /r/ sound in words. Then ask your student to name the colors in his or her rainbow. Ask him or her which color begins with the same sound as the word *rainbow*. [red] Break down the sounds in the word *red* and invite your student to repeat after you: /r/ /ĕ/ /d/. Have your student pronounce more words that begin with *r*, such as *run, rain, rope*, and *ride*.

9 **SING** Write the word *song* on a piece of construction paper. Say the word out loud as you point to it. Ask, *What is the first letter in the word* song? [s] Then ask, *Which sound do you hear at the beginning of the word* song? [/s/] Now invite your student to sing this sentence after you: *Sammy sings a song in the summer sun.* Have your student clap each time he or she hears a word that begins with the /s/ sound. Keep singing the sentence until your student identifies each /s/ word. You may want to continue this exercise with a common children's song that repeats the /s/ sound, such as "Here Comes Suzy Snowflake."

10 **EXPAND** Name each day of the week out loud. Point to each day's name on a calendar as you say it. Tell your student that each day of the week begins with a consonant letter. Then say, *There are two days of the week that begin with the /s/ sound. Help me find these days on the calendar.* Read out loud each day of the week in order. Ask your student to say *Stop!* when he or she hears a day that begins with the /s/ sound. [Saturday and Sunday]

11 **COUNT** Hold up two fingers. Ask, *How many fingers do you see?* [two] Then hold up four fingers and ask, *How many fingers do you see now?* [four] Ask, *Do the words* two *and* four *begin with the same sounds?* [no] Then have your student say which sound he or she hears at the beginning of the word *two*. [/t/] Tell your student that the letter *t* makes the /t/ sound in *two*. Then count from one to five. Ask your student to tell you the other number word that begins with *t*. [three] Name other simple words that begin with *t*, such as *tree, tall, toe*, and *turn*. Also include some words that don't start with *t*. Ask your student to turn around in a full circle when he or she hears a /t/ sound at the beginning of a word. Tell your student to put his or her head down if a word doesn't begin with a /t/ sound.

PROMOTING LITERACY **LESSON 1.3**

ENRICH THE EXPERIENCE

To help your student connect sounds to familiar things, take a walk around your neighborhood. Point to different things and have your student say the word that names each thing. Then ask your student which sound he or she hears at the beginning of the word.

12 READ As your student learns to read, it's important that he or she learn to identify sight words. These are words that occur frequently in different types of literature. Some frequently used words are *to, the, a, is, I, see, go, has, can, do,* and *for.* Write each of these sentences on a separate strip of construction paper:

> The boy has a bike.   The boy can go to the store.
> I can do a puzzle.   The girl sees a dog.
> The bone is for the dog.   The dog has spots.

Read each sentence out loud as you point to each word. Then invite your student to read each sentence after you as he or she also points to each word. Keep reading the sentences out loud until your student can read them on his or her own.

13 PRACTICE Distribute Student Learning Page 3.A to your student. Help him or her practice identifying sounds and reading high-frequency sight words. Read the directions to your student. Then encourage him or her to name the picture out loud to help him or her identify the correct initial consonant. Guide your student's work as needed.

14 CHALLENGE As your student shows readiness, help him or her spell some of his or her favorite words. Say aloud each letter as you write it. Then encourage your student to write the words.

15 CONCLUDE Give Student Leaning Page 3.B to your student. Read each activity out loud to your student. Invite him or her to do an activity of his or her choice.

Branching Out

TEACHING TIP

Make up riddles to help your student practice pronouncing the consonants in this lesson. For example, tell your student, *I shine in the sky. You see me more in the summer. What am I?* [the sun] Ask your student which sound he or she hears at the beginning of the riddle's answer.

CHECKING IN

To assess your student's understanding of the lesson, say some simple sentences while omitting one consonant. For example, say, *I can read a _____ook.* (Sound out the last three letters in the word *book* at the end of the sentence.) See if your student can guess the missing consonant sound, /b/.

FOR FURTHER READING

The War Between the Vowels and the Consonants, by Priscilla Turner and Whitney Turner, photographer (Farrar Straus and Giroux, 1999).

Word Wizard, by Cathryn Falwell (Houghton Mifflin, 1998).

Find the Letter

Read the sentence. Look at each picture. Then write the missing letters.

1. The _ _ _ ird sees a _ _ _ oad.

2. A _ _ _ an can go to the _ _ _ oon.

3. I can _ _ _ un.

4. The _ _ _ uck sees a _ _ _ ish.

5. The _ _ _ oy has _ _ _ ocks.

What's Next? You Decide!

Teacher: *Read aloud the directions and activities. Then have your student choose which activity to do next.*

Now it's your turn to choose what to do next in the lesson. Read the activities and decide which one you want to do—you may want to try them both!

Make a Letter Flag

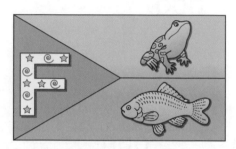

 MATERIALS

❏ 1 sheet construction paper

❏ markers or crayons

STEPS

Make a flag for one of these letters: *b, d, f, m, r, s,* or *t.*

❏ Write one letter on a sheet of construction paper.

❏ Make the letter look fun.

❏ Name some things that begin with the letter. Ask an adult to help you.

❏ Draw those things on the construction paper.

❏ Hang up your letter flag for people to see!

Create a Mobile

MATERIALS

❏ 5–10 sheets construction paper

❏ markers or crayons

❏ 1 pair scissors

❏ 1 hole puncher

❏ 5–10 lengths ribbon

❏ 1 hanger

STEPS

❏ Name some things that begin with *b, d, f, m, r, s,* or *t.*

❏ Draw the things on sheets of construction paper. Cut them out.

❏ Punch a hole through each picture. Ask an adult to help you.

❏ Tie a long piece of ribbon to the hole.

❏ Tie the other end of the ribbon to the hanger.

❏ Ask an adult to help you hang the mobile in your room or play area.

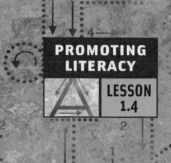

Comprehending the Initial Consonants
c, g, h, l, n, p, and w

*Phonics allows us to solve the riddle of language.
Without a system of phonics, we would be left with
literally thousands of words to memorize!*

OBJECTIVE	BACKGROUND	MATERIALS
To teach your student to identify initial consonants and sounds and to recognize additional high-frequency words	Your student is learning that every letter has a sound and that sounds are combined to form words. Understanding this basic principle of phonics will enable your student to experience success in reading and writing. In this lesson, your student will learn to recognize and pronounce the initial consonants *c, g, h, l, n, p,* and *w.* He or she will also learn more frequently used words in reading and writing.	■ Student Learning Pages 4.A–4.B ■ 1 cup ■ 1 set picture cards (optional) ■ 1 copy Web, page 356 ■ 18 index cards ■ markers or crayons ■ old magazines (optional) ■ 1 pair scissors (optional) ■ glue (optional)

Let's Begin

1 **INTRODUCE** Begin the lesson by reminding your student that each letter of the alphabet is either a vowel or a consonant. Recall that the letters *a, e, i, o,* and *u* are vowels and that all other letters are consonants. Then ask, *Can you name one word that begins with a consonant?* [answers will vary] Now invite your student to complete this sentence: *When we say words, we make* _____. [sounds]

2 **REVEAL** Tell your student that in this lesson he or she is going to learn the sounds of more consonants. Then show your student a cup and ask him or her to name the object. Ask, *What sound do you hear at the beginning of the word* cup? [/k/] Write the word *cup* on a sheet of paper. Point out the letter *c* and tell your student that this consonant makes the /k/ sound in *cup.* Then say the word *can.* Ask, *Does the word* can *begin with the same sound as the word* cup? [yes] Invite your student to repeat the words *cup* and *can* after you.

3 **IDENTIFY** Slowly read the rhyme below to your student. Clap once for each word that begins with a /k/ sound. Emphasize the initial /k/ sound to help your student identify it.

> Coolie the Cow went to catch a nap,
> When Casey the Cat began to stomp and snap.
> Snap, stomp, snap went Casey the Cat.
> Well, Coolie the Cow wasn't cool with that.

Next, say more words that begin with the consonant *c* and have the /k/ sound, such as *color, camel, curl,* and *cute.* Ask your student to say each word after you. Listen to be sure he or she correctly pronounces each initial consonant sound.

Girl

4 **COMPARE** Point to the photos and read each label out loud. Ask, *What sound do you hear at the beginning of the word* girl? [/g/] *What sound do you hear at the beginning of the word* boy? [/b/] *Do the words* girl *and* boy *begin with the same sounds?* [no] Point to the *g* in *girl* and explain that it makes the /g/ sound. Say the word *girl* while stretching the initial consonant sound. Then have your student repeat after you: /g/ /g/ /g/ /ŭ/ /r/ /l/, girl. Now have your student say these words after you: *go, goat, fan, gate, dish, guitar, gull,* and *moon.* Ask him or her to give a thumbs-up sign if a word begins with a /g/ sound and a thumbs-down sign if a word begins with a different sound. Continue with other commonly used sight words. Combining sight words with phonics concepts boosts your student's reading abilities.

Boy

5 **RECITE** Read out loud another silly rhyme to have your student practice the /g/ sound. Read it one or two times to your student. Then have him or her repeat the rhyme after you.

> Gish the Silly Goose likes to giggle, giggle, giggle.
> Gish gallops in the garden with a silly, little wiggle.
> Go on, Gish. Go on! Go on, giggle. It's not bad!
> You give the world a grin when you're silly and you're glad!

Now invite your student to name the words in the first three lines of the rhyme that begin with the /g/ sound.

+

ENRICH THE EXPERIENCE

Read the rhymes expressively to engage your student's interest. Act out some of the words to help him or her attach meanings to them and form images. Creating images from words will inspire your student as he or she learns to read.

---

6 **DISTINGUISH** Place your hand on your head. Ask, *What part of my body am I touching?* [head] Ask your student which sound he or she hears at the beginning of the word *head.* [/h/] Then have your student answer this riddle: *You put this on your head to keep it warm. What is it?* [hat] Ask, *Do the words* head *and* hat *begin with the same sounds?* [yes] Write the words *head* and *hat* on a sheet of paper. Tell your student that the consonant *h* makes the /h/ sound at the beginning of each word. Have your student say *head* and *hat* several times. Then say each of these words one at a time: *horse, bath, hair, hill,* and *rain.* Tell your student to put both hands on his or her head each time he or she hears the /h/ sound.

7 **EXPAND** Draw a tree on a sheet of paper. Include at least four large leaves. Then point to a leaf and ask your student to name it. Ask, *What sound do you hear at the beginning of the word* leaf? [/l/] Next, say the following pairs of words one at a time: *lamp/seal, ring/lion, tuna/lake,* and *bee/leg.* As you say each word pair, emphasize the /l/ sound. Ask your student to tell you the word in each pair that begins with the /l/ sound. Write the correct word in one of the leaves on the tree. Invite your student to pronounce each word on his or her own.

8   **COUNT** Write the number 9 on a sheet of paper. Then write the word *nine* below the number. Count from 1 to 9 as your student counts with you. When you get to the number 9, hold up the paper and stress the word *nine* while stretching the /n/ sound of the initial consonant. Tell your student that the consonant *n* makes the /n/ sound in the word *nine.* Then ask him or her to say *nine* on his or her own. Display picture cards (or draw pictures) of things that begin with the /n/ sound, such as a net, a nut, a noodle, a nose, or a neck. Mix in pictures of things that begin with other consonants. Name each picture and invite your student to say *No!* when he or she hears a word that doesn't begin with the /n/ sound.

9   **LISTEN** Slowly read out loud the rhyme below. Stress the initial /p/ sounds.

> *Here comes Punky Porcupine,*
> *Poking people with his pointy spines.*
> *Prick, prick, prick is Punky's trick.*
> *Here comes Punky—run real quick!*

Ask, *Which sound do you hear at the beginning of the word* porcupine? [/p/] Tell your student that the consonant *p* makes this sound. Then write each of the following words on a sheet of paper: *pig, pot, leg, pillow, jelly,* and *peach.* Point to the initial consonant as you say each word out loud. Then ask your student to tell you whether each word begins with a /p/ sound.

10   **LIST** Invite your student to answer this riddle: *A spider spins this around and around. What is it?* [web] Write the word *web* on a sheet of paper. Point to the first letter and tell your student that the consonant *w* makes the /w/ sound in the word *web.* Then use a copy of the Web found on page 356. Write "Web" in the center. Say the following pairs of words one at a time: *meal/worm, well/ball, wolf/lamp,* and *tall/wall.* Stress the /w/ sound for words beginning with *w.* For each word pair, ask, *Which word begins with the /w/ sound?* Write each correct response in a different surrounding oval. Then have your student pronounce each word.

11   **REINFORCE** Review the sight words your student learned in Lesson 1.3. Write each of these words on index cards: *to, the, a, is, I, see, go, has, can, do,* and *for.* Think of sentences that include one or more of the words. As you say each sentence out loud, flash the appropriate index card when you say a sight word. When you're finished, flash each of the index cards to your student. Invite him or her to read each word on his or her

,
TAKE A BREAK

Be sure to make time to read stories and poems to your student. Guide your student's pronunciation when he or she reads out loud with you. A good book to use for story time is *You Read to Me and I'll Read to You,* edited by Janet Schulman, or *The Random House Book of Poetry for Children,* by Jack Prelutsky.

   Comprehending the Initial Consonants *c, g, h, l, n, p,* and *w*

own. Then introduce these new words: *am, it,* and *some.* Write down some simple sentences that include these words. Slowly read each sentence with your student while pointing to each word. After you have read the sentences several times, point to each new sight word and invite your student to read it. As your student shows interest, encourage him or her to spell and write these words.

12 PRACTICE Distribute Student Learning Page 4.A and read the directions out loud. Ask your student to name the things in the picture and tell the sound he or she hears at the beginning of each word. Have your student color the thing if the sound matches one of the consonants listed in the directions. Then have your student circle the sight words that he or she knows in the caption.

13 CONCLUDE To end the lesson, distribute Student Learning Page 4.B. Read each activity out loud. Then invite your student to choose one or both of the activities to complete.

Branching Out

TEACHING TIP

You might want to make your own picture cards to help your student connect consonant sounds with picture names. Cut familiar pictures out of old magazines. Glue each picture to a large index card and label it. Have your student name each picture and listen for the initial sounds in words.

CHECKING IN

To assess your student's understanding of the lesson, write each of these consonants on a separate index card: *c, g, h, l, n, p,* and *w.* Choose two index cards at a time and show them to your student. Think of a word that begins with the initial consonant sound on one of the index cards you selected. Then ask your student to point to the letter that makes the sound he or she hears at the beginning of the word.

FOR FURTHER READING

Reading Success Mini-Books: Initial Consonants, by Mary Beth Spann (Scholastic Trade, 1999).

So Many Bunnies: A Bedtime ABC and Counting Book, by Rick Walton and Paige Miglio, ill. (Lothrop Lee and Shepard, 1998).

Color the Consonant Picture

PROMOTING
LITERACY

4.A

Name the pictures. Color things that begin with *c*, *g*, *h*, *l*, *n*, *p*, or *w*.

The girl can see some noodles.

What's Next? You Decide!

Teacher: *Read aloud the directions and activities. Then have your student choose which activity to do next.*

Now it's your turn to choose what to do next in the lesson. Read the activities and decide which one you want to do—you may want to try them both!

Play Consonant Hopscotch

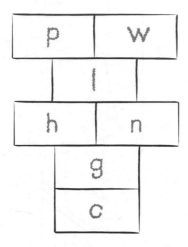

◣ MATERIALS

❏ chalk

◣ STEPS

❏ Draw boxes for hopscotch on the ground. Use chalk.

❏ Write a letter in each box. Use *c, g, h, l, n, p,* and *w.* The boxes should look like the picture.

❏ Hop on the first box. Look at the letter.

❏ Say a word that begins with the letter.

❏ Then hop to the next box and say a word that begins with that letter.

❏ Try to go through all the boxes!

Act Out Words

◣ MATERIALS

❏ 7 index cards

◣ STEPS

Play this game with a friend or family member.

❏ Ask an adult to write one word on each of seven index cards.

❏ Use these words: *curl, guitar, hop, laugh, nap, push,* and *wish.*

❏ Mix up the cards.

❏ Ask your partner to choose a card.

❏ Ask your partner to act out the word.

❏ Try to guess the word.

❏ Tell the first letter of the word.

❏ Now choose a card and act out the word for your partner.

Recognizing the Initial Consonants *j, k, q, v, x, y,* and *z*

Zippedy-doo-da, zippedy-ay. Teach the initial z sound today!

OBJECTIVE	BACKGROUND	MATERIALS
To teach your student to identify initial consonants and sounds and to recognize additional high-frequency words	Your student is learning to distinguish individual sounds within words. As he or she assimilates the phonetic principles of our language, he or she will naturally gain fluency in reading and writing. In this lesson, your student will learn to recognize and pronounce the initial consonants *j, k, q, v, x, y,* and *z*. He or she will also learn more frequently used words in reading and writing	▪ Student Learning Pages 5.A–5.B ▪ 1 key ▪ 8 index cards ▪ 1 quarter ▪ 1 penny

Let's Begin

1   **SING** Review some sounds your student has learned by singing a version of "Old McDonald." Replace the traditional line of animal sounds with letter sounds:

> *Old McDonald had a farm, E-I-E-I-O!*
> *And on this farm he had a cow, E-I-E-I-O!*
> *With a /k/ /k/ here and a /k/ /k/ there*
> */k/ here, /k/ there, /k/ /k/ everywhere*
> *Old McDonald had a farm, E-I-E-I-O!*

Repeat this version of the song using animal names and consonant sounds your student learned in previous lessons. Invite your student to sing with you. Then ask him or her to tell you the first letter of one of the animal names in the song.

2   **INTRODUCE** Tell your student that it's fun to play with the sounds we hear in letters and words. Then engage him or her in this knock-knock joke to introduce the /j/ sound:

> *Knock-knock.*
> *Who's there?*
> *Jo.*
> *Jo who?*
> *Jon't you wanna learn the /j/ sound today?*

A BRIGHT IDEA

If you have a cassette recorder, you might want to record your student singing. You can also record your student throughout the lesson. Using a different medium may increase your student's interest in the lesson. This may also inspire your student to listen to his or her own voice when pronouncing words.

3 **IDENTIFY** Say this sentence to your student and stress the /j/ sound of the consonant *j* in the words *just* and *joke: I just heard a silly joke.* Ask, *What sound do you hear at the beginning of* joke? [/j/] Then write the word *joke* on a sheet of paper. Point to the first letter and tell your student that the consonant *j* makes the /j/ sound in *joke.* Have your student say the word *joke* several times. Then hold your student's hand and invite him or her to jump up and down with you while you repeat the word *jump.* Ask, *Do the words* jump *and* joke *begin with the same sound?* [yes] Next, say these words one at a time: *toast, jelly, pig, jeans, jam, wiggle,* and *juice.* Ask your student to jump each time he or she hears a word that begins with the /j/ sound. Then have your student say the /j/ sound sight words *jelly, jeans, jam,* and *juice.*

4 **COMPARE** Show your student a key and have him or her name the object. Tell him or her that the word *key* begins with the letter *k.* Say the word *key* while stressing the /k/ sound. Then ask your student what sound the letter *k* makes. [/k/] Next, show your student the pictures below. Ask, *What do you see in the pictures?* [a kite, a balloon] Have your student point to the picture whose name begins with the same sound as the word *key.* [kite] Then give your student a key. Say these words and have your student repeat each one after you: *giraffe, kangaroo, king, leaf, kitchen,* and *kick.* Tell your student to "turn the key" if he or she hears a word that begins with the same sound as *key.*

5 **EXTEND** Write the word *quarter* on an index card. Set a quarter on the card. Slowly say the word *quarter* as you stretch the /kw/ sound in the initial consonant. Then invite your student to say which sound he or she hears at the beginning of the word *quarter.* [/kw/] Explain that the consonant *q* in *quarter* makes this sound. Then show your student a penny and name the coin out loud. Ask, *Do the words* penny *and* quarter *begin with the same sound?* [no] Next, write each of these words on a separate index card: *kind, queen, quilt, duck, quack,* and *tiger.* Say each word out loud as your student repeats each one. Be sure he or she blends each part of the initial *q* sound: /k/ /w/. Then have him or her put the index cards for each word with the /kw/ sound next to the quarter card.

6 **GUESS** Ask your student this riddle to introduce the consonant *v: This is a type of food that you should eat. It can look like spinach, or carrots, or even beets! What is it?* [vegetables] Say the word *vegetable* and invite your student to repeat after you. Write a *v* on a sheet of paper and tell your student that the consonant *v* makes the /v/ sound in *vegetable*. Stress the /v/ sound as you say the word *vegetable*. Then ask your student to say the word on his or her own. Listen to be sure that he or she can enunciate the /v/ sound. Next, say the following pairs of words one at a time: *vase/boat, radio/video, mail/vanilla,* and *volcano/quake*. Tell your student to hold up two fingers to make a V each time he or she hears the word in each pair that begins with the /v/ sound.

7 **DEFINE** Your student will be learning the /z/ sound of the letter *z* later in the lesson. Therefore, to avoid confusion use the word *X ray* (rather than a word such as *xylophone*) to focus on the /ĕks/ sound of the initial consonant *x*. Write *X ray* on a sheet of paper and say the word. Linger on the letter *x* and emphasize the initial /ĕks/ sound. Tell your student that an X ray is a picture that shows what's inside a person's body. Then invite your student to repeat the word *X ray* after you. Be sure your student enunciates the first /ĕ/ sound in /ĕks/.

8 **WRITE** Use pictures and sight words to help your student put together sentences with the word *X ray*. For example, use the sentence fragment *I can see the X ray of a . . .* Then end the sentence with a picture of a part of the body. Write one of these "picture sentences" for your student. Invite your student to copy the words and to add his or her own picture. Be sure to put periods at the end of the sentences. Then have your student read the sentences out loud.

I can see
the X ray of a

9 **REINFORCE** Put together more picture sentences to review high-frequency sight words. Use some new words, such as *my, with,* and *have*. Include any other words your student has learned, such as *to, the, a, is, I, see, go, has, can, do, for, am, it,* and *some*. Write a few sentences with pictures on a sheet of paper. Then have your student read each sentence with you. Challenge your student to use familiar sight words to come up with some sentences of his or her own. Be sure to praise your student's efforts to reinforce his or her interest in reading and writing.

Recognizing the Initial Consonants *j, k, q, v, x, y,* and *z* **29**

10 RECITE Slowly read out loud the rhyme below. Stress the initial /y/ sounds.

> *Yellow corn, green beans, and red beets, too.*
> *Orange yams and carrots and squash for stew.*
> *In the yard they grow and look so yummy,*
> *And Kelly says "Yum!" when they go to her tummy.*

Have your student say these words after you and tell which sound they start with: *yellow, yams, yard, yummy,* and *yuck.* [/y/] Stand up and hold up your hands in a V shape to form a *y.* Tell your student that the consonant *y* makes the /y/ sound. Then say these words out loud: *yawn, lamp, yes,* and *ham.* Ask your student to say *Yay!* when he or she hears the initial /y/ sound.

11 IDENTIFY Ask this riddle: *It has four legs, white stripes, and black stripes, too. You might see it when you go to the zoo! What is it?* [zebra] Slowly say *zebra* out loud. Then guide your student's hand and make the shape of a large *z* letter in the air. Tell your student that the letter *z* makes the /z/ sound in the word *zebra.* Next, say each of these words while stretching the initial /z/ sound: *zebra, zoo, zipper, zero,* and *zucchini.* Have your student repeat each word. Listen carefully to be sure he or she pronounces the *z* with a /z/ sound rather than an /s/ sound.

12 PRACTICE Distribute Student Learning Page 5.A to your student. Read the directions out loud. Have your student say the name of the picture. Then ask him or her to circle the letter the picture name starts with.

13 CONCLUDE To end the lesson, give Student Learning Page 5.B to your student. Read each activity out loud. Then invite your student to do an activity of his or her choosing.

Branching Out

FOR FURTHER READING

Reading Success Mini-Books: Sight Words, by Mary Beth Spann (Scholastic Trade, 1999).

Vowels and Consonants: 1st Grade (*Jumpstart*), by Audrey Carangelo and Duendes Del Sur, ill. (Cartwheel Books, 2001).

TEACHING TIP

This lesson may take one or more hours to complete, and it requires your student to process a lot of new sounds. You may want to break up the lesson into three parts that each consist of four to five steps. You could even intersperse a meal or an outdoor excursion between parts of the lesson.

CHECKING IN

To assess your student's understanding of the lesson, sound out each of the initial consonants covered in this lesson—*j, k, q, v, w, x, y,* and *z.* Then have your student complete the sound with a word. For example, /k/ /k/ /k/ . . . *king.* Ask your student to name the consonant the word begins with.

Circle the Letter

PROMOTING LITERACY

5.A

Name each picture. Circle the first letter in the name.

X   s

y   j

h   k

z   c

What's Next? You Decide!

Teacher: *Read aloud the directions and activities. Then have your student choose which activity to do next.*

Now it's your turn to choose what to do next in the lesson. Read the activities and decide which one you want to do—you may want to try them both!

Make Sticky Sentences

⚠ MATERIALS

- ❑ 2 index cards
- ❑ markers or crayons
- ❑ 3–8 large sticky notes
- ❑ tape

⚠ STEPS

- ❑ Draw two pictures of things you like on two index cards. Draw one picture on each index card.
- ❑ Write words you can read on sticky notes. Write one word on each sticky note.
- ❑ Ask an adult to help you write the words.
- ❑ Tape both pictures to the wall.
- ❑ Put some sticky notes around each picture to make a sentence.
- ❑ How many sentences can you make?

Name Body Parts

⚠ MATERIALS

- ❑ 1 large sheet paper
- ❑ 1 marker

⚠ STEPS

- ❑ Lie down on a large sheet of paper.
- ❑ Ask an adult to outline your body.
- ❑ Name some parts of your body.
- ❑ Write the names on the outline.
- ❑ Ask the adult to help you spell the words.
- ❑ Draw hair and a face on the body. Make it look like you!
- ❑ Read the names of the body parts out loud.
- ❑ What sounds do you hear at the beginning of the words?

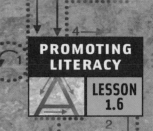

Identifying Middle Sounds

Help your student find the happy medium in the sounds of words.

OBJECTIVE	BACKGROUND	MATERIALS
To teach your student to identify the middle sounds of words and the letters that make those sounds	As your student practices blending the sounds that make up a word, he or she will learn to recognize the distinct sound of each letter in the word. In this lesson, your student will learn to identify the middle sounds of words. He or she will also learn to associate letters with those sounds.	■ Student Learning Pages 6.A–6.B ■ 6 index cards ■ 3 paper cups

Let's Begin

1 **REVIEW** Begin the lesson by briefly reviewing initial consonant sounds. Say the word *cat*. Ask your student which sound he or she hears in the beginning of the word. [/k/] Next, write each letter in the word *cat* on a separate index card. Arrange the three index cards on a flat surface to form the word *cat*. Ask, *Which letter in* cat *makes the /k/ sound?* [c] Then ask your student to point to the index card that shows the letter *c*.

2 **BLEND** Say the word *cat* again while stretching each sound into the next: /k/ /k/ /k/ /ă/ /ă/ /ă/ /t/ /t/ /t/. Invite your student to repeat the sound in each letter after you. Then ask, *Which sound do you hear after the /k/ sound?* [/ă/] Tell your student that the /ă/ sound in *cat* is the middle sound of the word. Then make the final /t/ sound in *cat* and tell your student that the letter *t* makes the last sound of the word. Finally, ask, *Which letter makes the middle /ă/ sound in* cat? [a] Have your student point to the index card that shows the letter *a*.

3 **SEQUENCE** Explain that the middle sound of a word comes after the first sound and before the last sound. Draw a sequence chart like the one on the next page on a sheet of paper. Point to the first box and make the /d/ sound. Invite your student to follow the arrow to find the next sound. Ask, *What is the middle letter in the word* dot? [o] Ask, *What sound does the middle letter make?* [/ŏ/] Next, point to the last box and make the /t/ sound. Finally, invite your student to say the word *dot* on his or her own.

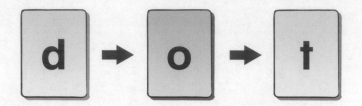

4 **COMPARE** Review the words your student has pronounced in this lesson: *cat* and *dot*. Hold each middle sound as you slowly say each word: /c/ /ă/ /ă/ /ă/ /t/, *cat*, and /d/ /ŏ/ /ŏ/ /ŏ/ /t/, *dot*. Then ask, *Do the words* cat *and* dot *have the same middle sounds?* [no] Next, say the word *hat* as you stress the middle /ă/ sound. Say, *Listen for the middle sound of the word* hat. *Now, tell me which word has the same middle sound as* hat—cat *or* dot? [*cat*]

5 **EXTEND** Introduce some common sight words with different middle sounds, such as *cup, pat, big,* and *hot.* Write each letter in the word *cup* on a separate index card. Arrange the cards in order to form the word *cup.* Then say the word while holding the middle /ŭ/ sound. Ask your student which sound he or she hears in the middle of the word *cup.* [/ŭ/] Then direct his or her attention to the index cards. Ask your student to point to the letter that makes the /ŭ/ sound. [*u*] Repeat the exercise with other middle sounds, such as the /ĕ/ sound in the word *red* and the /ĭ/ sound in the word *pig.* Remember to blend phonics concepts with sight words to help your student get prepared for reading.

6 **PRACTICE** Distribute Student Learning Page 6.A. Explain the directions to your student. To end the lesson, read the activities on Student Learning Page 6.B to your student. Then have your student complete an activity of his or her choice.

ENRICH THE EXPERIENCE

Use objects to help your student make a spatial connection to the sequence of letters and sounds in words. For example, use three paper cups to help your student sound out *cup.* Write each letter in the word on its own cup and arrange the cups in order. Point out that the letter on the middle cup shows the middle sound.

FOR FURTHER READING

Phonemic Awareness Activities for Early Reading Success, by Wiley Blevins (Scholastic Trade, 1999).

Phonics Learning Games Kids Can't Resist (*Grades K–2*), by Michelle Ramsey (Scholastic Professional Book Division, 2000).

Branching Out

TEACHING TIP

You can use words with long vowel sounds to help your student identify middle sounds. However, don't write these words down on paper; just say them out loud. Many words with a middle long vowel sound end in a silent *e,* such as *kite,* or have diphthongs, such as *boat.* Your student may become confused if he or she can't attach a distinct middle letter to a middle sound.

CHECKING IN

To assess your student's understanding of the lesson, say two words at a time and have your student tell whether or not the words have the same middle sound.

Match the Pictures

Name each picture. Match the names
with the same middle sound.

What's Next? You Decide!

Teacher: Read aloud the directions and activities. Then have your student choose which activity to do next.

Now it's your turn to choose what to do next in the lesson. Read the activities and decide which one you want to do—you may want to try them both!

Enjoy the Middle Sound

◤ MATERIALS

- ❏ 5 empty glass jars
- ❏ 5 each: peanuts, small pretzels, sunflower seeds, raisins, and small marshmallows
- ❏ 5 index cards
- ❏ markers or crayons
- ❏ tape

◤ STEPS

- ❏ Put each set of treats in each jar. For example, put all five peanuts in one jar, all seeds in one jar, and so on.
- ❏ On each index card, write a vowel: *a, e, i, o,* and *u.*
- ❏ Tape one card to each jar. These are your middle sounds.
- ❏ Have an adult say words with middle sounds for each vowel.
- ❏ Tell the adult what middle sound you hear.
- ❏ If you are correct, eat one treat from the jar with that letter.
- ❏ Keep playing until all the treats are gone.
- ❏ When you're ready to play again, refill the jars with other treats.

Make a Middle Sound Bug

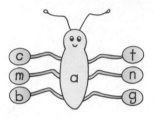

◤ MATERIALS

- ❏ 1 sheet construction paper
- ❏ markers or crayons

◤ STEPS

- ❏ Draw a big bug on a sheet of construction paper.
- ❏ Write one letter on the body. Use *a, e, i, o,* or *u.*
- ❏ Draw three legs on each side of the body.
- ❏ Make words on the bug.
- ❏ The letter on the body is the middle letter.
- ❏ Make three words.
- ❏ Write the first letter of each word at the end of a left leg.
- ❏ Write the last letter of each word at the end of a right leg.

PROMOTING LITERACY

LESSON 1.7

Recognizing Ending Sounds

The final sound in a word is the last but not least sound.

OBJECTIVE	BACKGROUND	MATERIALS
To teach your student to identify the ending sounds of words and the letters that make those sounds	Your student is learning that the sounds of a word are pronounced in the order of the letters from left to right. In this lesson, your student will learn to identify the ending sounds of words. He or she will also learn to associate letters with those sounds.	■ Student Learning Pages 7.A–7.B ■ 3 index cards ■ 1 copy T Chart, page 355

Let's Begin

1 **REVIEW** Begin the lesson by reviewing initial and middle letter sounds. Say the word *pig* to your student while emphasizing the initial consonant sound. Ask your student which sound he or she hears at the beginning of the word. [/p/] Write the letter *p* on an index card and place the card on a flat surface. Say the word *pig* again, this time stressing the middle vowel sound. Ask your student which sound he or she hears in the middle of the word. [/ĭ/] Write the letter *i* on an index card and place it to the right of the *p* card. Then ask your student to tell which letters make the first and middle sounds of the word *pig*. [*p* and *i*]

2 **CONNECT** Say the word *pig* a third time, this time holding the final sound in the word: /p/ /ĭ/ /g/ /g/ /g/. Ask your student which sound he or she hears at the end of the word *pig*. [/g/] Write the letter *g* on an index card and place it to the right of the *p* and *i* cards to form the word *pig*. Ask your student to tell which letter makes the /g/ sound in *pig*. [*g*] Then have him or her sound out each letter in the word on his or her own. Ask your student to point to each letter as he or she sounds the word out. Listen to be sure that your student correctly pronounces the ending /g/ sound.

3 **SEQUENCE** Draw a sequence chart like the one on the next page on a sheet of paper. Say the word *hen* out loud and ask your student to repeat after you. Ask him or her to point to the first and middle letters in the word *hen*. Invite your student to name the letters. Then ask, *What sounds do you hear in the beginning and middle of the word* hen? [/h/ /ĕ/] Next, tell your student that the ending sound of a word comes after the first and middle sounds. Explain that the last letter makes the ending

sound in the word *hen*. The last letter is at the right side of the word. Ask your student to point to the last letter in *hen* and name it. [*n*] Then say *hen* out loud while holding the ending /n/ sound. Ask, *What sound do you hear at the end of the word* hen? [/n/] Finally, invite your student to say *hen* on his or her own.

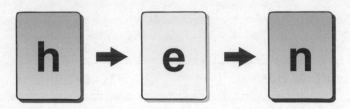

4 **IDENTIFY** Slowly say each of the following words one at a time while emphasizing the ending sound in each word: *mop, top,* and *hot*. Ask, *Do all the words have the same ending sound?* [no] If necessary, repeat the words to help your student answer the question. Ask, *Which words end with the same sound?* [*mop* and *top*] Ask, *Which word ends with a different sound?* [*hot*] Have your student tell which sound he or she hears at the end of the words *mop* and *top*. [/p/] Then have him or her identify the sound at the end of the word *hot*. [/t/]

5 **SORT** Use a copy of the T Chart found on page 355 to help your student identify additional ending sounds. Write the letter *d* as a left-column heading and the letter *m* as a right-column heading. Say the following common sight words and hold the ending sound: *jam, bed, lid, ham, red,* and *Sam*. After you say each word, ask, *Which sound do you hear at the end of the word?* Have your student tell which letter makes the ending sound. Then ask him or her to write the word in the correct column of the T Chart. Combining phonics concepts with the use of commonly used sight words can increase your student's ability to read.

6 **PRACTICE** Distribute Student Learning Page 7.A to your student. Name each picture. Tell your student to listen for the ending sound in each name. Then read aloud the activities on Student Learning Page 7.B.

ENRICH THE EXPERIENCE

Having your student listen to rhymes and poems is a great way to reinforce his or her understanding of ending sounds. You might want to check out a video or audio recording of nursery rhymes from the library.

Branching Out

TEACHING TIP

Model good reading habits by leaving some of your student's favorite books around the house. Regularly read in front of your student, and encourage him or her to look through the books at his or her leisure.

CHECKING IN

Say some words that your student knows. Be sure that the words end in consonants. Hold the final consonant sound. Then ask your student to name the letter the word ends with.

FOR FURTHER READING

The Great Big Book of Fun Phonics Activities, by Claire Daniel, Deborah Eaton, and Carole Osterink (Scholastic, 1999).

Rumpus of Rhymes: A Book of Noisy Poems, by Bobbi Katz (Dutton Books, 2001).

Make a Word

Write the last letter of each word.

s u _____

f o _____

w e _____

d o _____

What's Next? You Decide!

Teacher: *Read aloud the directions and activities. Then have your student choose which activity to do next.*

Now it's your turn to choose what to do next in the lesson. Read the activities and decide which one you want to do—you may want to try them both!

Put Words Together

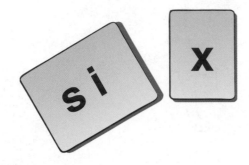

MATERIALS

- ❏ 6 index cards
- ❏ 1 pair scissors

STEPS

- ❏ Write a different word on each of the index cards.
- ❏ Use these words: *six, jam, bed, hop, big,* and *pad.*
- ❏ Say each word out loud.
- ❏ Cut each index card into two pieces. Ask an adult to help you.
- ❏ Cut between the first two letters and the last letter.
- ❏ Mix up the 12 pieces.
- ❏ Have a friend help you put the words back together.
- ❏ See what other words you can make with these letters.

Match Ending Sounds

MATERIALS

- ❏ old magazines
- ❏ 1 pair scissors
- ❏ glue
- ❏ several sheets construction paper
- ❏ markers or crayons

STEPS

- ❏ Look through old magazines.
- ❏ Cut out pictures of different things.
- ❏ Ask an adult to help you.
- ❏ Glue the pictures to sheets of construction paper.
- ❏ Write the name of each thing on a different sheet of construction paper.
- ❏ Mix up the pictures.
- ❏ Then mix up the names.
- ❏ Say the name of each picture out loud.
- ❏ Match each name with its picture.

Beginning to Write

You can't read and write without direction.

PROMOTING LITERACY

LESSON 1.8

OBJECTIVE	BACKGROUND	MATERIALS
To have your student write familiar words and to recognize the left-to-right and top-to-bottom directions of print	Your student has practiced making letter sounds in the order in which they appear within a word. In this lesson, your student will learn to read and write words from left to right and from top to bottom. He or she will also practice writing his or her own name as well as some common words.	■ Student Learning Pages 8.A–8.D ■ 1 favorite picture book ■ 4 index cards ■ 1 posterboard (optional) ■ markers or crayons ■ 1 copy Writing Lines, page 357 (optional)

Let's Begin

1 **INTRODUCE** Write the following sentence across a sheet of paper: "I am [your student's name]." Place the sheet of paper on a flat surface. Have your student place his or her left hand near the left side of the paper and his or her right hand near the right side of the paper. As you read the sentence out loud, move your finger from your student's left hand to his or her right hand. Explain that your finger is moving in the direction we read words in—from left to right. Have your student read the sentence while moving his or her finger below each word.

2 **EXTEND** Tell your student that many things we read have more than one line of words. Show your student an example of several lines of text from a favorite picture book. (Be sure there is at least one page with more than one line of text.) Explain that we read these words from left to right and from top to bottom. Without reading, move your finger in the direction in which all the words on the page would be read, starting with the first word and ending with the last. Then read the page out loud and scan your finger across the bottom of each word you say. When you're done, ask your student to point to the very first word on the page as well as the very last word. Then have your student choose a book for you to read aloud to him or her. Make sure that each page has more than one line of words. As you read aloud, point to the words to reinforce the left-to-right, top-to-bottom direction.

3 **WRITE** Print your student's name on an index card. Then write three different names on separate index cards. Display the four index cards and ask your student to select his or her name. Have your student identify each letter in his or her name from left to right. Then distribute a copy of Student Learning Page 8.A. Invite your student to practice writing his or her name on the lines. You might show your student how to write his or her middle name or last name on the second line. Then have your student draw a picture of himself or herself in the box using markers or crayons. Keep a master copy of the Student Learning Page so you can make additional copies for further practice. You may also use a copy of the Writing Lines found on page 357.

4 **JOURNAL** Distribute Student Learning Page 8.B. Tell your student that he or she is going to write on a journal page. Explain that a journal is a notebook in which we can tell about ourselves or the things we do. Then read out loud each sentence starter. Guide your student as he or she completes each sentence out loud. Help your student write each response. You might want to have him or her write phonetic spellings. At the end of the activity, invite your student to read the page with you. Praise him or her for having written from left to right and from top to bottom.

5 **READ** Leave some of your student's favorite books lying around for him or her to look through at his or her leisure. Even if your student isn't reading yet, this will promote reading as a fun and enjoyable activity.

6 **PRACTICE** Distribute Student Learning Page 8.C. Explain the activity to your student. Help your student sound out the letters in the words to connect them to the pictures. End the lesson by reading out loud the activities on Student Learning Page 8.D.

! A BRIGHT IDEA

Use a word processor and help your student type his or her name in different fonts, sizes, and colors. Type several lines of simple sentences in a large font. As you type, point out how the words in the sentences appear from left to right, top to bottom.

FOR FURTHER READING

Me, Myself, and I (Road to Writing: First Journals: Mile 4), by Sarah Albee and John Manders, ill. (Golden Books Publishing, 2000).

Write About It, Activities for Teaching Basic Writing Skills, Beginning Writers, by Imogene Forte, Mary C. Mahoney, ed., and Mary Hamilton , ill. (Incentive Publications, 1999).

Branching Out

TEACHING TIP

Read out loud some familiar examples of print to reinforce your student's understanding of left-to-right writing. You might want to read package labels, signs, and book titles to your student as you point to each word.

CHECKING IN

To assess your student's understanding of the lesson, together look at a page from a book. Ask your student to point to the first letter that should be read on the page and then point to the last letter that should be read.

Write Your Name

Write your name on the lines.

I can write my name!

PENDER COUNTY PUBLIC LIBRARY
BURGAW, NORTH CAROLINA

Tell About Yourself

Write on the journal page.

Journal Page

Date: _____

My name is _____ .

I am _____ years old.

I like _____ .

I can _____ .

Today I will _____ .

Write Picture Names

Write words for the pictures. Choose words from the box.

dog	boy	girl	book
cat	bike	ball	hat	cup

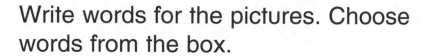

_____ _ _ _ _ _ _ _____	_____ _ _ _ _ _ _ _____	_____ _ _ _ _ _ _ _____
_____ _ _ _ _ _ _ _____	_____ _ _ _ _ _ _ _____	_____ _ _ _ _ _ _ _____
_____ _ _ _ _ _ _ _____	_____ _ _ _ _ _ _ _____	_____ _ _ _ _ _ _ _____

What's Next? You Decide!

Teacher: *Read aloud the directions and activities. Then have your student choose which activity to do next.*

Now it's your turn to choose what to do next in the lesson. Read the activities and decide which one you want to do—you may want to try them both!

Write a Name Poem

Likes soccer
Is nice
Silly
A good friend

MATERIALS

❏ 1 sheet construction paper

❏ markers or crayons

STEPS

Make a name poem for your name!

❏ Write the letters in your name from top to bottom.

❏ The first letter should be on top.

❏ The last letter should be on the bottom.

❏ Use your name to write other words from left to right.

❏ Begin each word with one letter in your name.

❏ Use a different color marker or crayon.

❏ Ask an adult to help you write words that describe you.

Make Stationery

MATERIALS

❏ several sheets blank paper

❏ markers or crayons

STEPS

You can write a letter on stationery. Make your own stationery!

❏ Write your name at the top of a sheet of blank paper.

❏ Use bright colors.

❏ Make the letters look fun.

❏ Ask an adult to help you write your address by your name.

❏ Draw pictures at the bottom and sides of the paper.

❏ Repeat the steps to make more stationery.

❏ Write a letter to a friend.

❏ Use your stationery!

❏ Ask an adult to help you address an envelope and mail the letter.

Introducing the Short *a*

Vowels are like bridges that help us move from consonant to consonant.

OBJECTIVE	BACKGROUND	MATERIALS
To help your student recognize and pronounce the short /ă/ sound	Your student has explored various vowel sounds in the middle of words. He or she is now ready to identify the sound a particular vowel can make and attach a letter to that sound. In this lesson, your student will learn to distinguish the short /ă/ sound in words. He or she will also practice using high-frequency words.	■ Student Learning Pages 9.A–9.B ■ sticky notes ■ markers or crayons

VOCABULARY
VOWELS the letters *a, e, i, o,* and *u*
CONSONANTS the letters in the alphabet that aren't vowels

Let's Begin

1 **REVIEW** Remind your student that all letters in the alphabet are either **vowels** or **consonants.** Tell your student that the letters *a, e, i, o, u,* and sometimes *y* are vowels. Every other letter is a consonant. Next, say the word *bat* out loud. Ask your student which sound he or she hears in the middle of the word. [/ă/]

2 **CONNECT** Write the word *bat* on a sheet of paper. Ask your student to tell which letter makes the short /ă/ sound in the word. [*a*] Confirm that the vowel *a* can stand for the short /ă/ sound in words. Explain to your student that this sound is called a short /ă/ sound. Have your student hum the short /ă/ sound with you.

3 **EXTEND** Say the word *at* out loud. Hold the short /ă/ sound as you say the word—/ă/ /ă/ /ă/ /t/. Ask your student which sound he or she hears at the beginning of the word. [/ă/] Then point out that the letter *a* can also make the short /ă/ sound at the beginning of a word. Say the following words out loud while emphasizing the initial letter sound: *out, ant, apple,* and *nut.* After you say each word, ask your student to raise his or her hand if it begins with the short /ă/ sound.

4 **BUILD** Pronounce the initial /h/ sound and ask your student which letter makes the sound. [*h*] Write the letter *h* on a sticky note and place the note on a sheet of paper. Repeat these steps for the letters *a* and *t.* Arrange the sticky notes to form the word *hat.* Read the word out loud. Then blend each sound in the

word and invite your student to repeat after you: *hhhăăăttt.* Ask, *Where do you hear the short /ă/ sound, in the beginning, middle, or end of the word?* [middle]

5 **SHOW** Draw a web like the one below on a sheet of paper. Help your student pronounce each word. Add as many outer circles as needed as your student calls out short *a* words. Say the words aloud when finished.

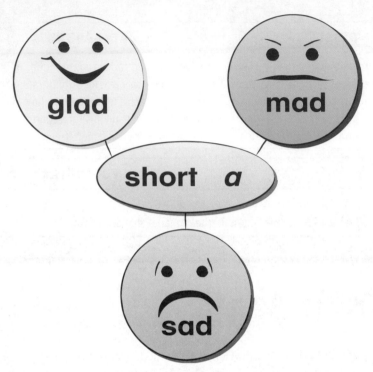

glad

mad

short *a*

sad

6 **WRITE** Help your student use familiar sight words and short *a* words to read and write sentences. Introduce the pronouns *he* and *she*. Write some sentences on a sheet of paper and read them with your student. You can use the following examples:

She is glad.   *He sat on a mat.*   *She can see the cat.*

7 **PRACTICE** Distribute Student Learning Page 9.A. Read the directions out loud for your student. To end the lesson, read the activities on Student Learning Page 9.B.

Branching Out

TEACHING TIP

Play a game called What's That? when you are out with your student. Point to things whose names have a short /ă/ sound and ask, *What's that?*

CHECKING IN

Read a list of words that have the short /ă/ vowel sound. Be sure to include some words that don't have this sound. Have your student clap his or her hands when he or she hears a short *a* word.

Color the Short *a* Word

Name the pictures. Color the picture if its name has a short *a* sound.

Student Learning Page 9.A: Color the Short *a* Word **49**

What's Next? You Decide!

Teacher: *Read aloud the directions and activities. Then have your student choose which activity to do next.*

Now it's your turn to choose what to do next in the lesson. Read the activities and decide which one you want to do—you may want to try them both!

Make a Picture Puzzle

MATERIALS

❏ 1 sheet construction paper

❏ markers or crayons

❏ 1 pair scissors

STEPS

Make a short *a* picture puzzle.

❏ Think of words that have a short *a* sound.

❏ Draw a picture to show one of the words on a sheet of construction paper.

❏ Use scissors to cut your picture into different pieces.

❏ Now you have pieces of a puzzle.

❏ Put your short *a* puzzle back together.

❏ Have a friend try it!

Guess the Short *a* Word

MATERIALS

❏ 1 hat

❏ 10 index cards

STEPS

❏ Think of words that have a short *a* sound.

❏ Write each word on a different index card.

❏ Ask an adult to help you.

❏ Place all the cards into a hat.

❏ Mix up the cards.

❏ Play a game with a partner.

❏ Choose one of the words from the hat. Don't say the word!

❏ Give clues to your partner about the word. For example, if you choose the word *fan* you can say, "It goes around and around. It helps you stay cool."

❏ Ask your partner to guess the word.

❏ Now let your partner choose a word. Ask him or her to give you clues.

❏ See if you can guess the word.

Identifying the Short *e*

Get set and encourage your student's effort when teaching the short /ĕ/ sound!

OBJECTIVE	BACKGROUND	MATERIALS
To help your student recognize and pronounce the short /ĕ/ sound	Every word in the English language has at least one vowel with a unique sound. Vowel sounds are distinguished from consonant sounds by the fact that they are more sonorous and open. In this lesson, your student will learn to recognize the short /ĕ/ sound in words. He or she will also practice using high-frequency words.	■ Student Learning Pages 10.A–10.B ■ 20 index cards ■ markers or crayons

Let's Begin

1 **REVIEW** Remind your student that *a, e, i, o, u,* and sometimes *y* are letters called vowels. Then tell your student that in this lesson he or she is going to learn about the sound of the vowel *e.* Write the number 10 on a sheet of paper. Ask your student to tell which number he or she sees. Then sound out each letter in the word *ten* while you hold the short /ĕ/ sound: /t/ /ĕ/ /n/. Ask, *Which sound do you hear in the middle of the word* ten? [/ĕ/]

2 **INTRODUCE** Hold up a pen and ask your student to name the object. Invite him or her to repeat after you as you sound out each letter in the word *pen.* Ask, *Are the sounds in the middle of the words* ten *and* pen *the same?* [yes] Write the words *ten* and *pen* on a sheet of paper. Ask, *Which letter makes the middle sound in both words?* [e] Then point out to your student that the vowel *e* can stand for the short /ĕ/ sound in words.

3 **EXPAND** Bend your arm and point to your elbow. Ask your student to say which part of your body you're pointing to. Then say the word *elbow* out loud while stretching the initial short /ĕ/ sound: /ĕ/ /ĕ/ /ĕ/ /l/ /b/ /ō/. Ask, *Which sound do you hear at the beginning of the word* elbow? [/ĕ/] Point out that the letter *e* can also make the short /ĕ/ sound at the beginning of a word. Have your student pronounce some words that begin with the short /ĕ/ sound. Say each word and invite your student to repeat it after you: *egg, enter,* and *elephant.* Next, say *end, wet, red,* and *empty.* After you say each word, ask your student to tell whether the short /ĕ/ sound is at the beginning or in the middle of the word.

4 **RHYME** Help your student come up with some rhyming words that have the short /ĕ/ sound. Begin by reading the following rhyme out loud:

> *Ten red hens went to see the vet,*
> *with aches and shakes, and dripping wet.*

Ask your student to name any rhyming words he or she heard. [*aches/shakes; vet/wet*] Then focus on the words *wet* and *vet*. Help your student come up with words that rhyme with *wet* and *vet*. Then help your student brainstorm some rhyming words for *ten* and *red*. Draw a chart like the one below on a sheet of paper. Review the pronunciation of each word with your student.

wet	ten	red
vet	Ben	bed
get	den	fed
let		

5 **PRACTICE** Distribute Student Learning Page 10.A. Help your student read the directions by reading any words he or she doesn't know. Then read out loud Student Learning Page 10.B.

Branching Out

TEACHING TIP

Help your student use sight words and short *e* words to write simple sentences. Write different high-frequency words your student knows on separate index cards. Then write individual short *e* words on index cards. Work with your student to put together the index cards to make different sentences.

CHECKING IN

Ask your student to say two words that have the short /ĕ/ sound. Then ask your student if the short /ĕ/ sound of each word comes at the beginning or in the middle of each word.

A BRIGHT IDEA

Challenge your student to make a simple rhyme. Point out two short *e* words that rhyme. Then help your student come up with two related sentences that each end with one of the rhyming words. Allow your student to express his or her creativity as he or she makes a rhyme.

FOR FURTHER READING

Ben's Pens: The Sound of Short E, by Alice K. Flanagan (Child's World, 1999).

Every Egg: Learning the Short E Sound, by Lynn Metz (PowerKids Press, 2002).

Short Vowel Word Machines, by Jo Ellen Moore, Marilyn Evans, ed., and Jo Larsen, ill. (Evan-Moor Educational Publishers, 2000).

Help the Hen Cross the Road

PROMOTING
LITERACY

10.A

Make a road for the hen. Color each box with a short *e* word.

pet	bed	cat
bug	men	sat
box	ten	hen

What's Next? You Decide!

Teacher: Read aloud the directions and activities. Then have your student choose which activity to do next.

Now it's your turn to choose what to do next in the lesson. Read the activities and decide which one you want to do—you may want to try them both!

Ride the Short *e* Elephant

MATERIALS

❑ 1 chair

❑ 1 sheet

STEPS

❑ Place the sheet over the chair.

❑ Sit in the chair.

❑ Suppose you are riding an elephant. His name is Enzo.

❑ The elephant lives in the land of short *e* words. Everything has a name with a short /ĕ/ sound.

❑ What do you see as you ride Enzo?

❑ Say the names of the things you see!

Make Short *e* Eggs

MATERIALS

❑ 12 hard-boiled eggs

❑ food coloring

❑ markers

❑ 1 egg carton

❑ tempera paints

STEPS

❑ Ask an adult to boil the eggs.

❑ Then have an adult show you how to use the food coloring.

❑ Color the eggs with food coloring.

❑ Use the markers to write a word that has a short *e* on each egg.

❑ You can draw a picture of the word, too!

❑ Paint the outside of the egg carton.

❑ Make it look fun!

❑ Keep your short *e* eggs in the egg carton until used in a recipe, such as for deviled eggs.

Understanding the Short *i*

Sit for a bit and take a short i *trip!*

OBJECTIVE	BACKGROUND	MATERIALS
To help your student recognize and pronounce the short /ĭ/ sound	Like other short-vowel sounds, the short /ĭ/ sound often appears at the beginning of words as well as in the middle of words that follow the consonant-vowel-consonant pattern. In this lesson, your student will learn to recognize the short /ĭ/ sound in words. He or she will also practice using high-frequency words.	■ Student Learning Pages 11.A–11.B ■ 1 map ■ 9 index cards ■ markers or crayons

Let's Begin

1 **REVIEW** Begin the lesson by reviewing the sounds of the short vowels *a* and *e*. Write the following sentence on a sheet of paper: "An elephant is big." Read the sentence out loud as you point to each word. Ask your student which sound he or she hears at the beginning of the word *an*. [/ă/] Have your student name the letter that makes the sound. [*a*] Repeat this exercise for the initial short /ĕ/ sound in the word *elephant*.

2 **INTRODUCE** Continue to focus on the sentence from Step 1. Point to the word *is* and stretch the initial short /ĭ/ sound as you say the word: /ĭ/ /ĭ/ /ĭ/ /s/, *is*. Ask, *Which sound do you hear at the beginning of the word* is? /ĭ/ Then have your student name the first letter of the word. [*i*] After your student responds, point out that the vowel *i* can stand for the short /ĭ/ sound in words. Next, point to the word *big* and hold the short /ĭ/ sound as you say the word: /b/ /ĭ/ /ĭ/ /ĭ/ /g/, *big*. Have your student repeat the word after you. Then ask, *Where do you hear the short /ĭ/ sound in the word* big, *at the beginning, middle, or end of the word?* [middle] After you correct or confirm your student's response, point out that the vowel *i* can stand for the short /ĭ/ sound at the beginning or in the middle of words.

3 **DISTINGUISH** Lightly scratch your chin as you say the word *itch*. Ask your student to repeat the word after you. Have him or her identify the sound at the beginning of the word. [/ĭ/] Then say these words one at a time: *dot, it, inch, from, igloo, can,* and *in*. Tell your student to scratch his or her chin if a word begins with the same sound as *itch*. Next, say another series of words: *pig, sat, in, with, ten,* and *six*. Ask your student to scratch his or

GET ORGANIZED

As your student learns vowel sounds, you might want to organize a short-vowel bulletin board. Arrange columns with the headings "Short *a*," "Short *e*," and so on. As your student learns new words, list some of them in the appropriate columns. Cut out pictures from old magazines or ask your student to draw pictures that show some of the words.

her chin if a word has the short /ĭ/ sound anywhere in the word. Be sure to emphasize the vowel sounds in each word to help your student distinguish the short *i* words from the others.

4   **RHYME** Use word pies like the ones below to brainstorm short *i* rhyming words. Start out by listing one word in each quadrant. Go through different consonants to come up with words that rhyme with each word listed. Ask your student if he or she can think of any rhyming words on his or her own. Then invite your student to pronounce each word that you wrote down.

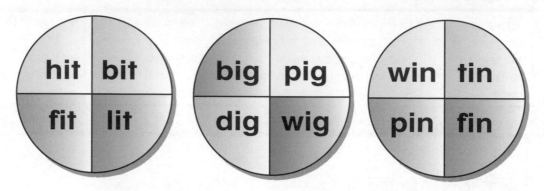

| hit | bit |
| fit | lit |

| big | pig |
| dig | wig |

| win | tin |
| pin | fin |

5   **WRITE** Help your student build sentences with sight words and short *i* words. Add the words *you, they, in,* and *are* to the list of high-frequency words your student has learned so far. Write the following sentences on a sheet of paper and read them with your student. Add any other sentences that you and your student can think of.

The pin is in the tin.   *A pig has a wig.*   *They have six wins.*

6   **PRACTICE** Distribute Student Learning Page 11.A. Explain the directions to your student. If necessary, guide him or her through one of the items on the page. Next, read Student Learning Page 11.B to your student.

FOR FURTHER READING

Little Bit: The Sound of Short I, by Peg Ballard and Cynthia Fitterer Klingel (Child's World, Inc., 1999).

Little Pigs, Big Pigs: Learning the Short I Sound, by Shelby Braidich (PowerKids Press, 2002).

Short I and Long I Play a Game, by Jane Belk Moncure (Child's World, 2001).

Branching Out

TEACHING TIP

You can use a map to help your student connect short *i* words to the world around him or her. Point to different regions or bodies of water and pronounce any names that have the short *i*. Invite your student to say the words after you.

CHECKING IN

Write a different word on nine separate index cards. Include words that have the short /ĭ/ sound and words that don't. Arrange the cards in three rows with three cards in each row. Then have your student turn over the cards that don't have the short /ĭ/ sound.

Match the Word

Draw a line from the picture to the word that names it. Then color each picture.

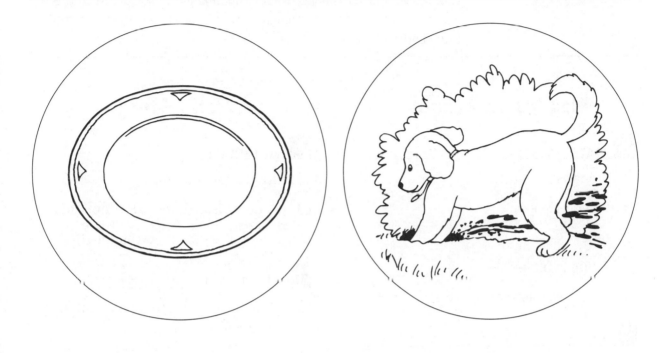

dig	fish	dish	win

Student Learning Page 11.A: Match the Word **57**

What's Next? You Decide!

Teacher: Read aloud the directions and activities. Then have your student choose which activity to do next.

Now it's your turn to choose what to do next in the lesson. Read the activities and decide which one you want to do—you may want to try them both!

Play Musical Chairs

MATERIALS

❑ 3 chairs

❑ 3 sheets paper

❑ tape

❑ 1 music player

❑ 1–2 audiocassettes or CDs

STEPS

❑ Put three chairs together in a row.

❑ Write a different consonant on each sheet of paper.

❑ Tape each sheet to a chair.

❑ Invite two people to walk around the chairs in a circle.

❑ Ask an adult to play music at the same time.

❑ Have the adult stop the music after a few seconds.

❑ Each player should sit in the chair closest to him or her when the music stops.

❑ Then have each player name a short *i* word that begins with the letter on the chair.

❑ Play again!

Tell a Story

MATERIALS

❑ clothes for costumes

❑ 1 audiocassette recorder (optional)

❑ 1 audiocassette tape (optional)

STEPS

❑ Think of a name of a person that has a short *i*.

❑ Suppose you're a person in a story. You have this name.

❑ Dress up to look like this person.

❑ Ask an adult to help you find a costume.

❑ Act like the person. Tell a story.

❑ Try to use words that have a short *i* in your story.

❑ Use the recorder to record the story if you want to.

❑ Ask an adult to help you.

❑ Tell your story to family and friends!

PROMOTING LITERACY

LESSON 1.12

Discovering the Short *o*

You can use the short /ŏ/ sound to say things such as "Phonics rock!"

OBJECTIVE	BACKGROUND	MATERIALS
To help your student recognize and pronounce the short /ŏ/ sound	At this point, your student may be learning that many short-vowel sounds follow a predictable pattern in words. In this lesson, your student will learn to recognize the short /ŏ/ sound in words. He or she will also practice using high-frequency words.	▪ Student Learning Pages 12.A–12.B ▪ 1 shoebox or other small box with lid ▪ several sheets construction paper ▪ 1 pair scissors ▪ glue ▪ markers or crayons ▪ 12 index cards ▪ 1 old sock ▪ beads, buttons, yarn, and so on for decoration ▪ glitter

Let's Begin

1 **INTRODUCE** Begin the lesson by showing your student a shoebox or another small box. Ask him or her to name the object. Then focus on the word *box*. Sound out each letter in the word as you hold the short /ŏ/ sound: /b/ /ŏ/ /ŏ/ /ŏ/ /ks/, *box*. Ask your student which sound he or she hears in the middle of the word *box*. [/ŏ/] Provide extra guidance to help your student distinguish the short /ŏ/ sound from the /ks/ sound of the final consonant *x*. Then write the word *box* on a sheet of paper. Point out the middle vowel *o*. Tell your student that the vowel *o* makes the short /ŏ/ sound in the word *box*.

2 **CREATE** Invite your student to make a short *o* box. Cover the box from Step 1 with construction paper. Help your student cut construction paper to fit the sides and lid of the box. Then help him or her glue the paper to the box. Next, use a marker or crayon to write the word *dot* on the box. Say the word *dot* out loud, stressing the short /ŏ/ sound. Invite your student to repeat the word after you. Listen to be sure he or she can enunciate the short /ŏ/ sound.

3 **EXPAND** Tell your student that the word *hop* has the short /ŏ/ sound. Then say the following words one at a time: *ox, net, pot, fit, mop, on, wax, job, fox,* and *bill*. Have your student hop each time he or she hears a word with the short /ŏ/ sound. Then ask him or her to write the short *o* word on the outside of the box.

Assist your student as necessary. You may also invite your student to draw pictures on the box of things with short *o* names.

4   **SORT**   Write each of the following words on separate index cards: *dot, hot, not, pot, spot, hop, mop, top, drop,* and *stop.* Put the cards in the box and mix them up. Then write the following two words on separate index cards and place them on a flat surface: *lot* and *pop.* Have your student go through the index cards in the box and place each one on top of the word it rhymes with. When your student has finished, ask him or her to pronounce each of the words on the index cards.

5   **WRITE**   Put the index cards back in the box. Ask your student to choose a few cards. Then direct him or her to use the words in sentences. Have your student say the sentence out loud first. Then see if he or she can write the sentence. Your student can write the other words in the sentence on individual index cards as well. He or she can also use pictures or phonetic spellings for more difficult words. Encourage your student to come up with new sentences, or help him or her rearrange words to make new sentences.

6   **PRACTICE**   Distribute Student Learning Page 12.A. Have your student point to each picture and name what's shown. Tell him or her to draw a square around the picture if what it shows has a name with a short /ŏ/ sound. Then read out loud the activities on Student Learning Page 12.B. Invite your student to do an activity of his or her choice.

Branching Out

TEACHING TIP

If your student is a tactile learner, use glitter to help him or her make the letter *o*. Draw the outline of an *o* on a sheet of construction paper and fill the outline with glue. Then cover all the glue with glitter. When the glue has dried, have your student trace the letter with his or her finger. He or she may also want to use the letter as a visual aid when learning the short *o* words in the lesson.

CHECKING IN

To assess your student's understanding of the letter, say each of these words out loud: *rap, ant,* and *fat.* After you say each word, ask, *What is the vowel in the word? Does the vowel make the first sound or the middle sound in the word? How do you spell the word?*

Take a Picture

Name the pictures. Draw a box around each picture that shows something with a short *o* name.

What's Next? You Decide!

Teacher: *Read aloud the directions and activities. Then have your student choose which activity to do next.*

Now it's your turn to choose what to do next in the lesson. Read the activities and decide which one you want to do—you may want to try them both!

Make a Clay Figure

▲ MATERIALS

- ❏ 1 package modeling clay
- ❏ 1 toothpick
- ❏ 1 index card
- ❏ 1 marker

▲ STEPS

- ❏ Think of things with short *o* names.
- ❏ Ask an adult to help you.
- ❏ Use modeling clay to make a figure of one of the things.
- ❏ Use a toothpick to carve the letter *o* onto the clay figure.
- ❏ Fold an index card in half.
- ❏ Write the name of your figure on the card.
- ❏ Put the card by your figure.
- ❏ Show your short *o* figure to your family and friends!

Play a Card Game

▲ MATERIALS

- ❏ 21 index cards

▲ STEPS

- ❏ Write each consonant on a separate index card.
- ❏ Ask an adult to help you.
- ❏ Mix up the index cards.
- ❏ Play a card game with one or two friends.
- ❏ Put the index cards facedown. Each player takes one card.
- ❏ Each player should name a word that begins with the letter on the card. The word should have a short *o* vowel sound.
- ❏ The player keeps the card if the word is correct.
- ❏ The player puts the card back if the word isn't correct.
- ❏ Play until all the cards are gone.
- ❏ The player with the most cards wins!

Recognizing the Short *u*

If you come up short on the short /ŭ/ sound, guessing just doesn't cut it.

OBJECTIVE	BACKGROUND	MATERIALS
To help your student recognize and pronounce the short /ŭ/ sound	Your student has been introduced to the first four short-vowel sounds of the alphabet. Understanding the various sounds that vowels make enables budding readers to decode new words. In this lesson, your student will learn to recognize the short /ŭ/ sound in words. He or she will also practice using high-frequency words.	<ul><li>Student Learning Pages 13.A–13.B</li><li>construction paper</li><li>markers or crayons</li><li>12 index cards</li></ul>

Let's Begin

1 **INTRODUCE** Begin the lesson by inviting your student to draw a picture of a sun. When your student has finished, label his or her picture with the word *sun*. Then invite your student to say the word *sun* after you. Stress the middle short /ŭ/ sound as you say the word: /s/ /ŭ/ /ŭ/ /ŭ/ /n/, *sun*. Ask, *Which sound do you hear in the middle of the word* sun? [/ŭ/] Ask, *Which letter makes this sound?* [u] Confirm that the vowel *u* can stand for the short /ŭ/ sound in words. Tell your student that this vowel sound is called the short /ŭ/ sound. Then invite him or her to chant the short /ŭ/ sound after you.

2 **EXPLAIN** To introduce the initial short /ŭ/ sound, draw a picture of an umbrella for your student. Label the picture with the word *umbrella*. Then invite your student to complete this sentence as you display the picture: *When it rains outside, we use an _____.* [umbrella] Guide your student as he or she pronounces the word. Say the word as he or she listens, holding the initial short /ŭ/ sound. Then ask, *Which sound do you hear at the beginning of the word* umbrella? [/ŭ/] Point to the label and ask, *Which letter makes the short /ŭ/ sound at the beginning of the word* umbrella? [u]

3 **DISTINGUISH** Write each of these short *u* words on separate index cards: *fun, bug, cub, up, jump,* and *nut.* Also write six words that don't have the short /ŭ/ sound on separate index cards. Display two index cards at a time—one with a short *u* word and one without. Read each word out loud as you stress the vowel sounds. Have your student point to the word that has a short /ŭ/ sound. Ask him or her to point to the vowel in the word that makes the sound. Then blend the sound of each letter

A TIME-SAVER

You might have picture cards or homemade pictures left over from previous lessons. Sift through the pictures to find images whose names have a short /ŭ/ sound. Reuse these materials to help you expedite this lesson. If necessary, hunt through old magazines with your student to find pictures of other things that have short *u* names. You may also add pictures with names that don't have a short *u* to help your student distinguish vowel sounds.

in the short *u* words and invite your student to repeat after you: *fffŭŭŭnnn, fun,* and so on. Listen to be sure that your student can clearly pronounce the short /ŭ/ sound.

4 **RHYME** Draw a three-column chart like the one below on a sheet of paper. Point out that the words in each column rhyme with the words in each heading. Help your student brainstorm more words that rhyme with each heading. Then assist your student as he or she writes each word in the correct column.

fun	bug	bump
bun	dug	jump

5 **WRITE** Use a fill-in-the-blank activity to help your student review high-frequency words. Include familiar sight words as well as words that have a short *u.* For example, write the following sentence on a sheet of paper: "I see _____ bug." Have your student complete the sentence with an appropriate word. Repeat this exercise using additional sentences.

6 **PRACTICE** Distribute Student Learning Page 13.A. Help your student read the words in the bubbles. Instruct him or her to color the bubbles that have a word with a short /ŭ/ sound. To end the lesson, read out loud the activities on Student Learning Page 13.B.

7 **SING AND DANCE** As your student learns more and more words, encourage him or her to pronounce and use words correctly. You can make learning words fun by checking out sing-along audiocassettes from the library.

Branching Out

TEACHING TIP

You might want to review words with other short-vowel sounds as you complete each step in the lesson for greater letter recognition.

CHECKING IN

Play a game of charades. Act out short *u* words: *jump, run,* and *hum.* Then act out words that don't have the short /ŭ/ sound. Have your student name each action and tell whether each word has the short /ŭ/ sound or another short-vowel sound.

FOR FURTHER READING

Fun! The Sound of Short U, by Peg Ballard and Cynthia Klingel (Child's World, 1999).

Just Bugs: Learning the Short U Sound, by Jeff Jones (PowerKids Press, 2002).

Words Their Way: Word Study for Phonics, Vocabulary, and Spelling Instruction, by Donald R. Bear, Francine Johnston, Shane Templeton, and Marcia Invernizzi (Pearson Education, 1999).

Blow Bubbles

Color the bubbles that have short *u* words.

What's Next? You Decide!

Teacher: Read aloud the directions and activities. Then have your student choose which activity to do next.

Now it's your turn to choose what to do next in the lesson. Read the activities and decide which one you want to do—you may want to try them both!

Spin a Word Wheel

MATERIALS

- ❑ 2 sheets construction paper
- ❑ 1 pair scissors
- ❑ 1 paper fastener

STEPS

- ❑ Cut a circle out of construction paper.
- ❑ Write the letters *ug* on the circle.
- ❑ Draw a box in front of the letters.
- ❑ Ask an adult to help you cut out the box.
- ❑ Cut a bigger circle out of construction paper.
- ❑ Put the smaller circle on top of the bigger circle.
- ❑ Ask an adult to help you put the circles together. Use a paper fastener.
- ❑ Write a letter inside the box. Make a short *u* word that ends with *ug*.
- ❑ Turn the bigger circle to make more words.

Make a Short *u* Book

MATERIALS

- ❑ 5 sheets construction paper
- ❑ markers or crayons
- ❑ 1 stapler

STEPS

- ❑ Think of four words that have a short *u*.
- ❑ Write each word on a sheet of construction paper.
- ❑ Draw a picture for each word.
- ❑ Make a cover for your book on construction paper.
- ❑ Write this title on the cover: "Short *u* Words."
- ❑ Decorate the letters to make them fun.
- ❑ Put the pages of the book together.
- ❑ Put the cover on top.
- ❑ Ask an adult to staple the pages together.
- ❑ Share your short *u* book with a friend or family member!

Exploring Rhyming Words

Use your regular story time to teach your student words that rhyme.

OBJECTIVE	BACKGROUND	MATERIALS
To help your student recognize repetition and rhyming words in a story	Teaching rhyming words is an effective way of helping an early reader memorize spelling and sound patterns. In this lesson, your student will read a story with repeated rhyming words. He or she will also learn to identify key words in text and will expand his or her vocabulary of high-frequency words.	■ Student Learning Pages 14.A–14.C ■ 3 index cards ■ markers or crayons ■ 1 copy Writing Lines, page 357

Let's Begin

1 **INTRODUCE** Distribute Student Learning Page 14.A. Tell your student that he or she will be reading a story together with you. Point to the title of the selection and read it out loud. Be sure that your student knows the meaning of each word in the title. Tell your student that a club is a group of people or animals who meet with each other, or get together. Then ask your student to guess what the story will be about.

2 **READ** Begin reading *The Bug Club*. Ask your student to read along with you. Be sure to read expressively, even exaggerating the mood or tone. Help your student with his or her reading by explaining the meaning of any words he or she doesn't know. Have your student sound out the individual letters of a word to help him or her learn to pronounce any words in the story that may be new to him or her. Be sure to also point out familiar sight words. Then explain to your student that some writers use the same words over and over to make stories more fun to read. Invite your student to point out three words that are repeated in *The Bug Club*. Write each of these words on a separate index card.

3 **IDENTIFY** Point out two words that rhyme in the story, such as *bug* and *rug*. Ask, *What do you notice about these words?* [they rhyme, or end with the same letters and sounds] Then invite your student to look through the selection with you to find more words that rhyme with *bug* and *rug*. On a sheet of paper, draw a diagram in the shape of a bug like the one on the next page. Note the rhyming words on the diagram and explain the meaning of the words listed to your student. Draw pictures or

ENRICH THE EXPERIENCE

You might want to read the selection as you and your student sit on a rug in your home. To help your student connect to the story, invite him or her to pretend that you're sitting on the rug where the bug club meets. If you don't have a suitable rug, use an old blanket and invite your student to imagine that it's an old red rug.

act out some of the words to help him or her make deeper connections to their meanings.

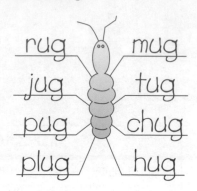

rug   mug

jug   tug

pug   chug

plug   hug

TAKE A BREAK

Encourage your student to make up a short, simple song with rhyming words.

4   **CONSTRUCT**   Ask your student to use words from the story to make new sentences. Use the index cards of repeated words from Step 2 as well as the rhyming words in the diagram from Step 3. Have your student say the sentences out loud.

5   **CONNECT**   Explain important ideas in the story about the bugs' points of view and feelings. Tell your student that the bugs are curious about, or want to know, what's in the jug. Also point out that the bugs work together to help their friend get out of the jug. Ask, *Can you think of a time when you wanted to find out about something? What did you do?*

FOR FURTHER READING

Chicka Chicka Boom Boom, by Bill Martin, John Archambault, and Lois Ehlert, ill. (Aladdin Paperbacks, 2000).

Get Ready, Get Set, Read! Teaching Short Vowels: A Phonetic Approach to Reading, by Gina Erickson, Kelli C. Foster, and Kerri Gifford, ill. (Barron's Juveniles, 1999).

Pigs, Pig, Pigs!, by Leslea Newman and Erika Oller, ill. (Simon and Schuster Children's, 2003).

Read to Me Grandma: Stories, Songs and Rhymes for You to Enjoy Together, by C. Repchuck (Barnes & Noble Books, 2002).

6   **RELATE**   Invite your student to use his or her experiences to think about the characters in *The Bug Club.* Ask your student to tell how the bugs felt as they saw Pug go down the jug. Then have your student describe how the bugs might have felt when they pulled Pug out of the jug. Encourage your student to express himself or herself in a journal. He or she can write letters or words or can draw. If your student is ready, you may wish to ask him or her simple questions about the story that can be answered in one word. Have him or her write the answer on a copy of the Writing Lines found on page 357.

7   **PRACTICE**   Distribute Student Learning Page 14.B. Help your student read the directions. To end the lesson, read out loud the activities on Student Learning Page 14.C.

Branching Out

TEACHING TIP

Scan your finger below words in the selection as you read. This will reinforce your student's understanding of the left-to-right direction of text.

CHECKING IN

To assess your student's understanding of the lesson, ask him or her to tell you the story in his or her own words.

Read a Story

The Bug Club

by Kelli C. Foster and Gina C. Erickson

The bug club met

on the old red rug.

Look up there.

What is in the jug?

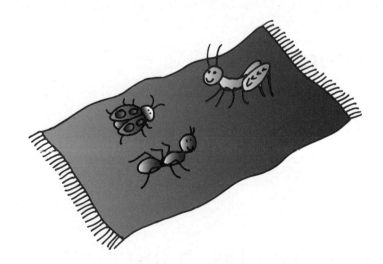

(CONTINUED) ▶

"Let's find out,"

said Pug the bug.

Away ran Pug . . . off the rug,

on the plug,

to the mug,

and up, up the jug.

There is Pug

at the top of the jug.

Pug, what is in the jug?

(CONTINUED)

Down, down went Pug

into the jug.

What is in the jug?

Pug is in the jug!

"Let's help Pug!"

said the bugs.

Away they ran off the rug,

(CONTINUED)

on the plug, to the mug,

and up, up the jug.

Pug?

With a tug

and a chug

up, up came Pug.

On top of the jug

the bug club hugs.

Make Sentences

Write a word on each line. Then draw
a picture to show one of the sentences.

jug	hugs	bug	Pug

1. The _____ club met.

2. Pug went down the _____.

3. The bugs helped _____.

4. The bug club _____.

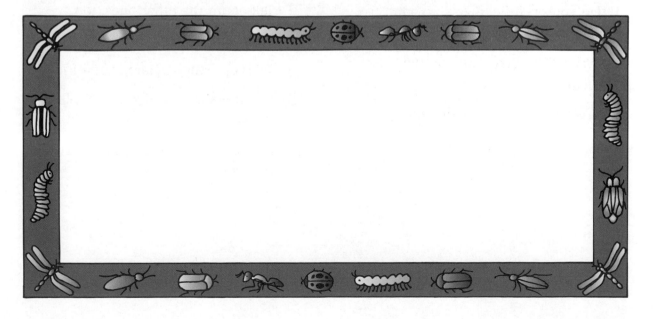

What's Next? You Decide!

Teacher: *Read aloud the directions and activities. Then have your student choose which activity to do next.*

Now it's your turn to choose what to do next in the lesson. Read the activities and decide which one you want to do—you may want to try them both!

Make a Bug Club Painting

MATERIALS

- ❏ 1 sheet white construction paper
- ❏ tempera paints
- ❏ pictures of bugs (optional)

STEPS

Suppose you're an artist. The bugs in the bug club called you. They want you to paint them!

- ❏ Use a pencil to draw the bug club on construction paper.
- ❏ Draw Pug and the rug.
- ❏ Draw other bugs, too.
- ❏ Do you need help? Ask an adult to show you pictures of bugs.
- ❏ Write "The Bug Club" on the picture.
- ❏ Color your picture with paint.
- ❏ Hang your picture in a place where your family and friends can enjoy it.

Tell a Bug Club Story

MATERIALS

- ❏ 1 rug or blanket
- ❏ 1 cassette recorder (optional)
- ❏ 1 cassette tape (optional)

STEPS

Tell a new story about the bug club!

- ❏ Sit on a rug or blanket with a friend or family member.
- ❏ Start with these words from the story: "The bug club met on the old red rug."
- ❏ Tell about Pug the bug.
- ❏ Tell about the other bugs, too.
- ❏ Try to use words that rhyme.
- ❏ Tell your story to family and friends.
- ❏ If you want, record yourself telling the story.
- ❏ Ask an adult to help you use a tape recorder.

Learning Opposites

Use opposites to attract your student's attention.

OBJECTIVE	BACKGROUND	MATERIALS
To teach your student words with opposite meanings	Antonyms are words with opposite, or completely different, meanings. Learning words with opposite meanings helps readers build context and background knowledge of individual word meanings. In this lesson, your student will learn high-frequency words that are opposites. He or she will also learn to use opposites in writing.	<ul><li>Student Learning Pages 15.A–15.B</li><li>1 children's thesaurus (optional)</li><li>10–15 index cards</li></ul>

VOCABULARY
OPPOSITES words that represent completely different things

Let's Begin

1 **INTRODUCE** Begin the lesson by writing this sentence on a sheet of paper: "An ant is little." Have your student read the sentence out loud. Ask him or her to think of another word for *little*. [*small*] Explain that the words *little* and *small* mean the same thing. Next, write this sentence on a sheet of paper and read it out loud: "An elephant is big." Ask, *Do the words* little *and* big *mean the same thing?* [no] Point out that the words *little* and *big* are **opposites.** Challenge your student to think of two other words that are opposites.

2 **CONNECT** Tell your student that a lot of stories have words that are opposites. To help your student identify opposites in stories, recall the selection entitled *The Bug Club* from Lesson 1.14. Remind your student that Pug went up the jug. Then ask your student to name the opposite, or completely different, thing that Pug did later in the story. [went down the jug] Explain to your student that the words *up* and *down* are opposites. Help him or her identify more examples of opposites from other stories he or she may remember.

3 **IDENTIFY** Draw the diagram on the next page on a sheet of paper. Explain that the lines should connect words that are opposites. Then say these words one at a time: *hot, stop, fast,* and *in*. Invite your student to tell you in which rectangle in the diagram to write the word.

Little

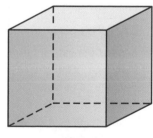

Big

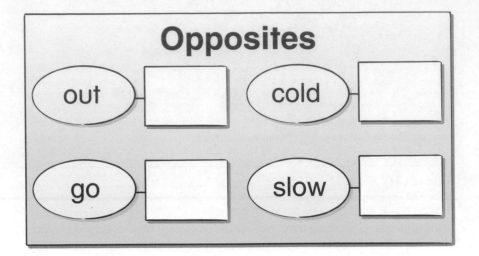

Opposites

out [ ] cold [ ]

go [ ] slow [ ]

4 **CONSTRUCT** Challenge your student to use each word in the diagram in a sentence. Have him or her focus on the sets of opposites by making up one sentence for each word of each set, such as *I go out to play* and *I come in the house.* Listen carefully to be sure that your student understands the concept of opposites. Then invite your student to act out each set of sentences to reinforce the concept of opposites.

5 **MODEL** Using new words, such as opposites, may be challenging to your student. Encourage him or her to use appropriate vocabulary to describe what he or she sees, hears, and feels. Be patient as your student learns new words. Then distribute Student Learning Page 15.A. Explain the directions to your student. To end the lesson, read the activities on Student Learning Page 15.B to your student.

Branching Out

TEACHING TIP

You may wish to use a children's thesaurus to teach your student more words that are opposites.

CHECKING IN

Show your student pairs of words on index cards. Some pairs should have similar meanings—such as *hot* and *warm*—and some pairs should have opposite meanings. Ask your student to point out the index cards that show opposites.

📖

FOR FURTHER READING

Alien Opposites, by Matthew Van Fleet (Hyperion Books for Children, 2001).

Elephant Elephant: A Book of Opposites, by Francisco Pittau and Bernadette Gervais (Abrams Books for Young Readers, 2001).

What's Up, What's Down?, by Lola M. Schaefer and Barbara Bash, ill. (Greenwillow, 2002).

Match Opposites

Draw a line between the pictures that show opposites.

What's Next? You Decide!

Teacher: Read aloud the directions and activities. Then have your student choose which activity to do next.

Now it's your turn to choose what to do next in the lesson. Read the activities and decide which one you want to do—you may want to try them both!

Act Out Opposites

MATERIALS

- ❏ 20 index cards
- ❏ 1 shoebox

STEPS

Play a game with a friend.

- ❏ Think of 10 sets of words that are opposites.
- ❏ Write each word on a separate index card. Ask an adult to help you.
- ❏ Put the index cards in the shoebox. Mix up the cards.
- ❏ Choose a card out of the box.
- ❏ Act out the opposite of the word on the card.
- ❏ Have your friend try to guess the word on your card.
- ❏ Now ask your friend to choose a card.
- ❏ Have your friend act out the opposite of the word on the card.
- ❏ Try to guess the word on your friend's card.
- ❏ Play until all of the cards are gone.

Make an Opposites Poster

MATERIALS

- ❏ 1 posterboard
- ❏ markers or crayons

STEPS

- ❏ Draw two big boxes on the posterboard.
- ❏ Think of two things that are opposites.
- ❏ Draw one thing in one box of the posterboard.
- ❏ Draw the opposite thing in the other box.
- ❏ Ask an adult to help you hang the poster where your family and friends can enjoy it.
- ❏ Make another poster if you have more ideas for opposites!

Using Descriptive Words

The joy of learning a language is having a way to express yourself.

OBJECTIVE	BACKGROUND	MATERIALS
To teach your student words that describe emotions and opinions	Learning words that allow us to express ourselves is an important part of building our vocabulary. In this lesson, your student will learn high-frequency words that describe emotions and opinions. He or she will also use these words in writing.	■ Student Learning Pages 16.A–16.B ■ 1 copy Web, page 356 ■ markers or crayons ■ 1 copy Writing Lines, page 357

VOCABULARY
EMOTION a feeling **OPINION** what someone thinks about something

Let's Begin

1 **INTRODUCE** Begin the lesson by inviting your student to talk about a time when he or she felt happy. Explain that when your student felt happy, he or she was experiencing an **emotion.** Define the word *emotion* as "a feeling." Next, use a copy of the Web found on page 356 and write "emotion" in the center. Together with him or her, brainstorm other emotions that people feel. Help your student write each word in an outer oval of the Web. Then invite your student to tell what each word means.

A BRIGHT IDEA

Encourage your student to keep a journal to express his or her feelings. Suggest that he or she write or draw how he or she feels about things.

2 **CONNECT** Write the sentences below on a sheet of paper. Be expressive as you read the sentences to your student. Have him or her circle the words that describe emotions. Then invite him or her to act out or illustrate the sentences.

The boy is glad. He can go play.   *That girl is sad. She is sick.*

Then help your student write the words in each sentence on a copy of the Writing Lines found on page 357.

    Using Descriptive Words   **79**

ENRICH THE EXPERIENCE

Many types of music can help people connect to their emotions. Play different styles of music for your student. Ask him or her to describe how the music makes him or her feel. You might even want to have your student dance to show his or her emotions.

3 **EXPLAIN** Ask your student to name a food that he or she likes. Write a sentence or sentences on a sheet of paper that reflects his or her response, such as "I like ice cream. I think ice cream tastes good." Inform your student that the sentences tell his or her **opinion** about ice cream. Explain that an opinion tells what someone thinks about something. Point to the words *like, think,* and *good* and explain that we can use these words to show our opinions. Then introduce opposites of *like* and *good, don't like* and *bad.* Write these sentences on a sheet of paper and read them out loud: "I don't like _____. I think _____ tastes bad." Ask your student to complete the sentence. Have him or her talk about other things he or she does and doesn't like. Help your student write about the opinions and draw pictures illustrating them.

4 **WRITE** Make a five-column chart on a sheet of paper. Draw a picture of a hand, a mouth, an eye, a nose, and an ear in the column headings to represent the five senses. Then say a few sentence starters that relate to each of the senses. Work with your student to complete each sentence with a descriptive word, such as *The bear feels fuzzy; The soup is hot; The building looks big; The cake smells yummy;* and *The music sounds soft.* Help your student brainstorm descriptive words for each sense. Then aid him or her in writing the words in the correct columns. Ask your student if he or she can think of new sentences using the words in the chart. Invite your student to say the sentences out loud. Provide encouragement by praising your student for using his or her creativity!

Remember to encourage your student to use appropriate vocabulary when telling you how he or she feels. This will build his or her language and reading skills. Be patient as your student learns new words.

5 **PRACTICE** Distribute Student Learning Page 16.A. To end the lesson, read out loud the activities on Student Learning Page 16.B. Allow time for your student to choose and complete one of the activities.

FOR FURTHER READING

The Feel Good Book, by Todd Parr (Little, Brown & Company, 2002).

Today I Feel Silly and Other Moods That Make My Day, by Jamie Lee Curtis (HarperCollins Canada, 2003).

When Sophie Gets Angry—Really, Really Angry, by Molly Garrett Bang (Scholastic Trade, 1999).

Branching Out

TEACHING TIP

Invite your student to look at himself or herself in a mirror. Ask him or her to make different facial expressions that relate to different emotions. You might want to join your student to help him or her think of more emotions to display.

CHECKING IN

To assess your student's understanding of the lesson, watch a video or television program featuring live actors. Have him or her name some of the emotions that the actors show.

Make Faces

Write each word on one of the lines. Then draw a face that shows each emotion.

glad   sad

mad   excited

1.

_____
_____
_____

3.

_____
_____
_____

2.

_____
_____
_____

4.

_____
_____
_____

What's Next? You Decide!

Teacher: Read out loud the directions and activities. Then have your student choose which activity to do next.

Now it's your turn to choose what to do next in the lesson. Read the activities and decide which one you want to do—you may want to try them both!

Make Masks

MATERIALS

❑ 4–5 paper plates

❑ markers or crayons

❑ 4–5 craft sticks

❑ tape

STEPS

❑ Draw a face that shows an emotion on the back of a paper plate.

❑ Use crayons or markers to decorate the face.

❑ Ask an adult to help you cut out the eyes on the plate to make a mask.

❑ Tape a craft stick to the other side of the mask.

❑ Hold the mask in front of your face.

❑ Act out the emotion that the mask shows.

❑ Tell why you might feel that emotion.

❑ Make three or four more masks. Show other emotions.

❑ Share your masks with family and friends and act out the emotions.

Make a Poster

MATERIALS

❑ 1 posterboard

❑ old magazines

❑ 1 pair scissors

❑ glue

STEPS

❑ Ask an adult for some old magazines.

❑ Cut out some pictures of things you like.

❑ Cut out some pictures of things you don't like.

❑ Draw a line down the middle of the posterboard.

❑ Glue pictures of things you like on one side of the poster.

❑ Glue pictures of things you don't like on the other side.

❑ Show your poster to family and friends.

❑ Talk about your poster.

❑ Tell about the things you like and don't like.

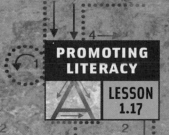

Reading Fiction

Foster a love of reading in your student and you will give him or her a gift to enjoy for a lifetime.

OBJECTIVE	BACKGROUND	MATERIALS
To help your student read and enjoy a fiction story	Fiction is a type of writing that includes made up characters and events. Reading fiction nurtures a child's imagination and teaches him or her about people's feelings and experiences. In this lesson, your student will read a fiction story with you. He or she will also learn about some elements of fiction stories.	■ Student Learning Pages 17.A–17.C ■ markers or crayons

Let's Begin

1 **DISTRIBUTE** Tell your student that in this lesson he or she is going to read a fun story with you about a silly cat and her poor little hat. Then distribute Student Learning Page 17.A. Invite your student to look at the picture and predict. Ask, *Who do you think some of the people or animals in the story will be?* [a cat and a fish] *What are the fish and the cat in the picture doing?* [flying in the air] Then help your student connect to the setting of the story by asking, *If you could fly in a hot air balloon above your home or neighborhood, what would you see?*

2 **INTRODUCE** Read out loud the title and the authors' names as you scan your finger below each word. Inform your student that the title is the name of a story. The people who write a story are called authors. Explain that the people who draw the pictures that go with the story are called illustrators or artists. Then begin reading the story as your student reads along with you. Be sure to read the text with an expressive and dramatic tone. Invite your student to read some parts of the story individually as you monitor his or her reading, giving help if needed.

3 **READ** As your student reads alone or with you, check his or her comprehension of high-frequency words. Also pay attention to your student's understanding of the key words in the story, such as *flying, hat, went, get, sped, up,* and *down.* Explain that the word *lop* can mean "drooping" or "flopping." This word can be used to describe how a bunny's ears hang down, so the lop is really a bunny in this story. Help your student sound out the letters of any words that he or she doesn't know. Praise your

ENRICH THE EXPERIENCE

To help your student connect to the story's setting, you might want to read the selection in a park. If bad weather doesn't permit this experience, use props as you read the story. For example, you might use a fan blowing on a hat to demonstrate the hat blowing away.

FOR FURTHER READING

From Pictures to Words: A Book About Making a Book, by Janet Stevens (Holiday House, 1999).

Ready to Read, by Rosemary Wells and Michael Koelsch, ill. (Penguin Putnam Books for Young Readers, 2001).

Story Starters Mysteries, by Q. L. Pearce (Lowell House, 1999).

student as you do this. Keep this instruction brief to avoid interrupting your student's enjoyment of the story. As you finish reading the story, have your student read the last two lines on his or her own.

4 IDENTIFY Tell your student that some authors use the same words over and over to help us remember the important things that happen in a story. Help your student identify and circle words and phrases that are repeated in the selection, such as *get my hat*, *went flying*, and *sped away*. Then tell your student that authors sometimes use rhyming words to make stories more fun to read. Invite your student to find words in the story that rhyme with *Pat, Ned,* and *lop.* Have your student use a different colored crayon to underline each set of rhyming words.

5 CONNECT Review the narrative arc of the story. Have your student tell you aloud what happened. Then discuss the main ideas and the characters' points of view. Explain that in the story Pat almost loses something she really likes—her hat. Invite your student to talk about a time he or she lost a favorite thing. Ask your student what he or she did to try to get that thing back.

6 INTRODUCE Now explore the punctuation in the story. Show your student the periods and exclamation points and explain why they are used. Then point out the commas and quotation marks. Explain that quotation marks are used to show what a character in a story is saying. Have your student circle the quotation marks and put an X over the exclamation points. The next time you read together, point out some of the punctuation in the story to get your student familiar with the marks.

7 PRACTICE Distribute Student Learning Page 17.B. Explain that the sentences tell about things that happened in the story. Tell your student to write the sentences in the order in which they happened in the story. To end the lesson, read out loud the activities on Student Learning Page 17.C. Allow time for your student to complete an activity of his or her choice.

Branching Out

TEACHING TIP

As your student begins to read, encourage him or her to look at the pictures in the books and predict what the story will be about.

CHECKING IN

To assess your student's understanding of the lesson, have him or her retell the important parts of the story. Be sure he or she can identify the main character and the problem in the story.

Discover Fiction

What a Day for Flying!

by Gina Erickson and Kelli Foster

What a day for flying!

Trish was in her dish.
Pat had on her hat.

"Just look," said Trish.
"It is a dream come true."

Swish . . .
Pat's hat went flying off.

"Oh, no!" said Pat.
"There goes my hat."

Pat's hat went flying . . .
by Ned and Ted.

(CONTINUED) ▶

"Help," said Pat.
"Please get my hat."

Ned and Ted sped away
to get Pat's hat.

Pat's hat went flying
by the bug club.

It went flying by
slim Jim and the lop.

"Please," said Pat.
"Help get my hat."

Slim Jim, Ned, the lop,
and Ted all sped away
to get Pat's hat.

The fat rat and Ed
saw Pat's hat.

(CONTINUED)

Pat's hat went down
with a plop and came to
a stop on the see-saw.

"Help, help," said Pat.
"Please get that hat."

But swish,
the hat went flying off.

Away they all sped—
slim Jim and Ned,
the lop and Ted,

the fat rat and Ed—
to get Pat's hat.

With a swish and a drop
the hat came to a stop
on top of Pop.

"Up there," said Pat.
"Let's get my hat."

(CONTINUED)

Slim Jim and Ned,
the rat and Ed,
the lop and Ted,

and Trish and Pat
went up, up, up
to get Pat's hat.

"Tug, Pat, tug," they said.
And she did.

The hat went down,
and Pat went down.

They all went down
on top of Pat's hat.

Pat's hat was flat.

What a day for Pat's
flying hat!

Be an Illustrator

Write the sentences in order. Then draw a picture showing each sentence.

Pat's friends went to get the hat.
Pat's hat was flat.
Pat's hat went flying.

1.

2.

3.

What's Next? You Decide!

Teacher: *Read out loud the directions and activities. Then have your student choose which activity to do next.*

Now it's your turn to choose what to do next in the lesson. Read the activities and decide which one you want to do—you may want to try them both!

Tell New Stories

▲ MATERIALS

❑ 1 shoebox

❑ 10 index cards

▲ STEPS

Play a game with friends.

❑ Write 10 different words on separate index cards.

❑ Write words about animals, people, and places.

❑ Put the index cards in a shoebox.

❑ Mix up the cards.

❑ Choose a card from the box.

❑ Start telling a story about the word on the card.

❑ Have each friend take a turn telling what happens next in the story.

❑ Choose a new card. Start a new story.

Make a Hat for Pat

▲ MATERIALS

❑ 1 brown paper bag

❑ construction paper

❑ 1 pair scissors

❑ glue

▲ STEPS

Suppose that Pat lost her hat. Make a new hat for Pat.

❑ Open the brown paper bag.

❑ Turn it upside down.

❑ Use the bag to make a hat.

❑ Draw parts of the hat on construction paper.

❑ Cut out the parts of the hat.

❑ Glue the parts to the paper bag.

❑ Try on the hat.

❑ Ask an adult to help you make sure that the hat will fit.

❑ Do you think Pat will like her new hat?

Enjoying Poetry

A favorite poem is like a song that lingers sweetly in one's memory.

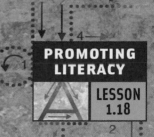

PROMOTING
LITERACY

LESSON
1.18

OBJECTIVE	BACKGROUND	MATERIALS
To help your student read and enjoy poetry	A poem is a type of writing that's made up of lines of text called stanzas. Poems often include descriptive words that help readers connect to their senses and make images in their minds. In this lesson, your student will read and enjoy a poem. He or she will also identify key words and rhyming words in the poem.	■ Student Learning Pages 18.A–18.B ■ 1 pair boots ■ 1 pair shoes ■ 1 pair gloves

Let's Begin

1 **DISTRIBUTE** Begin the lesson by distributing Student Learning Page 18.A. Read the title out loud and the name of the author of the selection. Tell your student that "Twos" is a special type of writing called a poem. Ask your student what he or she thinks the poem might be about based on the title. Then ask your student to look at the picture on the page. Invite your student to tell you what he or she sees in the picture. Explain that sometimes we can use pictures in poems and stories to make guesses about what we will read. Ask your student to look at the picture and guess some words that are in the poem. [possible answers: *seesaw, friend, up,* and *down*]

2 **ENJOY** Begin reading the poem with your student. Change the tone of your voice after you read the first sentence to show that it's a question. Read the entire poem at least once without reviewing any difficult words or monitoring your student's reading. This will allow your student to enjoy the poem without interrupting the rhythm of the verse. Then read the poem again while using props to demonstrate the text. Use a pair of boots, a pair of shoes, and a pair of gloves. When you read the last line, hold your hands out to form a diagonal line. Move them up and down to simulate a seesaw. Invite your student to join you. Then ask him or her to name something from the poem that comes in twos.

3 **REVIEW** Reread the poem to help your student memorize it. This will also allow you to monitor his or her reading. Invite your student to read parts of the poem on his or her own. Help your student sound out any difficult words, and explain to him

ENRICH THE EXPERIENCE

Play a game to help your student make up some poems of his or her own. Use the lines from "Roses Are Red, Violets Are Blue." Help your student come up with words that rhyme with *blue*. Begin by making up a poem for your student, such as *Roses are red, violets are blue. I have a shoe. I even have two!* Then invite your student to make up a poem using the same first two lines. Guide him or her as necessary.

FOR FURTHER READING

20th Century Children's Poetry Treasury, selected by Jack Prelutsky and Meilo So, ill. (Alfred A. Knopf, 1999).

Baby Einstein: Poems for Little Ones, concept by Julie Aigner-Clark, Nadeem Zaidi, ill., and J. D. Marston, photo. (Hyperion, 2001).

Writing Poetry with Children, by Jo Ellen Moore (Evan-Moor Educational Publishers, 1999).

or her any meanings as necessary. Then focus on the key word *twos*. Explain that the word *twos* in the poem means that there are two of something. Remind your student that the word *two* is a number. Next, use the props and the picture on the page to help your student make connections to other key words. Point to the words *boots, shoes, gloves,* and *seesaw* and say them out loud. After you say each word, ask your student to identify the prop or picture that matches the word.

4 **IDENTIFY** Tell your student that some poems have words that rhyme. Remind your student that rhyming words end with the same sound. Then challenge him or her to find two rhyming words in the poem without your help. Tell your student to look only at the last word in each line. Help your student identify each set of rhyming words: *twos/shoes; town/down;* and *friend/end.* Then invite your student to repeat these pairs of words after you.

5 **MODEL** Model good reading habits by reading together with your student regularly. Encourage him or her to look through books on his or her own, perhaps while you are reading silently.

6 **PRACTICE** Distribute Student Learning Page 18.B. Read out loud each activity to your student. Invite him or her to do an activity of his or her choice.

Branching Out

TEACHING TIP

You might want to sing the poem "Twos" with your student. Experiment with different tunes as you sing the words. If you play an instrument or have instrumental recordings, you can try singing the poem as you play music. Also, try clapping for each syllable in each line of the poem. This will allow your student to notice the rhyming pattern and beat of the poem.

CHECKING IN

To assess your student's understanding of the lesson, ask him or her to tell you how a poem is different from a story he or she has read. Name a familiar story to help your student compare the two types of writing.

Enjoy a Poem

Twos

by Lilian Moore

What comes in twos?
Old boots
And new shoes
And gloves to wear going to town
And you and your friend
One on each end
Of a seesaw that goes up and down.

What's Next? You Decide!

Teacher: Read out loud the directions and activities. Then have your student choose which activity to do next.

Now it's your turn to choose what to do next in the lesson. Read the activities and decide which one you want to do—you may want to try them both!

Make a Poem Book

MATERIALS

- ❑ 8 sheets construction paper
- ❑ markers or crayons
- ❑ 1 hole puncher
- ❑ 1 length ribbon

STEPS

Make a book for the poem "Twos"!

- ❑ Write each line of the poem on a different sheet of construction paper.
- ❑ Draw a picture showing each line.
- ❑ Now you have the pages of your book.
- ❑ Make a cover for your book. Write the name of the poem on the cover.
- ❑ Draw a fun picture on the cover, too.
- ❑ Put the pages of your book together. Put the cover on top.
- ❑ Punch a hole in the top left corner of your book. Ask an adult to help you.
- ❑ Put a length of ribbon through the hole. Tie the ribbon in a bow.
- ❑ Show your poem book to family and friends.

Write a Poem

MATERIALS

- ❑ markers or crayons

STEPS

Ask an adult to help you with this activity.

- ❑ Think of words that rhyme.
- ❑ Write the words on a sheet of paper.
- ❑ Write two lines of a poem.
- ❑ Make sure the last words in the lines rhyme.
- ❑ Use the list of rhyming words to help you.
- ❑ Now write two more lines for your poem.
- ❑ Use different words that rhyme.
- ❑ Draw a picture to go with your poem.
- ❑ Read your poem to family and friends.

In Your Community

To reinforce the skills and concepts taught in this section,
try one or more of these activities!

Go on an Alphabet Scavenger Hunt

Many towns and communities have a large number of signs. Whether they're road signs, signs in storefronts, or billboards, you can use these signs to reinforce several aspects of the alphabet for your student. Take a walk through your community and ask your student to find words on signs that begin with a specific letter. Start with the letter *a* and go through the entire alphabet. When moving on to the next letter, be sure to ask your student which letter comes next so as to develop his or her awareness of the sequence of letters. Also ask your student if the letter is a consonant or vowel to strengthen his or her understanding of each letter. Because of the time needed for this activity, you may want to progress through the whole alphabet over a series of walks with your student.

Take a Rhyming Walk

Help your student practice rhyming by taking a walk through your community. As you walk with your student, identify things that you see by name. Then ask your student to think of a word that rhymes with it. For example, if you see a dog, your student's response could be *log*. Expand the game to specific rhymes or letter-sound connections. For example, you could change from rhyming words to having your student think of words that begin with the same letter. Your student's response to *dog* could then be a word such as *door*. Take turns by having your student identify things on your walk. Have him or her ask you to name a word that rhymes or that starts with the same letter. Allow your student to display his or her knowledge of the words by saying if your responses are correct.

Use Nature to Expand Vocabulary

Nature can be described in many ways, so it's a great way for a child to learn words that describe things. Visit a local nature preserve or another natural setting with your student. As you walk, point out specific things to your student and ask him or her to describe them. For example, point out a tree and ask your student to think of words that describe the tree, such as *big, pretty, green, old,* or *tall*. Expand your question and your student's vocabulary by asking for opposites of the descriptive words your student states. For example, a "tall tree" could become a "short tree." Use your imagination to come up with other ways to use the natural setting to expand your student's vocabulary.

Attend a Story Reading

One of the most helpful literacy activities for students is reading to them. Most libraries or community centers will have readings of stories for children regularly. Contact your local library for upcoming events and take your student to a reading. If you know the selection or selections that will be read, obtain a copy and let your student look through it beforehand. Point out the special features of the book, such as the title, the author, and the illustrator. After the storytelling is over, ask your student questions about the sequence of events and about some details from the story. If he or she enjoyed the story, look in the library for more books by the same author or illustrator. You can take the activity to another level by acting out scenes from the story at home. Rather than memorizing the book, have your student act out scenes in his or her own way.

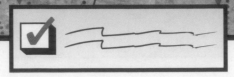

We Have Learned

Use this checklist to summarize what you and your student
have accomplished in the Promoting Literacy section.

❑ **The Alphabet**
❑ classifying and writing uppercase letters
❑ classifying and writing lowercase letters
❑ developing awareness of sequence of letters

❑ **Consonant Sounds**
❑ beginning sounds and initial consonants
❑ identifying initial sounds and initial consonants
❑ high-frequency words

❑ **Middle Sounds**
❑ identifying middle sounds
❑ letter recognition of middle sounds
❑ middle sounds in words

❑ **Ending Sounds**
❑ identifying ending sounds
❑ letter recognition of ending sounds
❑ ending sounds in words

❑ **Writing the Alphabet**
❑ recognizing and writing own printed name
❑ recognizing and writing familiar or common words
❑ recognizing and writing left to right and top to bottom

❑ **Vowel Sounds**
❑ short-vowel sounds: *a, e, i, o, u*
❑ identifying short-vowel sounds and words
❑ high-frequency words

❑ **Vocabulary Expansion**
❑ recognizing short-vowel and high-frequency rhyming words
❑ using and reading rhymes
❑ recognizing short-vowel and high-frequency words as opposites
❑ using opposites
❑ recognizing high-frequency words that describe emotions and opinions
❑ using describing words

❑ **Reading Fiction and Poetry**
❑ understanding key words
❑ using pictures to predict words
❑ recognizing sight words and rhymes
❑ making meaningful connections between text and experiences
❑ recognizing points of view and main ideas
❑ understanding print concepts (title, author, illustrator)
❑ understanding literary elements and how they can be used

We have also learned:

_____

_____

Math

Math

Key Topics

Sorting and Classifying

Patterns

Shapes

Numbers to 10

Greater Numbers

Addition

Subtraction

Money

Time and Measurement

Making the Grade: Everything Your Kindergartner Needs to Know

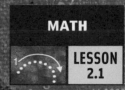

Exploring Positions and Sorting

Identifying similarities and differences is a fundamental part of exploration and discovery.

OBJECTIVE	BACKGROUND	MATERIALS
To help your student understand positions and sorting	Being able to tell how one thing is over or under another thing, or how one thing is the same or different from another thing, is an important skill. In this lesson, your student will learn to identify and describe things in relation to their position. Your student will also learn to sort items using the simple characteristics of color, size, and shape.	<ul><li>Student Learning Pages 1.A–1.B</li><li>1 three-shelf bookcase</li><li>1 chair</li><li>2 shoeboxes</li><li>1 length string, 5 feet long</li><li>1 toy that floats on water</li><li>1 bag or box</li><li>2 apples, 1 orange, 1 grapefruit, 1 banana</li><li>5 red and 5 black checkers</li><li>5 large and 5 small cups</li><li>5 marbles</li><li>5 dice</li><li>markers or crayons</li></ul>

VOCABULARY

SAME things that are alike

DIFFERENT things that aren't alike

SORTING putting things into groups based on their characteristics

Let's Begin

TOP, MIDDLE, AND BOTTOM

1 **MODEL** Tell your student that he or she will be learning about the positions top, middle, and bottom. Explain to him or her that these describe the place where something is. Model top, middle, and bottom for your student using a bookcase with three shelves. If you don't have a three-shelf bookcase, anything with a clear top, middle, and bottom level will work as your model. Place a book or another object on the top shelf. Say, *This is the top shelf.* Explain that the highest part of something is the top. Draw a picture of something tall, such as a mountain or a house. Have your student point to the top of the picture. Then ask your student to show you the top of his or her body. [top of head]

2 **CONTINUE** Now place a book or another item on the bottom shelf of the bookcase. Explain that the lowest part of something is called the bottom. Ask, *What is this shelf called?* [the bottom shelf] Have your student point out the bottom of various household items, such as a saucepan, a broom, a cup, and a lamp. Then ask your student to point out the bottom of his or her feet.

3 **EXPAND** Have your student point one finger in the direction of top [up] and one finger in the direction of bottom. [down] Explain that the middle of something is between the top and the bottom. Illustrate the concept of middle to him or her by using the middle shelf on the bookcase. Ask your student to point out the top shelf and the bottom shelf. Then give your student a book and ask him or her to put it on the middle shelf. Ask, *What is between the top and the bottom?* [middle] Use items in the home or room to model middle for your student. Show him or her the middle cushion of a couch, the middle of a sandwich [the peanut butter or lunchmeat] or the middle of a book. [the pages] Then have your student find the middle of his or her body. [stomach or belly]

4 **REVIEW** Reinforce the concepts of top, middle, and bottom for your student. Instruct him or her to point to the top, middle, and bottom shelves of the bookcase. Then have your student identify the top, middle, and bottom of another object, such as a ladder. You might also ask your student to draw a picture or build something with blocks that has a top, a middle, and a bottom.

IN FRONT AND BEHIND

1 **EXPLAIN** Talk about the meaning of the phrase *in front of* with your student. Tell him or her that things can be described by where they are in relation to other things. Explain to your student that if his or her face is toward something, then that thing is in front of him or her. Model this

The girl is in front of the chair.

concept with a chair. Place the chair in front of you. Say, *The chair is in front of me.* Then face the chair forward. Stand in front of the chair with your back to it. Say, *I am in front of the chair.* Have your student demonstrate his or her understanding of this concept by asking him or her to stand in front of the chair.

2 **EXPLORE** Use the chair again to model the meaning of the word *behind.* Stand in front of the chair with your back to it.

Explain to your student that when you have your body facing away from the chair, the chair is behind you. Now move the chair so that it's behind your student. Ask, *What is behind you?* [the chair] Place the chair in front of and facing away from your student. Ask, *What is behind the chair?* [your student]

The boy is behind the chair.

3 **REVIEW** Walk around the room with your student, and have him or her identify a pair of objects that are in front of and behind each other. For example, ask, *Is the table behind or in front of the chair?* Have your student sit down on the floor. Place a shoebox behind and in front of your student. Hand your student several small household items one at a time. Direct your student to place each item in the box that's behind or in front of him or her. Then reverse the activity and have your student take items out of each of the boxes or name items that are in front of and behind him or her.

OVER, UNDER, AND ON

1 **EXPLAIN** Introduce the concept of *over* to your student. Tell him or her that when one thing is higher than another thing it is said to be over it. Ask, *Can you name one thing in the room that is over us?* [the ceiling] Help your student understand the concept of over by discussing other examples, such as an airplane flying overhead or clouds moving over the land. Show your student the picture of the bridge. Ask, *What is over the river?* [a bridge]

The bridge is over the river.

> **!**
>
> **A BRIGHT IDEA**
>
> Give your student more practice identifying things in front of and behind him or her. Have your student stand in the middle of a room and slowly begin turning around. When you say *stop*, ask your student to stop spinning and name the things that are in front of him or her. See if your student can also name a few things that are behind him or her without turning around.

Exploring Positions and Sorting **101**

2 **MODEL** Keep your student's attention on the picture of the bridge. Ask, *What is under the bridge?* [a river] Explain that when one thing is lower than another thing it is said to be under it. Model the concepts of over and under using a table. Have your student hold one end of a piece of string while you hold the other end. Stand so that the string is over the table but not touching it. Ask, *What can you tell me about the string and the table?* [the string is over the table and the table is under the string] Now, together with your student, move the string so that it's under the table but not on the floor. Ask, *What can you say now?* [the string is under the table and the table is over the string]

3 **DEMONSTRATE** Tie the string to a chair or doorknob. Holding one end, ask your student to demonstrate over and under by crawling under or stepping over the string as you say *over* and *under*.

4 **EXPAND** Have your student bring you one of his or her favorite toys. Place it on the table. Tell your student that the toy is on the table, not over it. Point out that the string was over the table but the toy is on the table. Challenge him or her to tell you the difference between over and on. If your student needs help, explain that the string wasn't touching the table, but the toy is. Invite your student to talk about other examples, such as a book on a shelf, a person on a couch, or a radio on a counter. Then ask your student to put the toy under the table. Ask, *What is the toy on?* [the floor]

INSIDE AND OUTSIDE

1 **EXPLAIN** Introduce the concept of *inside* to your student. Ask, *What are we inside of right now?* [a house or another building] Tell him or her that you are also inside a room. Ask, *What room are we inside of?* Explore with your student the other ways that things can be inside. Model placing a toy or other object inside of a bag or a box. Have your student practice putting different things around the house inside of the bag or box. Each time he or she places an object in the box, have your student say, *The _____ is inside the box.*

2 **MODEL** Explain to your student that when something isn't inside, then it's outside. Model how you can be inside or outside a room. Stand up and say, *I am inside the room.* Then tell your student to stay where he or she is as you leave the room. From the other room say, *I am now outside the room.* Have your student practice identifying inside and outside by telling you where you are as you move inside and outside of the room. Ask, *If it's raining, where will you get wet?* [outside] *Where will you stay dry?* [inside]

3 **REVIEW** Reinforce the concepts of inside and outside for your student by playing a game. Build a playhouse or fort with your student. You can use large cardboard boxes, cushions, blankets, and so on for a playhouse inside. If there is snow, you can build the outline of a house in the snow. If there are autumn leaves on the ground, rake together leaf-house walls. You can both have fun walking through the house and announcing which rooms you are inside or outside of. Then try directing each other to go inside certain rooms or stay outside other rooms. Have other family members or friends join in as appropriate.

MATH

LESSON 2.1

A BRIGHT IDEA

Help your student explore the differences between learning inside and learning outside. If weather permits, teach several steps from the lesson at a park or in another outdoor setting. Or just visit the playground for an exercise break!

SAME AND DIFFERENT

1 **INTRODUCE** Explain to your student what the word **same** means. Show him or her two apples that are the same shape and size. Say, *These two pieces of fruit are the same. They're both apples.* Tell your student that when things are the same they usually look alike. Model some things that are the same, such as your socks or your shoes. Say, *My socks are the same. My shoes are the same.* Ask your student to look around the room or house to find pairs of things that are the same. [plates, silverware, pillow cases, windows, and so on]

2 **CONNECT** Use the concept of same to introduce the concept of **different** to your student. Contrast an apple with an orange. Point out that an apple is different from an orange. Ask, *What is different about the apple and the orange?* [they're different colors, maybe they're different sizes] Have your student choose two things in the room to compare. Have him or her name three ways that the two objects are different.

GROUPS BEING SORTED

1 **PREVIEW** Use an apple, an orange, a grapefruit, and a banana to introduce the concept of **sorting.** Show your student the apple and orange again. Remind him or her that an apple and an orange are different colors. Then compare a grapefruit to the apple and the orange. Explain that the grapefruit is a different color and also a different size than the other pieces of fruit. Finally, introduce a banana to the group. Tell your student that the banana is a different shape. Ask your student to pick two of the four pieces of fruit and tell you what is different about them in relation to their color, shape, and size.

2 **EXPLAIN** Practice sorting by color with your student. Give your student a pile of checker pieces, five red and five black. Ask, *What two colors are the checker pieces?* [red and black] Model how to sort the pieces by color. Place the five red pieces in one pile and the five black pieces in another pile. Point to the red pile and ask, *What is the same about these pieces?* [all red] Then point to the black pile and ask, *What is the same about these pieces?* [all black] Mix up the pieces and have your student sort them by color. Ask, *How many colors are there?* [2] *So how many piles will you have?* [2]

3 **MODEL** Model sorting by size. Place 10 cups on a table. Half of them should be the same large size and the other half should be the same in a small size. Ask, *How many different sizes are there?* [2] Model how to sort the cups by size. Say, *This is a big cup. I will start a big cup group here.* Then choose a small cup and start a small cup group, explaining to your student what you are doing. Continue to sort the cups by size. Then ask your student to explain what is the same about each group. [all big and all small] Mix the cups into one group. Then have your student re-sort the cups by size.

4 **CONTINUE** Model sorting by shape. Show your student five marbles and five dice. Ask, *What shapes do you see?* [round and square] Place the marbles and dice in one pile. Challenge your student to sort the objects by shape. Help him or her make one group of marbles and one group of dice. Guide your student to practice sorting by shape with other household items.

5 **EXPAND** Give your student a group of 10 objects. In the group, include at least two different shapes, sizes, and colors of objects. Have your student sort the group these three different ways. Give him or her help as necessary. For each way of sorting, have your student draw a picture of the groups the objects were sorted into. When your student has sorted and drawn the groups by color, size, and shape, use the drawings to point out how sorting in different ways puts objects in a different group each time.

6 **DISTRIBUTE** Give your student Student Learning Page 1.A. Have him or her color all the cars blue and all the bears red using markers or crayons. Have your student sort by size by marking an X on the small toys and circling the big toys. Then read the activities on Student Learning Page 1.B to your student and ask him or her to decide which one he or she would like to do.

Branching Out

TEACHING TIP

Have your student practice identifying positions by playing Simon Says. Give directions such as *Simon says stand in front of the window* or *Simon says go under the doorway.* Make up other commands for top, bottom, middle, inside, outside, over, under, on, in front of, and behind. If your student can complete 10 directions in a row correctly, he or she becomes Simon and gets to make up directions for you to follow.

CHECKING IN

To assess your student's understanding of the lesson, the next time you bring groceries home from the store, have your student help you sort them and put them away. Tell your student where to put each item using position terms. Say, *Put the lettuce inside the refrigerator; Put the bread above the fruit; Put the juice in the bottom cabinet;* and so on.

FOR FURTHER READING

Let's Sort, by David Bauer (Capstone Press, 2003).

Sorting and Sets, by Henry Arthur Pluckrose (Gareth Stevens, 2001).

Sort Toys

Color the cars blue. Color the bears red. Mark an X on the small toys. Circle the big toys.

What's Next? You Decide!

Teacher: Read aloud the directions and activities. Then have your student choose which activity to do next.

Now it's your turn to choose what to do next in the lesson. Read the activities and decide which one you want to do—you may want to try them both!

Hunt for Toys

MATERIALS

❏ 10 toys

STEPS

Go on a scavenger hunt for toys! Ask an adult to help you.

❏ Find 10 toys you can hide around the room or your home.

❏ Hide a toy.

❏ Give an adult a clue about where to find the toy. Be sure to use the words *top, bottom, middle, inside, outside, over, under, on, in front of,* or *behind.*

❏ Ask an adult to hide the next toy and give you the clue to find it.

❏ Take turns hiding the toys and giving clues.

❏ When all the toys are found, sort them by size, color, and shape.

Sort the Laundry

MATERIALS

❏ 1 load dried laundry

STEPS

Help sort the laundry the next time your family does the wash.

❏ After the laundry is dry, ask an adult if you can help.

❏ First sort the clothes by size. Make a pile of the big pieces of laundry and a pile of the small pieces.

❏ Then sort the large and small piles by shape. Make a pile of shirts, a pile of pants, and a pile of socks for each size.

❏ Finally, sort the clothes by color. Match clothes together by color. For example, put all of the small red shirts in one pile.

❏ Help fold the clothes. Then put them away.

❏ Ask an adult to tell you where to put the clothes. Notice if it's on the top, bottom, middle, inside, outside, over, under, on, in front of, or behind something.

Learning About Patterns

Patterns are the basis for understanding order in mathematics.

MATH

LESSON 2.2

OBJECTIVE	BACKGROUND	MATERIALS
To teach your student about the patterns he or she sees and uses every day	Learning about patterns using familiar objects will help your student understand order and patterns using numbers. In this lesson, your student will learn about patterns in rhythm, movement, color, shape, and size and how these patterns are translated.	■ Student Learning Pages 2.A–2.D ■ 5–6 sheets construction paper (assorted colors) ■ 5–6 pieces thick cardboard ■ 1 pair scissors ■ glue ■ markers or crayons

VOCABULARY

PATTERNS groups of sounds, movements, shapes, colors, or other things arranged in an order

RHYTHM a pattern of sounds

MOVEMENT an action in which the position of something changes

TRANSLATED something shown in another way using different words, shapes, or symbols

Let's Begin

PATTERNS

1 **EXPLAIN** Tell your student that **patterns** are all around us. Patterns can be made using sounds, movements, colors, and shapes. Explain that combinations of sounds, movements, colors, and shapes can also make patterns. Discuss with your student the different types of sounds, movements, colors, and shapes that he or she is familiar with.

2 **CREATE** Before continuing the lesson, work with your student to make colored shapes to use throughout the lesson. Cut different colors and sizes of shapes out of construction paper, and then cut the same shapes and sizes out of thick cardboard. Have your student help you glue the construction paper to the cardboard. This will create pattern pieces that you and your student can easily use to create patterns.

RHYTHM AND MOVEMENT PATTERNS

1 **EXPLAIN AND DEMONSTRATE** Tell your student that **rhythm** patterns are patterns made using sounds. Discuss with him or

A TIME-SAVER

If you don't have the time to create pattern pieces with your student, gather household items, such as buttons, dried beans, pasta, coins, colorful blocks, stuffed animals, or toy cars, that your student can use to create his or her own patterns.

her some of the ways that people make sounds. For example, demonstrate or tell your student about clapping, snapping, tapping, stomping, and playing musical instruments. Explain that a pattern with sounds is made by repeating the same or different sounds in a specific order. Tap and clap a pattern for your student. Follow this pattern or make up one of your own: tap, tap, clap, tap, tap, clap, and so on. Have your student tap and clap out the pattern with you. Then ask him or her to tap and clap the pattern on his or her own. Have your student create and describe another rhythm pattern.

2 **EXPLAIN AND DEMONSTRATE** Tell your student that **movement** patterns are made of a series of movements that are repeated in a specific order. These movements may include jumping, walking, hopping, and so on. Demonstrate a movement pattern by walking one step and then hopping one step. Continue this pattern and have your student join in. Then ask him or her to continue the pattern on his or her own. Have your student create and describe another movement pattern.

COLOR, SHAPE, AND SIZE PATTERNS

1 **INTRODUCE AND INVESTIGATE** Tell your student that patterns people can see can be made using different colors, shapes, and sizes of objects. Have your student investigate his or her surroundings and identify the things he or she thinks are patterns, such as the flooring, the carpet, or the wallpaper.

2 **DIRECT AND EXPLAIN** Direct your student to look at the color pattern shown in the pattern box. Explain to him or her that this pattern is made of different colors. Ask, *What colors do you see in the pattern?* [yellow and green] *What order are the colors in?* [yellow, green, yellow, green, yellow, green, yellow, green] *What color should come next in the pattern?* [yellow] Use the colored circles you created from construction paper and cardboard to make another color pattern and repeat the activity with your student. Have him or her tell you what colors should come next and place the colors to continue the pattern. Then have your student draw another color pattern.

3 **DIRECT AND EXPLAIN** Direct your student to look at the shape pattern shown in the pattern box. Explain to him or her that this pattern is made of different shapes. Ask, *How many different shapes do you see in the pattern?* [2] *What different shapes do you see in the pattern?* [squares and circles] *What order are the shapes in?* [square, square, circle, circle, square, square, circle, circle] *What shape should come next in the pattern?* [square] Use the cardboard shapes to make another shape pattern and repeat the activity with your student. Have him or her tell you what shapes should come next and place the shapes to continue the pattern. Ask your student to model another shape pattern using the cardboard shapes.

A BRIGHT IDEA

Create shape patterns using magnets and construction paper. Have your student create shapes using construction paper. Model how to make patterns using the paper shapes and magnets on a refrigerator or another metal surface.

Pattern Box

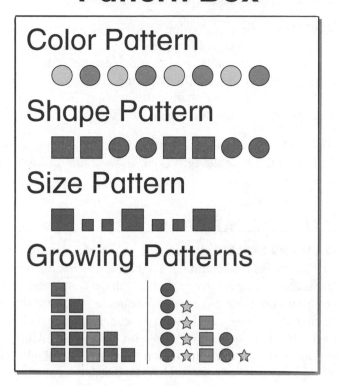

Color Pattern

Shape Pattern

Size Pattern

Growing Patterns

4 **DIRECT AND EXPLAIN** Direct your student to look at the size pattern in the pattern box. Tell your student that the size pattern is a pattern made of the same shape, but with different sizes. Ask, *What shape do you see in the pattern?* [squares] *What different sizes do you see?* [big and small] *What is the order of the sizes?* [big, small, small, big, small, small, big] *What size should come next in the pattern?* [small] Use the cardboard shapes to continue the activity using a new pattern. Have your student tell you what size shape should come next and ask him or her to place the shapes in the right place in the pattern. Then have your student draw or model another size pattern.

5 **DISTRIBUTE** Distribute Student Learning Page 2.A. Help your student by reading the directions out loud to him or her. Then direct your student to complete the activity.

6 **EXPAND** After your student has displayed an understanding of basic patterns, continue the lesson by creating patterns and covering up or leaving out colors, shapes, or objects from the middle of the pattern. Then have your student identify the missing pattern pieces and place the correct cardboard piece in the pattern.

PATTERNS THAT GROW

1 **EXPLAIN** Tell your student that patterns can grow. Explain that when a pattern grows, the number of objects in the pattern increases. The number of different objects in the pattern may also increase. Show your student the beginning of one of the

ENRICH THE EXPERIENCE

Plant a pattern of flowers in a garden space or planter box. Have your student decide on the types of flowers he or she would like to use. Then have your student help you plant the flowers in a pattern of his or her choosing.

MATH

LESSON 2.2

growing patterns shown in the pattern box. Then challenge him or her to describe the way the pattern is growing.

2 **DIRECT** Place one of the color, shape, or size pattern pieces in front of your student. Have him or her continue the pattern using any different colors, shapes, or sizes of pattern pieces. Guide your student to use the pattern pieces to make a growing pattern. Help him or her change the number, color, or size of the pattern pieces to create a growing pattern.

3 **DISTRIBUTE** Give Student Learning Page 2.B to your student. Help him or her read the directions and ask him or her to complete the activity.

TRANSLATION OF PATTERNS

1 **REVIEW AND EXPLAIN** Review the letters of the alphabet with your student before beginning this part of the lesson. Then tell your student that patterns of rhythm, shapes, and sizes can be **translated** into other patterns. For example, a pattern that shows shapes that are blue, red, blue, red, blue, red, and so on can also be shown as A, B, A, B, A, B, and so on. This AB pattern can also be shown using two different shapes or two different sizes of shapes. Have your student look at the color, shape, and size patterns in the pattern box. Ask him or her to describe each pattern to you using A and B.

2 **EXPAND** Give your student an example of a letter pattern, such as A, B, C, A, B, C. Have him or her demonstrate the pattern using the color, shape, or size pattern pieces.

3 **DISTRIBUTE** Distribute Student Learning Page 2.C. Help your student read the directions and have him or her complete the activity. Then distribute Student Learning Page 2.D. Read the directions out loud to your student and have him or her choose and complete one (or both) of the activities.

+

ENRICH THE EXPERIENCE

For more games and activities on patterns and other math concepts, go to http://www. lessonplanz.com/grades. shtml. Click on Grades K–2 and then click on Mathematics.

FOR FURTHER READING

Let's Look at: Patterns, manufactured by Lorenz Books, (Anness Publishing, Ltd., 2002).

What's Next, Nina?, by Sue Kassirer and Page Eastburn O'Rourke, ill. (Kane Press, 2001).

Zoo Patterns, by Patricia Whitehouse (Heinemann Library, 2002).

Branching Out

TEACHING TIP

Take your student on a walk around his or her neighborhood. Ask him or her to identify patterns. These might include the bricks on buildings, the flowers in gardens, or the pattern of a traffic signal. Point out any patterns that you see that your student doesn't describe.

CHECKING IN

To assess your student's understanding of patterns, have him or her use toys to create one of each of the patterns that he or she learned in the lesson. Then ask your student to translate the patterns using A and B.

Circle What Comes Next

Follow the steps.

1. Circle the color that comes next.

       _____

2. Circle the shape that comes next.

        _____

3. Circle the size that comes next.

        _____

Draw the Pattern Pieces

Show how the pattern grew. Draw the missing pieces.

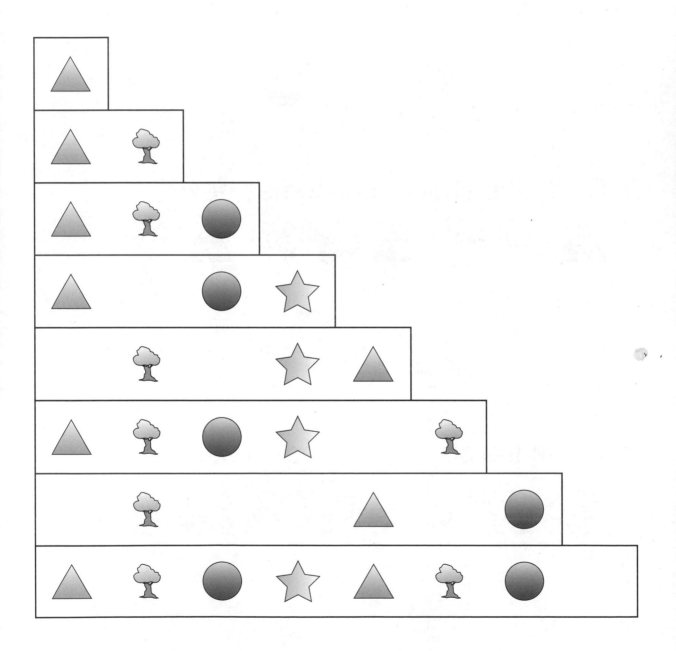

Find Your Way

Begin at the arrow. Find your way through the maze. Follow an AB pattern. Draw a line to mark your path. End at the star.

A is   B is

START

END

What's Next? You Decide!

Teacher: *Read aloud the directions and activities. Then have your student choose which activity to do next.*

Now it's your turn to choose what to do next in the lesson. Read the activities and decide which one you want to do—you may want to try them both!

Make a Rock Garden

MATERIALS

❏ 1 shallow square pan or plastic container

❏ sand

❏ pebbles, rocks, or marbles in a variety of colors and sizes

STEPS

Make your own patterned rock garden.

❏ Put a layer of sand in the pan.

❏ Use your hand to make the surface smooth.

❏ Choose the pebbles, rocks, or marbles you want to use.

❏ Arrange the pebbles, rocks, or marbles in a pattern.

❏ Share your rock garden with a friend. See if he or she can identify the pattern.

❏ Move and change the rocks to make new patterns.

Make a Flag

MATERIALS

❏ 1 large posterboard

❏ several sheets construction paper

❏ markers or crayons

❏ glue

❏ 1 pair scissors

STEPS

Make a patterned flag to hang up for a special day.

❏ Decide what you want your flag to show. Do you want to make a flag for a birthday or a holiday?

❏ Decide on a pattern for the flag.

❏ Draw pictures on the construction paper. Use scissors to cut out shapes.

❏ Glue the shapes to the posterboard in the pattern you chose.

❏ Share your flag with a friend or family member.

❏ Display the flag on the special day.

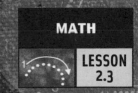

Exploring Shapes

The world around us is made up of shapes.

OBJECTIVE	BACKGROUND	MATERIALS
To teach your student about the shapes that people see and use every day and the way in which these shapes are separated into equal halves	The things that we see around us are shapes or made up of a combination of shapes. In this lesson, your student will learn about four basic shapes as well as space shapes. He or she will also learn how these shapes and other items can be made into two equal parts.	■ Student Learning Pages 3.A–3.D ■ models of space shapes, such as a ball, block, cereal box, oatmeal container, and party hat ■ several sheets construction paper ■ glue ■ 1 package modeling clay (optional) ■ markers or crayons

VOCABULARY

SHAPES the forms of things

EQUAL exactly the same amount

HALVES two equal amounts or parts from one whole

Let's Begin

CIRCLES, SQUARES, RECTANGLES, AND TRIANGLES

1 **DIRECT AND IDENTIFY** Direct your student to look at the **shapes** in the basic shapes section of the shape box on the next page. Then draw his or her attention to the things that have those shapes. Begin with the circle and work your way through the shapes. Tell your student the name for each shape and have him or her repeat each name. Then point to the shapes and have him or her name each shape to demonstrate his or her understanding. Have your student identify aspects about each shape. Say, *Describe a circle.* [possible answer: it's round] *Describe a square.* [possible answer: it has straight sides] *Describe a rectangle.* [possible answer: it has straight sides] *Describe a triangle.* [possible answer: it has a point at the top and a flat bottom]

Shape Box

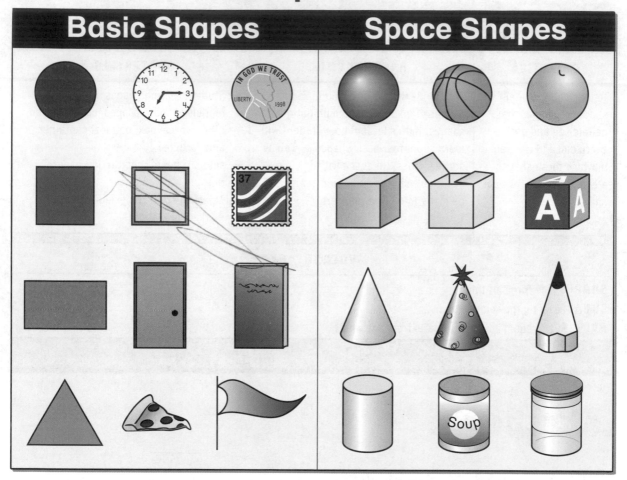

| **Basic Shapes** | **Space Shapes** |

2 **EXPAND** Direct your student to look at all the shapes in the left side of the shape box. Guide him or her to examine what is the same and different about the shapes. Ask, *How are the square and the rectangle the same?* [possible answer: they both have four straight sides] *How are the square and the rectangle different?* [possible answer: the rectangle has some sides that are longer] *How is the circle different from the other shapes?* [possible answer: it's the only shape that's round] *How is the triangle different from the square and the rectangle?* [possible answer: it has a different number of sides]

3 **INVESTIGATE** Tell your student that the shapes he or she just learned about can be seen in the things we look at every day. Direct your student to look around the room he or she is in and think of the things he or she uses every day. Ask, *What are some things that are shaped like circles?* [possible answers: a clock, a table, a plate, a coin] *What are some things that are shaped like* *squares?* [possible answers: a window, a box] *What are some things that are shaped like rectangles?* [possible answers: a sheet of paper, a rug, a door] *What are some things that are shaped like triangles?* [possible answers: a piece of pizza, a tile]

4   **DISTRIBUTE** Give Student Learning Page 3.A to your student. Help him or her with the directions. Then have your student complete the page.

SPHERES, CUBES, CONES, AND CYLINDERS

1   **INTRODUCE AND EXPLAIN** Direct your student to look at the shapes in the space shapes side of the shape box. Begin with the sphere and work your way through the space shapes. Tell your student the name for each space shape and have him or her repeat each name. Then point to the different space shapes and have him or her name each shape. Have your student look at the shapes and the objects he or she may be familiar with that have the same shape. Then point to each picture and have him or her name the shape.

2   **EXPAND** Explain to your student that circles, squares, rectangles, and triangles can be seen in the faces, or flat surfaces, of the space shapes. Point out how a sphere looks like a circle, a cube looks like a square, a cone looks like a triangle, and the top or bottom of a cylinder looks like a circle. Have your student look at the shape box and identify the basic shapes he or she sees in the space shapes.

3   **EXPLORE** Help your student explore his or her surroundings and identify items that are space shapes. Gather items that represent space shapes, such as blocks, cereal boxes, oatmeal containers, cans, party hats, balls, marbles, and so on. Have your student identify each item. Then have him or her describe each kind of space shape and match each item with its space shape in the shape box.

4   **CREATE** Work with your student to build space shapes. Create patterns for space shapes using construction paper. For example, a net of six squares in the shape of a cross can be folded to create a cube. Include tabs at the edges. Have your student help you glue the tabs together to make each space shape. Encourage your student to be creative as the two of you experiment and create the space shapes.

5   **DISTRIBUTE** Distribute Student Learning Page 3.B to your student. Have him or her complete the activity. Give assistance with the directions as necessary.

SEPARATE INTO HALVES

1   **EXPLAIN AND DEMONSTRATE** Tell your student that shapes can be cut to make two parts that are **equal** in size, or two **halves.**

Exploring Shapes   **117**

> **TAKE A BREAK**
>
> Take your student on a walk around your neighborhood and have him or her identify the shapes he or she sees.

Cut a sheet of paper in half. Then demonstrate that a whole sheet of paper and the two halves are the same size. Stack the two halves on top of each other to show your student that each half is the same size. Continue this lesson by cutting circles, squares, rectangles, and triangles from paper into halves and into parts that aren't halves. Have your student stack the two pieces of each shape. Then ask him or her to decide whether or not each shape has been separated into equal parts.

2   **EXPAND**   Gather food items, such as oranges, slices of bread, and vegetables. Cut some of the items in half and others into two unequal parts. Have your student match the pieces together. Then ask him or her to identify which items have been separated into two equal parts and which have not.

3   **DISTRIBUTE**   Give Student Learning Page 3.C to your student. Help him or her read the directions. Then have him or her complete the activity using markers or crayons. If your student is having trouble figuring out which shapes are divided into halves, repeat the activity from Step 1 of this section. After you have reinforced the concept with your student, invite him or her to complete the activity.

4   **CONCLUDE**   To finish the lesson, distribute Student Learning Page 3.D to your student. Read the directions out loud to him or her. Then ask your student to choose and complete one of the activities on the page. If time permits, your student may wish to complete both of the activities.

ENRICH THE EXPERIENCE

Have your student make space shapes using modeling clay. Then help him or her separate the clay shapes into halves to show two equal parts.

Branching Out

TEACHING TIP

Take your student on a trip to an art museum to look at art. Many paintings and sculptures, especially ones that are abstract, will help your student see the ways shapes are used to create designs and figures. If a trip to an art museum isn't possible, visit art sites on the Internet or get an art book from your local library and investigate the artwork with your student.

CHECKING IN

To assess your student's understanding of shapes and sharing, cover the first column in each section of the shape box and have him or her identify the shape of each object. Then have your student draw a line to show where each shape or object should be separated to make two equal parts.

FOR FURTHER READING

Shapes, by Robert Crowther (Candlewick Press, 2002).

Shapes to Go, by Lola M. Schaefer (Heinemann Library, 2003).

Zoo Fair Shares, by Patricia Whitehouse (Heinemann Library, 2002).

Build the House

Follow the dots to draw each shape in the box. Then draw a picture of a house. Use all of the shapes in the box.

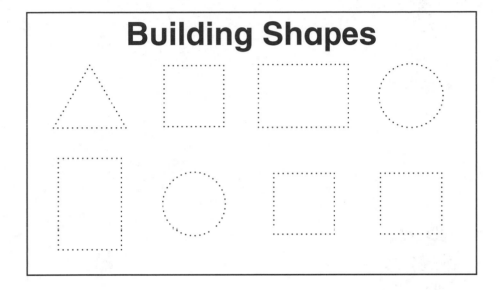

Building Shapes

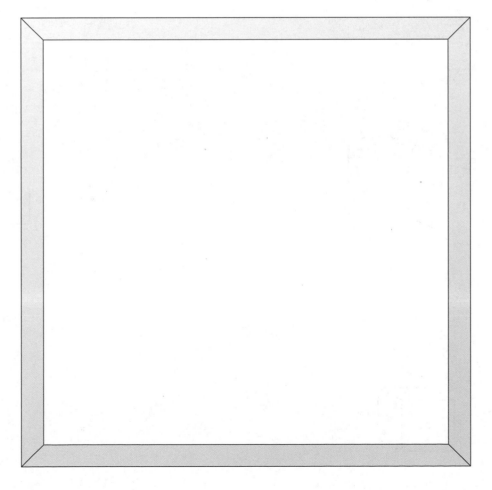

Match the Shapes

Draw a line. Match the objects with the shapes.

1.

A.

2.

B.

3.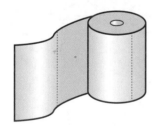

C.

4.

D.

Color the Halves

Each shape has been cut in two. Color the shapes red that show two equal parts. Color the shapes blue that show unequal parts.

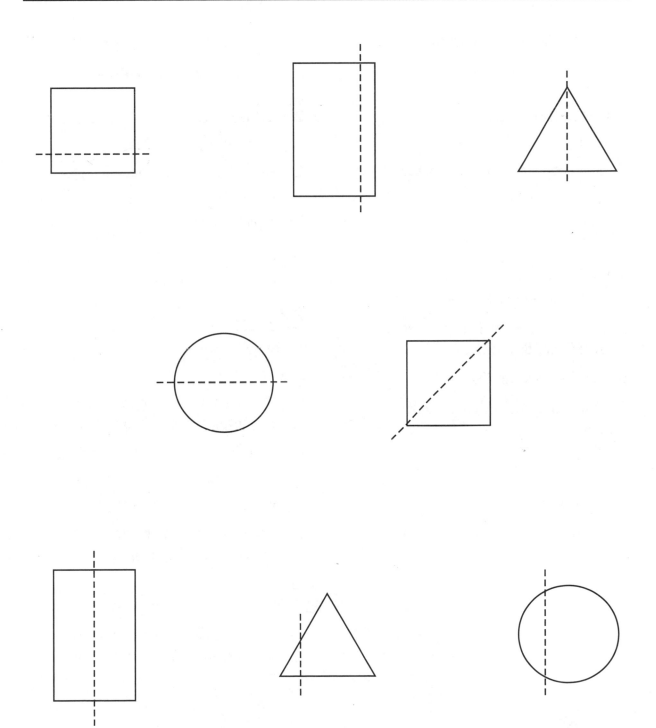

What's Next? You Decide!

MATH 3.D

Teacher: Read aloud the directions and activities. Then have your student choose which activity to do next.

Now it's your turn to choose what to do next in the lesson. Read the activities and decide which one you want to do—you may want to try them both!

Make a Shape Sun Catcher

MATERIALS

- ❏ 1 sheet waxed paper
- ❏ 3–4 sheets construction paper
- ❏ 1 pair scissors
- ❏ glue

STEPS

Make a sun catcher with a shape design.

- ❏ Cut the waxed paper into a square, rectangle, or triangle.
- ❏ Decide on your design.
- ❏ Cut shapes out of construction paper.
- ❏ Glue the shapes to the waxed paper. Make sure to leave spaces for the sun to shine through.
- ❏ Hang your sun catcher in a bright window.

Make a Shape Collage Shoebox

MATERIALS

- ❏ 1 shoebox
- ❏ several old newspapers and magazines
- ❏ 1 pair scissors
- ❏ glue
- ❏ crayons or markers

STEPS

Decorate a shoebox with a collage of pictures of shapes.

- ❏ Cut colorful pictures of shapes from old newspapers and magazines.
- ❏ Glue the pictures to the shoebox.
- ❏ If you'd like, color your shoebox with crayons or markers.
- ❏ Use your shoebox to store space shapes or art supplies.
- ❏ Show your collage shoebox to friends or family members.
- ❏ If you'd like, decorate another shoebox for a friend or family member to store something.

Learning About the Numbers Zero to 5

Basic numbers are the only way to start understanding the world of mathematics.

OBJECTIVE	BACKGROUND	MATERIALS
To teach your student about numbers from zero to 5	All numbers start from zero. The basic numbers of zero to 5 are an essential foundation for building a knowledge of math. In this lesson, your student will learn to count the numbers zero through 5 forward and backward, identify groups with one more and one less, recognize and make groups of objects, and write the numbers zero through 5.	■ Student Learning Pages 4.A–4.B ■ 30 buttons of the same shape and size ■ markers or crayons ■ 6 copies Writing Lines, page 357 ■ 12 index cards

VOCABULARY

EQUAL exactly the same number or amount
MORE a greater number or amount
FEWER a lesser number or amount

Let's Begin

FORWARD AND BACKWARD COUNTING

1 **DEMONSTRATE AND COUNT** Begin the lesson by modeling how to count from zero to 5. Show your student how he or she can count from zero to 5 using the fingers on one hand. Begin at zero with your hand in a fist, then raise one finger and say each number until you reach 5. Have your student say each number after you. Continue until he or she is able to repeat all of the numbers in order after you. Then have him or her count from zero to 5 on his or her own.

2 **EXPAND** Once your student has mastered counting forward from zero, begin at 5 and count backward to zero. Model this by holding your hand with the fingers out and closing one finger as your count backward. Have your student say each number after you and then count from 5 back to zero on his or her own.

TAKE A BREAK

Play a number game with your student. Give him or her instructions such as *Walk forward five steps* and *Walk backward zero steps.* Have your student count out the numbers as he or she takes each step. Alternate directions. If you have the time, let your student call out directions and take your turn as the walker.

EQUAL GROUPS AND MORE OR FEWER

1   **EXPLAIN** Use objects, such as buttons, to make **equal** groups. Explain to your student that the same number of objects is in each group. Have him or her compare the number of items by lining them up.

2   **EXPAND** Create two new groups of objects. The two groups should be noticeably different in size. Tell your student that the two groups have different numbers of objects. Have him or her compare the number of items by lining them up to show that there is a different number in each group. Have your student identify which group has **more** and which group has **fewer.**

3   **EXPAND** Rearrange the objects to create two equal groups. Make sure your student sees that the groups are now equal. Take one button from one group and add it to the other group. Ask, *Are the groups still equal?* [no; one group has more] Have your student identify which group has more and which group has fewer. Point to the group with one more. Ask, *How many more buttons are in this group?* [one more] Point to the group with one fewer. Ask, *How many fewer buttons are in this group?* [one fewer]

GROUPS OF ZERO TO 5

1   **MODEL AND RELATE** Set up six sheets of paper in an area where your student can watch. Don't place any objects on the first sheet of paper and say *zero*. Place one button on the second sheet of paper and say *one*. Continue placing objects and saying the numbers until you reach 5. Then have your student go from one sheet of paper to the other and say the number of objects in each group.

2   **DIRECT** Set up another six sheets of paper. Write each number from zero to 5 on one sheet of paper. Give your student 15 buttons. Direct him or her to make one group for each of the numbers.

3   **EXPAND** After your student has demonstrated an understanding of the number of objects shown by the numbers zero to 5, explain that groups of objects can be arranged differently and still have the same number. Show your student the sample arrangements on the next page. Help him or her to see that each group is grouped in a different way, but that the same number of objects is in each group. Then have your student create his or her own arrangements for each of the number groups from 2 to 5.

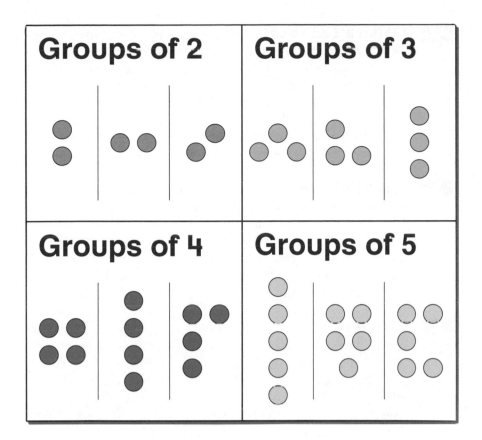

WRITE ZERO TO 5

1 **EXPLAIN AND DEMONSTRATE** Tell your student that we use symbols to show the numbers zero to 5. Show your student the numbers below. Explain the shape of each number as you guide your student's hand in the direction in which each number should be written. Tell your student that the number 0 is like drawing a circle and the number 1 is like drawing a straight line. The number 2 has a curve and a straight line. The number 3 has two curves, one on top of the other. There are two separate lines in the number 4. The first is like drawing two sides of a square and the second is like the number 1. The number 5 is another number with two lines. After explaining the number shapes, have your student trace each number path on his or her own.

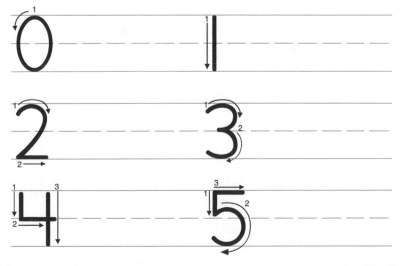

2 **DISTRIBUTE AND MODEL** Make six copies of the Writing Lines found on page 357. Beginning with zero, write each number for your student. Then hold your student's hand and guide him or her to write the number. Finally, have him or her practice writing the number on the rest of the page. Continue this exercise for each of the numbers through 5. Have your student write the numbers until he or she is able to demonstrate an understanding of the basic shape of each number.

3 **DISTRIBUTE** Distribute Student Learning Page 4.A to your student. Help him or her read the directions and then have him or her complete the activity. To complete the lesson, give Student Learning Page 4.B to your student. Read the directions out loud and have him or her choose one of the activities on the page. If time permits, your student may wish to complete both of the activities.

4 **CHALLENGE** Together with your student explore which learning methods work best for him or her. You may find that he or she would benefit from watching educational math videos from your local library. Or you may find that your student learns best when he or she can hold and count objects. Still, you may recognize that saying the numbers, steps, and instructions aloud to your student and having him or her repeat them is helpful. You may wish to incorporate some of these methods and check out http://www.funbrain.com for fun math activities and games.

Branching Out

TEACHING TIP

Take your student on a nature hike to find groups of "treasure." Make a list of items that your student must collect. There should be six items on the list. For example, direct your student to collect five leaves, four twigs, three stones, two blades of grass, one pine cone, and zero flowers. Give your student six different labeled containers and start the hunt.

FOR FURTHER READING

1, 2, 3 to the Zoo, by Eric Carle (Putnam Publishing Group, 1998).

Five Green and Speckled Frogs, by Priscilla Burns, ill. (Scholastic, 2003).

More, Fewer, Less, by Tana Hoban (Greenwillow Books, 1998).

CHECKING IN

To assess your student's understanding of the numbers zero to 5, play a game of matching cards. Make number and group cards using index cards. Write the numbers zero to 5 on six of the cards. Then draw groups of items numbering zero to 5 on another set of six cards. Mix up the cards and instruct your student to match the number cards to the cards that show the same numbers of items in a group. Then have your student line up the cards in order from zero to 5. Then ask him or her to make two groups of buttons arranged in different ways for the numbers 2 to 5.

Draw and Write Numbers

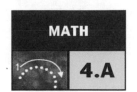

Draw a group for each number on the left. Write the number for each group on the right. Draw a line to match the groups that have the same number.

1. 0

2. 1

3. 2

4. 3

5. 4

6. 5

A. _____

B. _____

C. _____

D. _____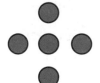

E. _____

F. _____

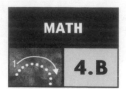

MATH
4.B

What's Next? You Decide!

Teacher: *Read aloud the directions and activities. Then have your student choose which activity to do next.*

Now it's your turn to choose what to do next in the lesson. Read the activities and decide which one you want to do—you may want to try them both!

Create a Mobile

MATERIALS

- ❏ 1 hanger
- ❏ 1 hole puncher
- ❏ several sheets construction paper
- ❏ 1 pair scissors
- ❏ glue
- ❏ string or yarn

STEPS

Make a mobile to show the numbers zero to 5.

- ❏ Cut the numbers 0 to 5 out of construction paper.
- ❏ Cut shapes out of construction paper.
- ❏ Have an adult help you punch a hole at the top and bottom of each number and shape.
- ❏ Use string or yarn to tie the shapes in each group to each number.
- ❏ Use string or yarn to tie each number to the hanger.
- ❏ Have an adult help you hang your mobile. Share it with your friends.

Make Place Mats

MATERIALS

- ❏ several sheets construction paper
- ❏ markers or crayons
- ❏ 1 pair scissors

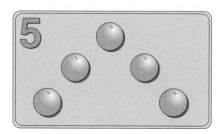

STEPS

Make place mats showing groups.

- ❏ Choose a sheet of colored construction paper for each place mat.
- ❏ Ask an adult to help you cut a fun design around the edge.
- ❏ Write the number for the group you want to make.
- ❏ Draw pictures of food items. Draw the number in the group.
- ❏ Make a place mat for each number group.
- ❏ Share your place mats with your family to use during mealtimes.

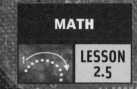

MATH

LESSON
2.5

Comprehending the Numbers Zero to 10

Everyone can count on math.

OBJECTIVE	BACKGROUND	MATERIALS
To teach your student about numbers through 10	Expanding your student's understanding of numbers to 10 will quickly produce fruit as his or her mathematical prowess develops. In this lesson, your student will learn to count to 10, to write and make groups of the numbers from 6 to 10, to combine and compare groups of numbers, and to order the numbers from 0 to 10.	<ul><li>Student Learning Pages 5.A–5.B</li><li>tape or chalk</li><li>40 buttons of the same color</li><li>5 clear plastic cups</li><li>5 copies Writing Lines, page 357</li><li>5 copies Web, page 356</li><li>5 red and 5 blue buttons</li><li>markers or crayons</li><li>11 index cards</li></ul>

VOCABULARY

COMBINATIONS the orders of digits to make numbers

COMPARE to look at two numbers to determine which is greater or lesser

Let's Begin

FORWARD AND BACKWARD COUNTING

1 **REVIEW** Together with your student review counting from zero to 5. Have him or her count out the numbers in order both forward and backward.

2 **INTRODUCE AND EXPAND** Explain to your student that 6, 7, 8, 9, and 10 are the numbers that come after 5. Count out the numbers and have him or her repeat each number after you. Begin with zero and count forward to 10. Then start at 10 and count backward to zero. Model for your student how he or she can use the fingers on both hands to count from zero to 10 and back from 10 to zero. Then ask your student to count from zero to 10 and back again on his or her own.

WRITING THE NUMBERS 6 TO 10

1 **EXPLAIN AND DEMONSTRATE** Direct your student to look at the numbers on the next page. Explain the shape of each number as

ENRICH THE EXPERIENCE

Make a number line using pieces of tape on the floor or by writing with chalk outside on a paved surface. Make 11 marks and label them from zero to 10. Have your student walk the number line as he or she counts from zero to 10 and back again.

you hold his or her hand and follow the direction in which each number should be written. Then have your student trace each number path without your help.

2 **DISTRIBUTE AND MODEL** Distribute five copies of the Writing Lines found on page 357 to your student. Begin with the number 6 and write the number one time for your student as he or she watches. Then guide your student's hand as he or she writes the number. Finally, have him or her complete the activity by writing the number on his or her own to fill the page. Direct your student to continue the activity with the rest of the numbers through 10.

GROUPS OF NUMBERS: 6 TO 10

1 **REVIEW AND MODEL** Review groups of zero to 5 with your student. Explain that groups can be made with 6, 7, 8, 9, or 10 objects, just like they were made with smaller numbers. Set five clear plastic cups right side up on a table. Write the numbers 6 to 10 on the cups. Have your student watch as you count out and place the correct number of buttons or other counters in each cup. Then have him or her remove the buttons from each cup and count out the numbers. Remove all the buttons from the cups and direct your student to count out and put the correct number of buttons in each cup.

2 **EXPLORE** Create several groups of buttons of different quantities on blank sheets of paper. Have your student count out the buttons in each group and identify the number in each.

3 **EXPAND** Refer your student to the groups on the next page. Tell him or her that groups can have the same number of objects even if they are organized in different ways. Have your student count the number of objects in each of the arrangements. Make sure he or she understands that the same number of objects are in each arrangement.

4 **DISTRIBUTE** Give your student five copies of the Web found on page 356. Write each number from 6 to 10 in the center of one copy of the Web. Direct your student to draw a different arrangement for the number in each of the outer ovals (a total of five arrangements for each number).

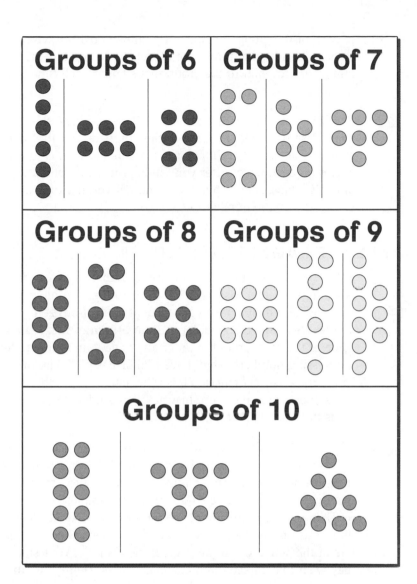

NUMBER COMBINATIONS

1   **EXPLAIN** Tell your student that a whole group of numbers can be made of smaller groups of numbers. Use different colors of buttons to model this concept for your student. Write each of the numbers 2 to 10 on a separate sheet of paper. Place one red button and one blue button on the page that has the number 2. Tell your student that this group of 2 is made of one red button and one blue button. Continue this activity with all of the numbers through 10. Show your student many different possible **combinations** for each number. Have your student count the numbers of different colored buttons that made each group.

2   **DIRECT** Clear the buttons from each page and have your student make each group using different combinations.

NUMBER COMPARISONS

1   **MODEL** Set up groups of buttons for your student to **compare.** Begin with two equal groups—one and one. Then add buttons

    Comprehending the Numbers Zero to 10   **131**

to each of the groups to compare numbers to 10. Have your student identify the number of objects in each group. Then ask him or her to point to the group that's larger each time you add buttons.

2 **DIRECT** Draw different numbers of circles on nine sheets of paper. Use one sheet for each of the numbers 2 to 10. Have your student use two different colored markers or crayons to color the circles on each page. After your student has colored each group of circles, have him or her count and tell you the total number of circles and the number of each color.

ORDER OF NUMBERS ZERO TO 10

1 **EXPLAIN** Explain to your student that numbers can be used to put things in order. Use 11 index cards to make number cards showing zero to 10. Have your student count from zero to 10 and lay the cards out in order in front of him or her. Remove some of the cards from the order and have your student identify the missing numbers. Then have him or her place the missing cards in the correct places. Finish the activity by gathering the cards and mixing them up. Instruct your student to place the cards in the correct order.

2 **DISTRIBUTE AND PRACTICE** Distribute Student Learning Page 5.A to your student. Help him or her read the directions and then direct him or her to complete the activity to practice working with the numbers 6 to 10. Then complete the lesson by giving Student Learning Page 5.B to your student. Read the directions out loud and have him or her choose and complete one of the activities on the page. If there's time, your student may wish to complete both of the activities. Help your student create the cards needed for both activities if necessary.

Branching Out

TEACHING TIP

Take your student on a walk around his or her neighborhood. Have him or her identify groups of objects, such as the number of trees in a yard, the number of cars in a parking lot or driveway, or the number of windows on a building.

CHECKING IN

To assess your student's understanding of the lesson, have him or her use buttons to count and compare the numbers from 6 to 10. Then ask him or her to use the buttons to count and compare all of the numbers from zero to 10.

FOR FURTHER READING

Counting Crocodiles, by Judy Sierra and Will Hillenbrand, ill. (Harcourt, 2001).

What's Cookin'?, by Nancy Coffelt (Chronicle Books LLC, 2003).

Order the Jars

Write the number in each jar. Then put the jars on the shelves in order. Draw a line to show where each missing jar should go.

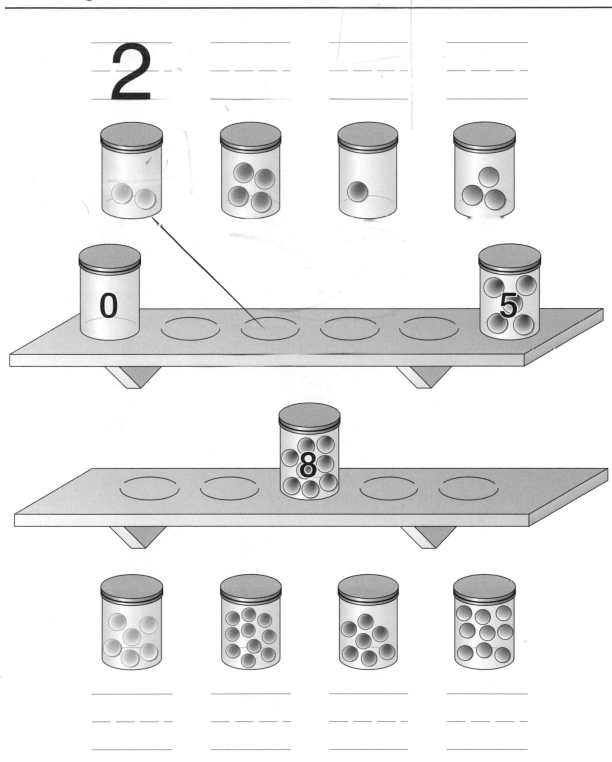

What's Next? You Decide!

Teacher: *Read aloud the directions and activities. Then have your student choose which activity to do next.*

Now it's your turn to choose what to do next in the lesson. Read the activities and decide which one you want to do—you may want to try them both!

Play a Counting Game

MATERIALS

❑ 11 index cards

❑ markers or crayons

STEPS

❑ Use markers or crayons to write 0, 1, 2, 3, 4, 5, 6, 7, 8, 9, and 10 on the index cards.

❑ Play the game with a friend.

❑ Mix up the cards and lay them in a pile facedown.

❑ Choose the top card.

❑ If the card has a number between 0 and 5, count up to 10. If the card has a number between 6 and 10, count down to 0.

❑ If you count correctly, keep the card.

❑ If you forget any numbers, put the card at the bottom of the pile.

❑ Your friend's turn is next.

❑ After the pile is gone, the game is over. The player with the most cards wins.

❑ Mix up the cards and play again.

Match the Cards

MATERIALS

❑ 22 index cards

❑ markers or crayons

STEPS

❑ Write 0, 1, 2, 3, 4, 5, 6, 7, 8, 9, and 10 on the index cards using markers or crayons.

❑ Draw pictures showing groups of 0 to 10 on index cards.

❑ Mix up the cards. Spread them out on a table, laying them facedown.

❑ Choose two cards at each turn.

❑ If the number on one card matches the group on the other card, keep the cards.

❑ If the cards don't match, lay them back down. Remember where each card is!

❑ When you've matched all the cards, put all the pairs in order.

❑ Play the game with a friend or family member.

Exploring Greater Numbers

The world is filled with greater numbers.
Learning to work with them is great!

OBJECTIVE	BACKGROUND	MATERIALS
To teach your student about greater numbers	The numbers zero to 10 serve to lay a foundation for greater numbers. Knowledge of the order from zero to 10 helps a student understand numbers greater than 10. In this lesson, your student will learn to count, read, write, order, and compare numbers from zero to 20. He or she will also learn about number patterns and become familiar with greater numbers by using a hundred chart.	■ Student Learning Pages 6.A–6.B ■ 41 index cards ■ 100 buttons of assorted colors ■ 1 cup ■ 20 small toys ■ markers or crayons ■ 3 copies Writing Lines, page 357 ■ 1 paper bag

VOCABULARY
ORDINAL NUMBERS number words that show places in order

Let's Begin

ZERO TO 20 AND BACK AGAIN

1 **REVIEW** Review counting from zero to 10 and back again with your student. Explain that he or she will use this knowledge to learn about more numbers.

2 **EXPLAIN** Tell your student that he or she is now going to learn to count to 20. Explain to him or her that 11, 12, 13, 14, 15, 16, 17, 18, 19, and 20 are the numbers that come in order after 10. Use index cards to make number cards that show the numbers zero to 20. First, display the numbers 11 to 20 in order. Count out the numbers for your student. Then have him or her count forward and backward from 11 to 20. Then add the numbers zero to 10 to the activity. Have your student count from zero to 20 and back again until he or she is able to count without skipping any numbers. If necessary allow your student to count in stages until he or she has mastered counting to 20 and back.

NUMBERS 11 TO 20

1 **EXPLAIN** Tell your student that each of the numbers from 11 to 20 is made of one group of 10 and another number between 1 and 10.

Model this concept by making a group of 10 red buttons. Have your student count the buttons and identify that there are 10 in the group. Then add one more button and say *eleven*. Have your student count the buttons to the number 11. Continue this activity through the number 20. Have your student count the buttons and identify the number that was added to the group of 10 to create each new number. Write each number as your student says it.

2 **EXPAND** Have your student use buttons to count and make groups from 11 to 20. Ask him or her to place the group of buttons for each number in a cup as he or she counts.

WRITING NUMBERS 11 TO 20

1 **DISPLAY AND ASK** Display the numbers below to your student. Ask, *How do these numbers look like the numbers you already learned to write?* [possible answer: they're all the same numbers I learned to write before] *How are they different?* [possible answer: they're all made of two numbers instead of just one]

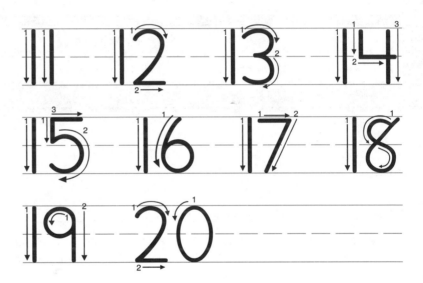

2 **GUIDE** Hold your student's hand as you trace each number as it's shown in the box. Have your student identify the numbers he or she has already learned that make up each of the new numbers.

3 **DISTRIBUTE AND MODEL** Distribute three copies of the Writing Lines found on page 357 to your student. Begin with the number 11. Demonstrate how to write the number for your student. Then guide your student's hand as he or she writes the number. Finally, have your student write the number three times, or until he or she demonstrates an understanding of the shape of the number on his or her own. Direct your student to continue writing the numbers 12 to 20.

NUMBER COMPARISONS TO 20

1 **EXPLAIN AND MODEL** Explain to your student that the numbers 11 to 20 can be compared just as the numbers 1 to 10 were compared. Make groups of buttons for your student to compare. Set each group on a sheet of paper and write the number of items in each group on the paper. Have your student count the number in each group and line up the buttons to tell which group is more and which group is less.

2 **EXPAND** Now give your student the buttons. Tell him or her to make groups of two numbers between 11 and 20. Have him or her use the counters to compare the numbers. Ask, *Which number is greater? How do you know?* [more buttons]

ORDER AND ORDINAL NUMBERS

1 **EXPLAIN** Tell your student that now that he or she has learned to count forward and backward to 20, he or she can put the numbers in order. Use the index cards numbered zero to 20 that you made at the beginning of the lesson. Put the cards in a paper bag and have your student pick out one card. Then have him or her count up from the number to 20 and then back down from the number to zero. After he or she has drawn all of the cards, have your student put them in order from zero to 20. If your student has a difficult time ordering the cards, create a number line on a large sheet of paper with spaces for all 21 cards. Your student may also wish to use buttons as counters to compare the numbers and find the correct order.

2 **EXPAND** Explain to your student that he or she can use other words to tell the order of objects. Set up a group of 20 small toys in a straight line. Write the **ordinal numbers** 1st through 20th on 20 index cards. Help your student think of a time when he or she waited in a line. Tell your student that each of the toys is waiting in line for its turn to play. Explain that the toy at the front of the line is in the 1st place. Place the index card with "1st" written on it next to the toy at the front of the line. Continue identifying each place and laying down cards until you reach the end of the line. Then go through the line and have your student repeat each ordinal number after you. Then have your student say each ordinal number in order on his or her own.

3 **ENRICH** Continue the activity by removing two of the cards at a time and having your student replace them next to the correct toys. Repeat this activity until you have removed, and your student has replaced, each of the cards at least once. Then remove all the cards and ask your student to place the cards in the correct order next to the toys.

4 **PRACTICE** Have your student choose 20 objects from around the house, such as a shoe, a book, and so on. Have him or her put them in a line. Point to one of the objects and have your

student identify its place, such as first, fourth, and so on. Continue pointing to other objects in the line. Be prepared to give lots of encouragement for correct answers. Then have him or her rearrange the line of objects. Encourage him or her to point to one of the objects and ask you to identify its position. As your student shows interest, you may wish to continue this throughout the week and periodically engage your student in identifying what's first, second, and so on with various objects.

NUMBER PATTERNS

1 **REVIEW** Review patterns of colors, shapes, and sizes with your student. You might wish to revisit Lesson 2.2 and have your student identify the patterns shown in the examples.

2 **EXPAND** Tell your student that patterns can also be made with numbers. First, use different colors of buttons to create a pattern for your student. For example, make a pattern showing red, yellow, blue, red, yellow, blue, red, yellow, blue, and so on. Tell your student that this is an A, B, C pattern. Write A, B, and C below each colored button. (Red is A, yellow is B, and blue is C.) Tell your student that patterns can also be shown with numbers. Write the numbers 1, 2, and 3 under each corresponding letter. (A is 1, B is 2, and C is 3.) So the number pattern is 1, 2, 3. Set up other consecutive number patterns for your student to identify. Include some patterns that have a number missing from the middle and have your student identify the missing number.

3 **EXPAND** Teach your student to skip count by using number patterns. Explain that in the number pattern 1, 2, 3, the numbers were counted in order by ones. Say that he or she can also count by twos to make patterns. Line up the index cards numbered 1 to 20. Put a button on the number 2. Explain to your student that to count by twos he or she will skip every other number. Place buttons on the numbers 4, 6, 8, 10, 12, 14, 16, 18, and 20. Then count the numbers for your student. Finally, have him or her count by twos on his or her own. Remove the buttons and have your student count by twos as he or she places the buttons on the number cards.

4 **CONTINUE** After your student has completed the activity for counting by twos, use the same number card line to show your student how to count by fives. Have him or her complete the same steps used for learning to skip count by twos.

5 **DISTRIBUTE** Give Student Learning Page 6.A to your student. Help him or her read the directions and complete the activity. After your student has finished the page, ask, *What numbers did both the frog and the kangaroo land on?* [10 and 20]

1 **EXPLAIN AND ASK** Direct your student to look at the number chart. Explain that the chart shows all of the numbers from 1 to 100. Ask, *What numbers look familiar to you?* [possible answer: the numbers 1 through 20] Have your student count from 1 to 20 as he or she points to each of those numbers in the chart.

Hundred Chart

1	2	3	4	5	6	7	8	9	10
11	12	13	14	15	16	17	18	19	20
21	22	23	24	25	26	27	28	29	30
31	32	33	34	35	36	37	38	39	40
41	42	43	44	45	46	47	48	49	50
51	52	53	54	55	56	57	58	59	60
61	62	63	64	65	66	67	68	69	70
71	72	73	74	75	76	77	78	79	80
81	82	83	84	85	86	87	88	89	90
91	92	93	94	95	96	97	98	99	100

2 **EXPAND** Point to the last column of numbers in the hundred chart. Explain to your student that all the numbers in this line stand for groups of 10. Point to 10 and say, *There is one group of 10 in 10.* Point to 20 and say, *There are two groups of 10 in 20.* Continue pointing to and describing the number of tens in each

multiple of 10 until you reach 100. Then model for your student how you can point to the numbers to help you count by tens to 100. Cover the last column of the hundred chart and have your student count by tens on his or her own.

3 **EXPLORE** Help your student explore the numbers on the hundred chart. Count with your student from 1 to 100 as you point to each number. If your student has trouble understanding the numbers, explain the groups of other numbers they are made of. For example, say, *In the number 36, there are three groups of 10 and one group of 6.* Help your student use buttons to create groups of objects for some of the greater numbers on the hundred chart.

4 **MODEL** Make several groups of 10 using buttons. Combine the groups to make the multiples of 10 from 10 through 100. Then add one button at a time to each tens group as you say the new number. Use this technique to help your student see how each number is formed. Say, *When I put one more button in the group that has 72, it makes 73.* After you have identified the groups to show the numbers 1 to 100, point to a number and have your student say the names of the numbers that come before and after. Then point to two numbers that have one number between them. Ask your student to tell you the name of the number that comes in between.

5 **DISTRIBUTE** To complete the lesson, distribute Student Learning Page 6.B to your student. Read the directions out loud to him or her and have your student choose and complete one of the activities on the page. If there's time, your student may wish to complete both of the activities.

A BRIGHT IDEA

Encourage your student to notice numbers as he or she goes about his or her day. For example, numbers are on street signs, on price tags, on food cartons, and so on.

Branching Out

TEACHING TIP

Have your student count out the number of the date of the month. Each day ask him or her to collect a group of household objects showing the number of the date of the month. Simple items, such as pieces of paper or pencils, will work best.

CHECKING IN

To assess your student's understanding of the lesson, use a hundred chart. Have him or her count from 1 to 100 and discuss the different groups that make up each number. Encourage your student to create patterns on the hundred chart using buttons. Ask him or her to count to 100 by twos, fives, and tens.

FOR FURTHER READING

Eating Pairs: Counting Fruits and Vegetables by Twos, by Sarah L. Schuette (Capstone Press, 2003).

Robert Crowther's Most Amazing Hide-and-Seek Numbers Book, by Robert Crowther (Candlewick Press, 1999).

Ten Friends, by Bruce Goldstone and Heather Cahoon, ill. (Henry Holt and Company, 2001).

Find the Patterns

Write the missing numbers. The frog jumps by twos. Color the rocks the frog lands on blue. The kangaroo jumps by fives. Color the rocks the kangaroo lands on yellow.

START

1 2 4 5

7 8 9

11 12 14 15 16

20 19

FINISH

What's Next? You Decide!

Teacher: *Read aloud the directions and activities. Then have your student choose which activity to do next.*

Now it's your turn to choose what to do next in the lesson. Read the activities and decide which one you want to do—you may want to try them both!

Create Number Pictures

MATERIALS

❑ 155 buttons, beads, or other objects to use as counters

❑ 10 sheets construction paper

❑ glue

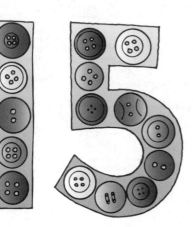

STEPS

❑ Draw a number from 11 to 20 on a sheet of construction paper. Write the number big!

❑ Count out the number of counters to show the number.

❑ Glue the counters around the shape of the number.

❑ Display your picture.

❑ Make pictures for all of the numbers from 11 to 20.

Make a Counting Book

MATERIALS

❑ 2 sheets construction paper

❑ markers or crayons

❑ 1 hole puncher

❑ 2 lengths string or yarn

STEPS

❑ Write the numbers 0 to 20 on one side of a sheet of construction paper. This will be your book's cover.

❑ Write the number 0 on a sheet of paper. Do not draw anything for zero.

❑ Write the number 1 on a sheet of paper. Draw one of your favorite objects or use stickers or rubber stamps instead.

❑ Write the number 2 on a sheet of paper. Draw two more objects.

❑ Write the numbers and draw pictures until you get to 20.

❑ Stack the drawings in order from 0 to 20. The cover should be on top. Add another sheet of construction paper for the back.

❑ Have an adult help you punch two holes at the top edges of each sheet.

❑ Use the string to tie the pages together.

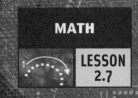

Understanding Addition

Everything adds up!

OBJECTIVE	BACKGROUND	MATERIALS
To teach your student basic addition concepts and methods	Now that your student has a solid understanding of numbers, it's time to put them together. In this lesson, your student will learn to join groups, to recognize and use the plus sign and the equal sign, and to add numbers to 6 horizontally and vertically.	■ Student Learning Pages 7.A–7.D ■ 10 counters, such as red and blue buttons ■ 6 wooden blocks (cubes) ■ 1 pair scissors ■ tape or glue

VOCABULARY
ADD to put two or more numbers or parts together to find the total **SUM** the total of two or more numbers added together

Let's Begin

JOINING PROBLEMS

1   **REVIEW** Review with your student the different combinations of numbers that make up groups from 2 to 6. Use the groups of buttons shown in the box on the next page. Cover the first two columns of the box with a blank sheet of paper. Begin with the section labeled "2 in all." Ask, *How many buttons are in the group?* [2 buttons] *How many red buttons are in the group?* [1 red button] *How many blue buttons are in the group?* [1 blue button] Continue until you have reached the last group in the "6 in all" section of the box. For each group, have your student identify the number of each color button that's part of the total number.

2   **EXPLAIN** Explain to your student that he or she can put smaller groups together to make one group. Use the box again. Cover the last column of the box with a blank sheet of paper. Begin with the section labeled "2 in all." Ask, *How many red buttons are there?* [1 red button] *How many blue buttons are there?* [1 blue button] *How many buttons are there in all?* [2 buttons] Continue through the "6 in all" section of the box. Have your student tell you how many buttons of each color there are. Then ask him or her to tell you how many buttons there are in all for each group.

Joining Groups

2 in all

3 in all

4 in all

5 in all

6 in all

3 **DISTRIBUTE** Distribute Student Learning Page 7.A to your
student. Help him or her read the directions and have him or
her complete the activity.

4 **CONNECT** Show your student how math is connected to things he
or she does. Incorporate addition into everyday activities with your
student. For example, during snack time invite your student to use
food items, such as raisins or crackers, to make and join groups.

PLUS AND EQUAL SIGNS

1 **EXPLAIN** Draw a large plus sign for your student. Tell him or
her that when he or she sees this sign it means to **add,** or to put

two numbers or groups together. A plus sign goes between the two numbers that should be added. Illustrate this concept by writing a plus sign between the first two groups of buttons in the box on the previous page. Then use buttons as counters or draw pictures of circles to make number groups. Have your student tell you the two numbers or groups that should be put together. Then have your student draw a plus sign between the two groups. (Save the counters or pictures with plus signs to use in the next step.)

2   **EXPLAIN** Draw a large equal sign for your student. Tell him or her that an equal sign means that the number written after it shows how many there are altogether. Illustrate this concept by writing an equal sign between the second and last groups of buttons in the box. Continue the activity started in the previous step by having your student write the equal sign after the two numbers that should be added. Then have him or her write the total number after the equal sign for each addition problem.

SUMS

1   **CREATE AND MODEL** Use wooden blocks to make number and symbol pieces to use in this section. Cut out 30 squares of paper the same size as one side of a block. Write each of the numbers from 1 to 6 on three sets of six squares for a total of 18 squares. Draw six plus signs on six of the squares. Draw six equal signs on six of the squares. Tape or glue each set of numbers from 1 to 6 on three of the blocks. Then cover the six sides of one block with plus signs and the six sides of another block with equal signs. If you have number blocks that show the numbers 1 to 6, use these and just make the plus and equal sign blocks. Use the blocks to set up horizontal addition problems (with sums of 6 or less) for your student to examine. Have him or her tell you what each number and symbol in the problem means.

2   **CONTINUE** Use the number and symbol blocks to set up the addends and the plus and equal signs for several addition problems. Have your student use the third number block to show the **sum.** Encourage your student to use buttons as counters to solve the addition problems. Be sure that none of the sums are greater than 6.

3   **EXPAND** Make one more number block to use in this section. This block should be covered on each side with the number zero. Use this block to show your student that adding zero to a number doesn't change the number. Set up addition problems that add zero to each number from 1 to 6. Have your student find and place the sum for each problem.

4   **DISTRIBUTE** Distribute Student Learning Page 7.B to your student. Help him or her read the directions and have him or her complete the activity.

MATH

LESSON 2.7

VERTICAL ADDITION

1 **EXPLAIN** Tell your student that he or she has just learned to read, write, and find the answer to addition problems that are written across in a straight line. Write a horizontal addition problem on a full sheet of paper with a plus and an equal sign. Then write the same addition problem vertically, using a bar under the bottom number in place of the equal sign. Show your student the two problems. Ask, *How are the two problems the same?* [they both have the same numbers and a plus sign] *How are they different?* [the first problem has an equal sign and the second problem has a line] *What do you think the line under the bottom number in the second problem means?* [equal]

2 **EXPAND** Tell your student that although the two example problems were written in different ways, they show the same thing. Work through the problems, comparing each number and sign to show your student that the problems are the same. Have your student use counters or draw pictures to find the answer to each of the addition problems. Use the blocks from the previous section to make new horizontal addition problems. Have your student write each problem vertically. Then invite him or her to use counters to model and solve each problem.

3 **PRACTICE** Give Student Learning Page 7.C to your student. Read the directions out loud to him or her and invite your student to finish the page.

4 **DISTRIBUTE** To complete the lesson, distribute Student Learning Page 7.D. Read the instructions out loud to your student and have him or her choose and complete one of the activities (or both!) on the page.

FOR FURTHER READING

Adding It Up at the Zoo, by Judy Nayer, Johanna Kaufman, and Claudine Jellison (Capstone Press, 2002).

Addition Annie, by David Gissler and Sarah A. Beise, ill. (Scholastic Library Publishing, 2002).

Animals on Board: Adding, by Stuart J. Murphy and R. W. Alley, ill. (HarperCollins Children's Books, 1998).

Branching Out

TEACHING TIP

Children at this age often play "teacher." Encourage your student to teach you about math.

CHECKING IN

Use a group of counters to show your student the number made by adding two groups. Have your student write the numbers shown by the counters, the plus and equal signs, and the sum.

Draw Groups

1. Draw 1 circle. Now draw 2 more. Write how many you drew in all.

----- ---- ----
_____

2. Draw 3 squares. Now draw 2 more. Write how many you drew in all.

----- ---- ----
_____

3. Draw 5 triangles. Now draw 1 more. Write how many you drew in all.

----- ---- ----
_____

Add Across

Write the number in each group.
Then write the number in all.

1. ____ + ____ = ____

2. ____ + ____ = ____

3. ____ + ____ = ____

4. ____ + ____ = ____

Add Down

Write the number in each group.
Then write the number in all.

1.   _ _ _ _ _ _ _

+ _ _ _ _ _ _ _

_ _ _ _ _ _ _

3.  _ _ _ _ _ _ _

+ _ _ _ _ _ _ _

_ _ _ _ _ _ _

2.  _ _ _ _ _ _ _

+ _ _ _ _ _ _ _

_ _ _ _ _ _ _

4. _ _ _ _ _ _ _

+ _ _ _ _ _ _ _

_ _ _ _ _ _ _

What's Next? You Decide!

Teacher: *Read aloud the directions and activities. Then have your student choose which activity to do next.*

Now it's your turn to choose what to do next in the lesson. Read the activities and decide which one you want to do—you may want to try them both!

Make a Book About Adding

MATERIALS

- ❏ 7 large sheets construction paper
- ❏ markers or crayons
- ❏ several old magazines
- ❏ 1 pair scissors
- ❏ glue
- ❏ 1 hole puncher
- ❏ yarn

STEPS

- ❏ Think of one way to show each of the numbers 1 to 6.
- ❏ Write a number on each sheet of construction paper.
- ❏ Write an addition sentence to show how to add to get each number.
- ❏ Cut out pictures from old magazines that show the groups of numbers. Ask an adult to help you. Glue the pictures near the addition sentences.
- ❏ Make a cover for your book on a sheet of construction paper.
- ❏ Stack the papers together with the cover on top.
- ❏ Have an adult punch two holes on the top edges and tie the pages together with yarn.

Play an Addition Game

MATERIALS

- ❏ 18 index cards
- ❏ markers or crayons

STEPS

Make playing cards to play an addition game with a friend.

- ❏ Write each of the numbers 1 to 6 on three sets of index cards.
- ❏ Turn the cards facedown and mix them up.
- ❏ Take three cards for yourself. Then have your friend take three cards.
- ❏ If you can, make an addition sentence and lay your three cards down.
- ❏ If not, take turns drawing cards with your friend until you can.
- ❏ The first player who makes three correct addition sentences wins the game.

Investigating Subtraction

When do you subtract?

OBJECTIVE	BACKGROUND	MATERIALS
To teach your student basic subtraction methods and concepts	Complementing the skill of addition is the skill of subtraction. A basic knowledge of subtraction is necessary in everyday life. In this lesson, your student will learn how groups and numbers are separated to find the difference, how the minus and equal signs are used in subtraction problems, and how to subtract from numbers up to 6 horizontally and vertically.	■ Student Learning Pages 8.A–8.D ■ 10 counters, such as red and blue buttons ■ 2 clear plastic cups ■ markers or crayons

VOCABULARY

SUBTRACT to take a number away from another number

DIFFERENCE the number that's left over when one number is subtracted from another number

Let's Begin

SEPARATING PROBLEMS

1 **MODEL AND ASK** Remind your student that in Lesson 2.7 he or she just learned to put two groups together to find the total number. Explain that groups can also be separated, or taken apart, to find the number that's left. Demonstrate this concept by using two clear plastic cups. Put 6 button counters in the first cup. Ask, *How many buttons are in the cup?* [6 buttons] Take out 2 of the counters and put them in the second cup. Ask, *How many buttons were moved to the second cup?* [2 buttons] *How many buttons are left in the first cup?* [4 buttons]

Step 1

Step 2

MATH

LESSON 2.8

2 EXPLAIN Tell your student that he or she can count to find the number of objects left over. Make different groups of buttons to show different separating problems. Have your student tell you the starting number, the number that was moved, and the number that was left over for each problem.

3 DISTRIBUTE Distribute Student Learning Page 8.A. Help your student read the directions. Then have your student complete the activity.

MINUS AND EQUAL SIGNS

1 MODEL AND EXPLAIN Draw a large minus sign. Tell your student that when he or she sees this sign, it means to take away, or **subtract.** The minus sign is put between two numbers. The number before the minus sign is what you start with, and the number after the minus sign is what should be taken away. Draw several groups of one to six circles on sheets of paper. First have your student write the number in the whole group. Then cross out some of the circles and have him or her write the number that was crossed out. Finally, instruct your student to draw a minus sign between the two numbers.

2 REVIEW AND EXPAND Draw a large equal sign for your student. Remind him or her that he or she learned about equal signs in addition problems. Tell him or her that in subtraction problems the equal sign also shows the final amount. In a subtraction problem the equal sign is used to show the **difference,** or the number that's left over. Return to the groups of circles you drew on paper in the previous step. Have your student draw an equal sign after the second number in each problem. Then help him or her write the difference in each problem.

DIFFERENCES

1 EXPLAIN Tell your student that the problems he or she wrote in the step above are known as subtraction sentences. These problems include one number that's subtracted from another number. They also include a minus sign, an equal sign, and the number showing the difference. Write more sets of horizontal subtraction problems for your student to complete. Have him or her draw and cross out circles or use buttons as counters to find each difference. Then have your student write the difference in each problem.

2 EXPAND Draw circles or use counters to demonstrate subtraction problems. Have your student write the entire subtraction sentence for each problem.

3 DISTRIBUTE Distribute Student Learning Page 8.B to your student. Begin with the first exercise. Have your student write the number in the group. Cross out one of the toy cars as your student watches.

ENRICH THE EXPERIENCE

Throughout the lesson, make up or have your student make up subtraction stories about the problems. For example, say, *Sam had 5 buttons on his coat. One of the buttons fell off. How many buttons are left on Sam's coat?* [4 buttons]

---

152 Making the Grade: Everything Your Kindergartner Needs to Know

Have your student write the number you crossed out. Then have him or her write the number left over. Continue crossing out and giving your student directions to write each number for the other three exercises: [2] cross out four toy rockets; [3] cross out two toy planes; and [4] cross out three toy boats.

VERTICAL SUBTRACTION

1   **EXPLAIN** Tell your student that he or she has learned to read, write, and solve subtraction problems that are written across from left to right. Now he or she is going to learn to read, write, and solve subtraction problems that are written downward from top to bottom. Write one horizontal subtraction problem on a sheet of paper. Then write the same problem vertically. See the examples shown below. Tell your student to look at and compare the two problems. Ask, *How are the two problems the same?* [they have the same numbers and a minus sign] *How are they different?* [the problem that goes across has an equal sign; the problem that goes down has a line] *What does the line under the second number in the problem that goes down mean?* [equal]

$$5 - 3 = 2$$

$$\begin{array}{r} 5 \\ -3 \\ \hline 2 \end{array}$$

$$6 - 2 = 4$$

$$\begin{array}{r} 6 \\ -2 \\ \hline 4 \end{array}$$

2   **EXPAND** Go through each number and symbol in the horizontal problem and show your student the corresponding number or symbol in the vertical problem. Be sure your student realizes that the problems are the same. Then write several horizontal subtraction problems on sheets of paper. Don't include the difference for any of the problems. Leave room at the bottom of each sheet. Have your student write each problem vertically. Then have your student use counters to find the difference for each vertical subtraction problem.

3   **DISTRIBUTE** Distribute Student Learning Page 8.C. Begin with the first exercise. Have your student write the number in the

ENRICH THE EXPERIENCE

For more math activities for your kindergartner, go to http://www. funbrain.com and click on Age 6 and Under.

Investigating Subtraction   **153**

MATH

LESSON 2.8

group. Cross out three of the seals as your student watches. Have your student write the number you crossed out. Then have your student write the number left over. Continue crossing out and giving your student directions to write each number for the last three exercises: [2] cross out one sea horse; [3] cross out three fish; and [4] cross out five penguins.

4 **DISTRIBUTE AND COMPLETE** Complete the lesson by distributing Student Learning Page 8.D to your student. Read the activity choices out loud and have him or her choose which activity to do next.

Branching Out

TEACHING TIP

Encourage your student to find and use subtraction in everyday situations and activities. For example, if he or she helps with housework, say, *There are 5 windows in this room. Three windows have been cleaned. How many are left to clean?* [2] You could also pose a problem such as *There were 4 squirrels in the tree. Four squirrels jumped to the ground. How many are left in the tree?* [0] Or, after the mail has arrived, say, *Six letters came in the mail today. After I open 1 letter, how many will be left to open?* [5]

CHECKING IN

To assess your student's understanding of subtraction, demonstrate a subtraction problem using counters. Then have him or her write the subtraction sentence for the problem horizontally. Finally, have your student write the problem vertically. Continue this activity using several other subtraction problems. This should help you identify any problem areas you might want to review with your student.

FOR FURTHER READING

Good-Bye Pie! A First Book of Subtraction, by Tim Healy and Jan Lewis, ill. (Reader's Digest Children's Publishing, 2003).

I Can Subtract, by Anna Nilsen and Mandy Stanley, ill. (Houghton Mifflin Company, 2000).

Math Games, by Vicky Shiotsu and Sean Parkes, ill. (Lowell House Juvenile, 2000).

Subtraction Fun, by Betsy Franco, Johanna Kaufman, and Claudine Jellison (Capstone Press, 2002).

Draw Differences

1. Draw 2 circles. Cross out
1 circle. Write how many
are left.

— — — —

2. Draw 5 squares. Cross out
3 squares. Write how many
are left.

— — — —

3. Draw 3 triangles. Cross out
2 triangles. Write how many
are left.

— — — —

Subtract Across

Write the number of the whole group. Watch as some of the objects are crossed out. Write the number of things crossed out. Then write the difference.

1. _____ − _____ = _____

2. _____ − _____ = _____

3. _____ − _____ = _____

4. _____ − _____ = _____

Subtract Down

Write the number of the whole group.
Watch as some of the objects are
crossed out. Write the number of things
crossed out. Then write the difference.

1.

$$\begin{array}{r} \text{-----} \\ - \text{-----} \\ \hline \\ \text{-----} \\ \text{-----} \end{array}$$

3.

$$\begin{array}{r} \text{-----} \\ - \text{-----} \\ \hline \\ \text{-----} \\ \text{-----} \end{array}$$

2.

$$\begin{array}{r} \text{-----} \\ - \text{-----} \\ \hline \\ \text{-----} \\ \text{-----} \end{array}$$

4.

$$\begin{array}{r} \text{-----} \\ - \text{-----} \\ \hline \\ \text{-----} \\ \text{-----} \end{array}$$

What's Next? You Decide!

Teacher: *Read aloud the directions and activities. Then have your student choose which activity to do next.*

Now it's your turn to choose what to do next in the lesson. Read the activities and decide which one you want to do—you may want to try them both!

Play a Matching Game

MATERIALS

❑ 20 index cards

STEPS

Make cards and play a subtraction matching game.

❑ Write the first part of 10 subtraction sentences on 10 index cards.

❑ Write the 10 differences on another set of 10 cards.

❑ Ask an adult to help you.

❑ Place one set of cards facedown on your left.

❑ Place the other set on your right.

❑ Choose one card from each set and see if you can make a subtraction sentence.

❑ If you can, keep the cards. If not, put the cards back where you found them.

❑ After all of the cards are matched, the game is over.

❑ Play the game again with a friend. The player with the most matches wins!

Make a Subtraction Kite

MATERIALS

❑ 1 sheet construction paper

❑ 1 pair scissors

❑ glue

❑ markers or crayons

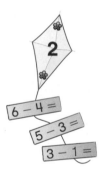

STEPS

Make a kite to show differences.

❑ Cut a kite shape from construction paper like the one in the picture.

❑ Cut out rectangles to make the tail.

❑ Glue the rectangles to the end of the kite.

❑ Choose a number from 1 to 6. Write it on the large part of the kite.

❑ Write subtraction sentences that have your number as the difference.

❑ Write each subtraction sentence on a rectangle of the kite's tail.

❑ Have an adult help you display your kite in your room or play area.

Counting Money

Money is something you can always count on!

OBJECTIVE	BACKGROUND	MATERIALS
To teach your student about the value of pennies, nickels, and dimes	Knowledge of money is essential to your student. Being able to recognize and count coins is an important life skill. In this lesson, your student will learn the value of pennies, nickels, and dimes as well as how to identify the three different coins.	■ Student Learning Pages 9.A–9.B ■ 10 pennies, 10 nickels, and 10 dimes ■ markers or crayons

VOCABULARY
PENNY a copper-colored coin with a value of 1 cent **NICKEL** a silver-colored coin with a value of 5 cents **DIME** a silver-colored coin with a value of 10 cents

Let's Begin

INTRODUCTION TO COINS

1 **EXPLAIN** Show your student a **penny,** a **nickel,** and a **dime.** Tell him or her that pennies, nickels, and dimes are money. Each coin stands for a different amount of money. Explain that these coins can be used to buy many different items. Ask, *Have you ever spent a penny, a nickel, or a dime?*

2 **MODEL AND EXPLAIN** Draw a large cent sign and show it to your student. Tell him or her that this sign means "cent." Now write "1¢" on a sheet of paper. Show this to your student and tell him or her that when a number is written next to a cent sign, it shows a money amount. Explain that 1¢ means "1 cent." Have your student practice writing cent signs after different numbers from 1 to 10 to show money amounts.

3 **SHOW** Line up two pennies, two nickels, and two dimes in front of your student. Each kind of coin should have one heads up and one heads down. Ask, *How are the first two coins the same?* [they are the same shape, color, and size] *How are they different?* [they each have a different picture] Ask your student the same questions about the nickels and the dimes. Have him or her recognize the similarities and differences between both sides of each coin. Explain that the side showing the head of a person is called the heads side, and that the other side is called the tails

A BRIGHT IDEA

Encourage your student to begin saving coins in a bank. Have him or her make a bank out of a jar or a small box. Have your student keep track of the number of each coin and the total amount of money in his or her bank.

FOR FURTHER READING

Deena's Lucky Penny, by Barbara de Rubertis; Joan Holuband Cynthia Fisher, ills. (Kane Press, 1999).

Monster Money (*Hello Reader! Math Series*), by Grace Maccarone, Marilyn Burns, and Margaret A. Hartelius, ill. (Scholastic, Inc., 1998).

Pennies, by Suzanne Lieurance and Tom Payne, ill. (Scholastic Library Publishing, 2003).

You Can't Buy a Dinosaur with a Dime, by Harriet Ziefert and Amanda Haley, ill. (Handprint Books, 2003).

side. Now make groups of pennies, nickels, and dimes. Arrange the coins so that some are heads up and some are heads down. For each coin, have your student tell you whether the heads or tails side is facing up.

VALUE OF COINS

1 **EXPLAIN** Show your student a penny. Explain to him or her that the penny is worth 1¢. Tell your student that he or she can find the total amount in a group of pennies by counting by ones. For example, three pennies are worth 3¢. Make groups of pennies from 1 to 10 for your student to count. Begin with groups that show all of the coins heads up or heads down, then mix up the positions of the coins. Have him or her tell you the total amount, in cents, for each group of pennies.

2 **EXPAND** Show your student a nickel. Explain to him or her that a nickel is worth 5¢. Ask, *How many pennies are worth 5¢?* [five pennies] Explain to your student that he or she can combine a nickel with pennies to make amounts from 6¢ to 10¢. Demonstrate to your student that he or she can start counting at 5¢ and then add 1¢ for each penny. Write the amounts 6¢ to 10¢ on paper. Help your student use a nickel and pennies to make each money amount. Tell your student that two nickels are worth 10¢. Have your student make two groups of nickels, one that's worth 5¢ and one that's worth 10¢.

3 **EXPAND** Show your student a dime. Explain to him or her that a dime is worth 10¢. Ask, *How many pennies are worth 10¢?* [10 pennies] *How many nickels are worth 10¢?* [two nickels] Have your student make four different groups of coins equaling 10¢. Direct him or her to use dimes [one dime], nickels [two nickels], pennies [10 pennies], or a combination [one nickel and five pennies]. Be sure your student recognizes that the four groups all show the same money amount. Ask him or her to count out the amounts to you. Then distribute Student Learning Page 9.A. Help your student complete the activity. Then complete the lesson by distributing Student Learning Page 9.B to your student. Read the activities out loud to your student.

Branching Out

TEACHING TIP

When you are out shopping with your student, have him or her count the pennies, nickels, and dimes you receive in change. Quiz him or her about the number of each coin you received and the total value of the coins.

CHECKING IN

To assess your student's understanding of pennies, nickels, and dimes, have him or her use coins to reteach each part of the lesson to you.

Match the Money

Draw a circle around the two groups of coins that show 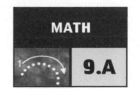 5¢ . Draw a square around the two groups of coins that show 8¢ . Draw a triangle around the two groups of coins that show 10¢ .

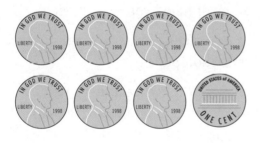

What's Next? You Decide!

Teacher: Read aloud the directions and activities. Then have your student choose which activity to do next.

Now it's your turn to choose what to do next in the lesson. Read the activities and decide which one you want to do—you may want to try them both!

Play a Coin Game

MATERIALS

❑ 5 pennies, 5 nickels, and 5 dimes

❑ 1 paper bag

❑ 1 bandana or scarf

STEPS

Play a guessing game with a partner using pennies, nickels, and dimes.

❑ Put all the coins in the bag.

❑ Have your partner tie the bandana or scarf around your head covering your eyes.

❑ Choose one coin from the bag.

❑ Use the size, shape, and feel of each coin to guess what the coin is.

❑ If you can't figure it out, have your partner give you a clue.

❑ Take turns choosing coins and guessing what they are.

Make a Catalog

MATERIALS

❑ 6 sheets construction paper

❑ old magazines

❑ 1 pair scissors

❑ glue

❑ markers or crayons

❑ 1 stapler

STEPS

Make a catalog selling items for 10¢ or less.

❑ Cut out from old magazines five pictures of items you want to sell.

❑ Glue one picture to each sheet of construction paper.

❑ Decide how much each item will cost. Write the amount in cents on each page.

❑ Draw coins to show each amount.

❑ Design a cover for your catalog.

❑ Stack the pages together with the cover on the top.

❑ Have an adult help you staple the pages together to make your catalog.

❑ Share your catalog with a friend or family member.

Examining Time

It's always a good time to learn!

OBJECTIVE	BACKGROUND	MATERIALS
To teach your student about time	Time is how people divide the parts of a day. Knowing the time helps people organize when they do things each day. In this lesson, your student will learn about the different parts of a day, how to measure the time of activities in relation to one another, and how to tell time on analog and digital clocks.	■ Student Learning Pages 10.A–10.B ■ 3 sheets construction paper, 1 brightly colored ■ 1 paper fastener ■ 12 index cards

VOCABULARY
DAYTIME the part of day when it's light out **NIGHTTIME** the part of day when it's dark out **MORNING** the time between sunrise and noon **AFTERNOON** the time between noon and sunset **EVENING** the time between sunset and bedtime

Let's Begin

PARTS OF A DAY

1 **EXPLAIN** Tell your student that each day is separated into different parts. **Daytime** is the part of the day when it's light out. **Nighttime** is the part of the day when it's dark out. Ask, *During what time of the day is the sun out?* [daytime] *During what time of the day can you see the moon?* [nighttime] *What are some of the things you do during the daytime?* [eat breakfast, eat lunch, take a walk, go shopping, and so on] *What are some of the things you do during nighttime?* [eat dinner, read, watch television, go to bed, and so on]

2 **EXPAND** Tell your student that the time that most people are awake is also divided into different parts. **Morning** is the time between sunrise and noon, or the time between waking up and eating lunch. Ask, *What are some of the things you do in the morning?* [eat breakfast, exercise, and so on] **Afternoon** is the time between noon and sunset. Ask, *What are some of the things you do in the afternoon?* [watch television, take a nap,

and so on] **Evening** is the time between sunset and bedtime. Ask, *What are some of the things you do in the evening?* [eat dinner, play games, and so on]

MORE OR LESS TIME

1   **EXPLAIN**   Tell your student that some of the things we do every day take a long time and other things take only a little while. Ask, *What are some things that take you a long time to do?* [clean my room, go shopping, and so on] *What are some things that take you only a little while to do?* [brush my teeth, get dressed, and so on]

2   **EXPAND**   Explain to your student that the things that take a long time take more time than the things that take only a little while. Ask, *Does it take you more time to brush your teeth or to eat breakfast?* [eat breakfast] *Does it take you less time to clap your hands three times or to read a book?* [clap my hands three times]

3   **DISCUSS**   Discuss with your student the activities in his or her daily schedule. Have him or her identify the things that take a long time and the things that take only a little while. Record each of the activities your student mentions. Then have him or her compare sets of two activities and tell which activity takes more or less time.

ANALOG CLOCKS—TELLING TIME

1   **INTRODUCE**   Tell your student that there are 24 hours in each day. Explain that clocks tell people what the time is using numbers. Show your student the analog clocks in the box below. Then have your student identify analog clocks in his or her surroundings. Tell your student that the little hand, or the short hand, shows the hour, and that the big hand, or the long hand, shows the minutes. Point to the different parts on the clock as you tell your student about them. Explain that the numbers on the clock show the number name for each hour.

Analog Clocks

2   **CREATE AND MODEL**   Make an analog clock model with moveable hands to use throughout the lesson. Cut out a circle from a sheet of construction paper. Write the numbers 1 to 12

ENRICH THE EXPERIENCE

Have your student think of a favorite story. Ask him or her to tell you about some of the activities that took place in the story. Then have your student draw pictures of the activities and tell whether each took place in the morning, afternoon, or evening.

around the clock face. Then make one hour hand and one minute hand out of brightly colored construction paper. Punch holes in the center of the clock face and the ends of the hands. Use a paper fastener to attach the hands to the clock face. Have your student identify each part of the analog clock.

3   **EXPAND** Explain to your student that when he or she tells the time of day shown on a clock, he or she should say the number that the little hand is pointing to and add the word *o'clock* to the end. Demonstrate this for your student. Begin with 12. Set the moveable hands to show 12 o'clock, say *12 o'clock*, and have your student repeat after you. Continue moving the hour hand, saying the time, and having your student repeat after you all the way around the clock. Then point to different hours and have your student tell you the time. Finally, give your student a time and have him or her move the hour hand on the clock face to show the time.

DIGITAL CLOCKS—TELLING TIME

1   **EXPLAIN** Tell your student that digital clocks are another type of clock that people use to tell the time. These clocks don't have hands and usually have a face that's shaped like a rectangle. Show your student the pictures of the digital clocks in the box below. Then have him or her compare the digital clocks to the analog clocks. Have your student identify digital clocks in his or her surroundings.

Digital Clocks

2   **CREATE AND EXPAND** Make a digital clock using construction paper and index cards. Draw a digital clock face on a sheet of construction paper. Include the two dots and two zeros after the two dots. Write the numbers 1 to 12 on index cards as they would appear on a digital clock face. Tell your student that on a digital clock the time is shown using numbers. The first number shows the hour and the number that comes after the two dots shows the minutes. Explain to your student that he or she tells the time the same way when using a digital clock—say the hour followed by the word *o'clock*. Use the index cards to change the hour shown on the clock. Begin with 12 o'clock and work in order through the times. Have your student repeat each time after you say it.

3   **DIRECT** Mix up the cards and place them on the digital clock face one at a time. Have your student tell you each time that's

! A BRIGHT IDEA

As you work through the lesson at different parts of the day, tell your student the time at each hour. Then have him or her move the hands on the analog clock and use the index cards on the digital clock to show the time.

shown. Then give the cards to your student and have him or her put the hour on the clock face as you indicate times in random order.

4 **DISTRIBUTE** Distribute Student Learning Page 10.A. Help your student read the directions and have him or her complete the activity. To complete the lesson, distribute Student Learning Page 10.B. Read the directions out loud to your student and have him or her choose which activity to complete next.

5 **SING AND DANCE** Help your student remember important times in his or her day by making up a song about what time is bedtime, lunchtime, and lesson time. Think of a song together—it can be silly and fun—and sing it out loud together during the day.

Branching Out

TEACHING TIP

Take a walk with your student around the neighborhood. Visit local stores and look for signs that tell the opening and closing hours. Have your student show the times by moving the hands on the analog clock you made for the lesson.

CHECKING IN

To assess your student's understanding of the lesson, have him or her go through each section and tell you about the things he or she learned. Guide your student in this retelling by asking questions about each topic, such as, *What do you know about the parts of the day?* If your student has a difficult time remembering any part of the lesson, review the material from that section.

FOR FURTHER READING

Bunny Day: Telling Time from Breakfast to Bedtime, by Rick Walton and Paige Miglio, ill. (HarperCollins Publishers, 2002).

How Long Did I Sleep?, by Jim Pipe (Millbrook Press, 2003).

What Time Is It?, by P. D. Eastman (Random House, 2002).

What Time Is It?: A Book of Math Riddles, by Sheila Keenan and Kayne Jacobs, ill. (Scholastic, Inc., 1999).

Match the Clock Times

Draw a line to match the time to the clock with hands. Then draw a line to match the clock with hands to the clock that only has numbers.

---

8 o'clock

8:00

3 o'clock

11:00

11 o'clock

3:00

1 o'clock

1:00

What's Next? You Decide!

Teacher: *Read aloud the directions and activities. Then have your student choose which activity to do next.*

Now it's your turn to choose what to do next in the lesson. Read the activities and decide which one you want to do—you may want to try them both!

Make Wall Art

MATERIALS

❏ 2 sheets construction paper, 1 white and 1 yellow

❏ 1 pair scissors

❏ old magazines

❏ glue

STEPS

❏ Cut out a large sun shape from yellow construction paper. Then cut out a large moon shape from white construction paper.

❏ Find and cut out pictures of things that show daytime from old magazines.

❏ Find and cut out pictures of things that show nighttime from old magazines.

❏ Glue the pictures that show daytime to the sun cutout.

❏ Glue the pictures that show nighttime to the moon cutout.

❏ Have an adult help you hang your wall art.

Make a Day Poster

MATERIALS

❏ 1 large posterboard

❏ markers or crayons

STEPS

Make a poster about your day.

❏ Think of the things you do every day.

❏ Draw a picture on the posterboard showing each thing.

❏ Draw a sun or a moon near each picture to show whether it's daytime or nighttime.

❏ Draw a clock face showing the time you do each thing.

❏ Ask an adult to help you if you're not sure what time you do each thing.

❏ Use the poster to tell a friend about your day.

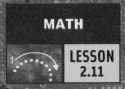

Comprehending Measurement

Everything around us comes in different shapes and sizes.

OBJECTIVE	BACKGROUND	MATERIALS
To teach your student about measurement	Measurement helps people decide on the sizes of things. Knowing how to measure is a skill your student will use in many ways. In this lesson, your student will learn about the measurements of length and weight and how to use objects to measure and compare different lengths and weights.	■ Student Learning Pages 11.A–11.B ■ string, ribbon, or yarn ■ masking tape ■ 50 or so buttons ■ 1 copy T Chart, page 355 ■ markers ■ 1 wire clothes hanger ■ 2 clear plastic cups ■ 2 pipe cleaners ■ assortment of objects of varying lengths and weights

VOCABULARY

LENGTH the measure of how long something is

WEIGHT the measure of how heavy something is

Let's Begin

LENGTH

1 **EXPLAIN** Tell your student that the things around us are of different sizes. One way that the differences among a set of objects can be seen is by measuring the **length** of each object. Discuss the definition of *length* with your student. Have him or her look at the objects in his or her surroundings. Ask him or her to explore length by looking at and comparing the lengths of different objects or areas. For example, direct your student to look at a window and note the length from top to bottom. Then have him or her look at a wall from the floor to the ceiling. Ask your student which is longer. Continue this activity by pointing out items with easily visible differences in length. Have your student identify which item is longer in each group.

2 **EXPAND** Help your student use string, ribbon, or yarn to measure the lengths of 7 to 10 items in his or her surroundings. Cut each piece of string to the correct length. Write the name of each item on a piece of masking tape and attach it to the end of the string. Then help your student line up the pieces of string to show the order of the objects from the least to the greatest length. Show your student the pieces of tape and read out loud the names of the objects in order according to their lengths. Then group the pieces of string into sets of three. Have your student line up each set and identify which piece is longest and shortest in each group.

3 **DISTRIBUTE** Distribute Student Learning Page 11.A to your student. Help him or her read the directions. If needed allow your student to measure the doorways and animals using string or buttons. Then have him or her complete the page.

4 **EXPAND** Have your student use buttons and markers to measure the lengths of string that were cut in Step 2 above showing the lengths of different objects. Make a copy of the T Chart found on page 355. Write the name of each object to the left of the chart. Then draw a button at the top of the left column and a marker at the top of the right column. Distribute the T Chart to your student. Have him or her write the number of buttons and markers he or she needed to equal the length of each object.

WEIGHT

1 **EXPLAIN** Read the definition of **weight** to your student. Tell him or her that the objects he or she uses every day have different weights. Also tell your student that people and animals have weights, too. Give him or her several different everyday objects. Have your student hold one object in each hand. Then have him or her tell you which object weighs more and which object weighs less.

2 **CREATE AND MODEL** Build a scale that your student can use to compare the weights of different objects. Gather a wire coat hanger, two clear plastic cups, 2 pipe cleaners, and tape. Punch holes in opposite sides of the plastic cups. Attach the cups to the coat hanger using the pipe cleaners. Use tape to secure the pipe cleaners so that the cups can't slide. Demonstrate for your student how to use the scale. Hold the scale level with one hand or hang it from a shower-curtain rod, wall hook, doorknob, or other similar thing. Place one object in each of the cups. Explain to your student that the cup that dips down holds the heavier object. Have your student select small objects that will fit into the cups and compare their weights.

3   **EXPAND** Tell your student that he or she can also use the scale to compare the weights of three objects. This process is shown below. First, have your student use the scale to weigh and compare two objects. Then remove the lighter object and have your student replace it with the third object. If the third object is heavier, have your student tell you the order of the objects from lightest to heaviest. If the third object is lighter, remove the heavier object from the first round and replace it with the object that was lighter in the first round. Then help your student find the order of the objects by weight. Have your student continue practice weighing and ordering the weights of groups of three objects.

> **! A BRIGHT IDEA**
>
> Follow a recipe with your student. Measure out the ingredients into equal-sized bowls. Have your student compare which is more and which is less.

Comparing Weights of Three Objects

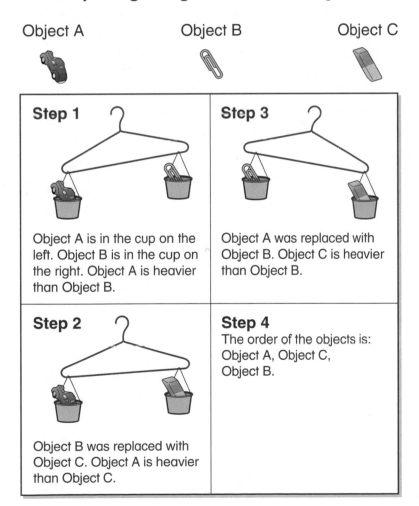

Object A   Object B   Object C

Step 1
Object A is in the cup on the left. Object B is in the cup on the right. Object A is heavier than Object B.

Step 2
Object B was replaced with Object C. Object A is heavier than Object C.

Step 3
Object A was replaced with Object B. Object C is heavier than Object B.

Step 4
The order of the objects is: Object A, Object C, Object B.

MATH

LESSON 2.11

4 **MEASURE** Encourage your student to have fun with taking measurements by having him or her measure some of his or her favorite toys. For example, he or she can weigh and measure the length of a toy truck or his or her favorite book.

5 **DISTRIBUTE AND COMPLETE** To complete the lesson, distribute Student Learning Page 11.B. Read the directions aloud to your student and have him or her choose which activity to do next. If there's time, your student may wish to complete both activities.

Branching Out

TEACHING TIP

Use the Internet or reference books, such as encyclopedias, to find pictures of some of your student's favorite animals. Ask him or her to compare the weights of animals such as elephants, lions, dogs, cats, mice, and so on.

CHECKING IN

To assess your student's understanding of measurement, have him or her measure and compare the lengths and weights of groups of three objects from around the home. Tell your student to find three objects. Ask him or her to compare the lengths of the objects. Then direct him or her to use the scale to compare the weights of the objects.

FOR FURTHER READING

Size: Many Ways to Measure, by Michele Koomen (Capstone Press, 2001).

So Big: My First Measuring Book, by Keith Faulkner and Stephanie Hinton, ill. (Simon and Schuster Children's, 2000).

Tell Me How Much It Weighs, by Shirley Willis (Scholastic Library Publishing, 1999).

Order Lengths and Weights

Circle the animals in each set that will fit through the doorway.

Student Learning Page 11.A: Order Lengths and Weights **173**

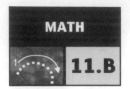
What's Next? You Decide!

Teacher: *Read aloud the directions and activities. Then have your student choose which activity to do next.*

Now it's your turn to choose what to do next in the lesson. Read the activities and decide which one you want to do—you may want to try them both!

Create Family Art

MATERIALS

❏ 1 posterboard

❏ 1 sheet construction paper for each family member

❏ markers or crayons

❏ glue

STEPS

Trace outlines of your family members' hands and make a poster to show the lengths.

❏ Gather the members of your family.

❏ Trace each person's right hand on a separate sheet of construction paper.

❏ Write the name of each family member on his or her hand.

❏ Cut out the hands.

❏ Then decorate the cutouts.

❏ Glue the hand cutouts to the posterboard in order from shortest to longest.

❏ Show your family your finished hand art.

Make a Wall Chart

MATERIALS

❏ 1 large sheet craft paper (taller than you)

❏ tape

❏ 1 measuring tape

❏ 1 marker

STEPS

Record your height on a wall chart.

❏ Get permission from an adult to tape a large sheet of craft paper to a wall.

❏ Stand against the wall and have an adult or friend mark your height on the paper.

❏ Have an adult use the tape measure to find how tall you are.

❏ Write your height and the date next to the mark.

❏ Record your height once each month.

❏ After a few months have passed, compare the marks to find out how much you've grown.

❏ How much have you grown?

❏ Ask an adult to help you write down your height each month and keep track.

In Your Community

To reinforce the skills and concepts taught in this section,
try one or more of these activities!

Hunt for Color

Help your student learn to sort and classify objects by going on a color hunt. Begin by labeling two paper bags with specific colors your student will classify objects by. Then place an object in each bag for your student to use as a model. For example, you can place a yellow crayon in a bag labeled "yellow." Take your student on a walk through your community. Ask him or her to place things in each bag that match the color of the model. Your student could place such objects as a yellow dandelion or a yellow leaf in the bag labeled "yellow" to match the yellow crayon. Be sure to ask your student to explain why he or she thinks each object should go in the bag.

Play Miniature Golf Math

Your student can play a fun game and learn math at the same time by playing a round of miniature golf. Look in a community directory or on the Internet to find a miniature golf course near you. Then go play! Allowing your student to keep score for the both of you can teach and strengthen several math skills. Primarily, if your student keeps score he or she will have an opportunity to practice counting. Your student can practice counting backward as well. Ask him or her to try to complete a hole in a certain number of shots, counting back one for each shot. Comparing length can also be addressed. Ask your student to estimate which player has a longer or shorter shot to the hole. You can bring string or ribbon for your student to use to check his or her answers.

Add and Subtract the Groceries

The grocery store—or any other store you buy various quantities of items at—is a good place for your student to strengthen his or her addition and subtraction skills, and using the items you will buy as symbols in addition and subtraction problems will help your student visualize the problems. For addition problems, ask your student to retrieve a certain amount of an item that's less than what you really need. Then tell him or her to retrieve an additional amount. For example, if you need five apples, ask your student to take three. Then tell your student to add two more to the total and ask how many $3 + 2$ is. For subtraction problems, have your student retrieve more items than you really need. Then ask him or her to return some of the items and solve for the items that remain.

Search for Shapes

Increase your student's familiarity with shapes by going on a shape search. Before you go, make sure that your student is familiar with the circle, square, rectangle, and triangle shapes. Then go somewhere in your community, such as a park or playground, and ask your student to look for and identify shapes in the surrounding area. As your student locates shapes, ask him or her to explain why the object is the shape he or she stated. For example, if your student finds a triangle, the answer to your question should be that the object has only three connecting sides. Feel free to point out objects to your student and ask him or her to explain what shape it is and why.

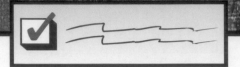

We Have Learned

Use this checklist to summarize what you and your student
have accomplished in the Math section.

❑ **Sorting and Classifying**
❑ top, middle, bottom
❑ in front, behind, over, under, on
❑ inside, outside, same, different
❑ sorting by color, size, and shape

❑ **Exploring Patterns**
❑ rhythm, movement, color, shape, size, and growing patterns
❑ translating and creating patterns

❑ **Shapes and Sharing**
❑ shapes in the real world: square, circle, rectangle, triangle
❑ building space shapes
❑ dividing objects into equal parts (halves)

❑ **Exploring Numbers to 5**
❑ counting forward and backward to 5
❑ equal groups and more and fewer
❑ number arrangements from zero to 5

❑ **Exploring Numbers to 10**
❑ counting forward and backward to 10
❑ groups, arrangements, and combinations from 6 to 10
❑ comparing and ordering numbers to 10

❑ **Exploring Greater Numbers**
❑ counting forward and backward to 20
❑ comparing and ordering numbers to 20
❑ finding patterns and ordinal order to 20
❑ exploring greater numbers to 100

❑ **Understanding Addition**
❑ solving joining problems
❑ using the plus sign, finding sums, vertical addition
❑ using concrete materials or pictures to support addition problems

❑ **Understanding Subtraction**
❑ solving separating problems
❑ using the minus sign, finding differences, vertical subtraction
❑ using concrete materials or pictures to support subtraction problems

❑ **Money**
❑ pennies, nickels, dimes
❑ identifying and recognizing coins

❑ **Time**
❑ exploring the time of day
❑ more time and less time
❑ telling time with an analog and a digital clock

❑ **Measurement**
❑ sorting and comparing by length and weight
❑ measuring length and weight with nonstandard forms of measurement

We have also learned:

_____

_____

Science

Science

Key Topics

Learning About Living and Nonliving Things

All things change, but only living things grow.

OBJECTIVE	BACKGROUND	MATERIALS
To teach your student about living and nonliving things	Understanding the nature of living and nonliving things helps us appreciate the things around us. In this lesson, your student will learn how to tell the difference between living things and nonliving things. He or she will also learn about what's necessary for living things to stay alive and grow.	■ Student Learning Pages 1.A–1.B ■ 1 houseplant ■ 1 rock ■ 1 series of photos of your student from infancy to present ■ several nonliving household items that show signs of wear ■ 1 picture of a canyon or of the ruins of an ancient building ■ 1 drawing paper ■ markers or crayons ■ 1 picture of a tree ■ 1 picture of a bird ■ 6 index cards

VOCABULARY

LIVING THINGS things that grow and need air, water, food, and shelter

NONLIVING THINGS things that don't grow, eat, drink, or breathe

GROW to get bigger and stronger

CHANGE to become different over time

SHELTER a place where living things can be protected from bad weather and danger

Let's Begin

1 **INTRODUCE** Explain to your student that everything he or she sees in the world belongs to one of two groups: living things and nonliving things. Tell him or her that **living things** need food, water, and air to stay alive. **Nonliving things** don't need any of these. They can't eat, drink, or breathe. Place a rock and a houseplant on a table for your student to observe. Ask, *Which of these things do you think is nonliving?* [rock] *Which of these things is living?* [plant] *How do you know?* [possible answers: the rock doesn't breathe or drink, the plant needs water and air] Point out that all plants and animals are living things.

2 **EXPAND** Explain that living things need air, food, and water because they **grow.** Point out that when something grows it usually gets bigger and stronger. An oak tree grows from an acorn, a very small seed. Cows, bears, and dogs grow from tiny baby animals into big adult animals. All living things grow. Nonliving things don't grow. Tell your student that even if a rock was given water and food, it still wouldn't grow because it isn't alive. Ask, *Do you need air, food, and water to grow?* [yes] *Are you a living thing?* [yes] Show your student a series of pictures of himself or herself from infancy to the present. Together, talk about how your student has grown since birth.

3 **DISCUSS** Have your student practice naming living and nonliving things. Ask, *Can you name five things that need food, water, and air?* [people, plants, dogs, cats, birds, fish, and so on] Walk around your home together. Have your student point to different things. Ask, *Is it living or nonliving?* Talk about whether your student finds more living or nonliving things.

4 **REVEAL** Point out to your student that although nonliving things don't grow, they do **change.** Collect several household items that show signs of wear, such as an old book, a ragged towel, a broken toy, and a dirty shoe. Present the items to your student. Ask, *Are these things living or nonliving?* [nonliving] Ask your student to picture what each of the items looked like when it was new. Have him or her describe the changes that have happened to each item.

ENRICH THE EXPERIENCE

Weathering and erosion are good examples of how nonliving things change over time. Show your student a picture of a canyon or of the ruins of an ancient building and explain that it's a nonliving thing that changed over time to look like it does today.

Pennies are nonliving things. They can change but they don't grow.

5 **EXPLAIN** Reinforce with your student the differences between living things and nonliving things. Ask, *When you get a scratch on your hand or leg, what happens after a few days?* [the scratch starts to get better and goes away] *If the table gets a scratch on it, does the scratch get better?* [no] Explain to your student that the ability to make a scratch get better and go away is part of being alive. Ask your student to describe a time that he or she got hurt but then got better.

6 **RELATE** Mention to your student that although living things grow and heal, they need to be treated with care. Point out that it's important to be gentle with living things that are smaller than us, such as pets and babies. Explain that pets and houseplants need food and water every day to grow. Have your student help feed your family pet or a friend's pet for a day to become more aware of the food and water it eats and drinks.

7 **EXPAND** Talk about the ways different living things get food and water. Have your student name some of the foods he or she likes to eat. Discuss some of the things that animals eat, such as squirrels eating nuts and acorns, birds eating seeds and worms, cats eating cat food and mice, and so on. Point out to your student that since people and animals can move, they can go to places to get water and food. Ask, *When you need water, where do you get it from?* [a water bottle, the kitchen faucet, the drinking fountain, and so on] *Where do animals that live outside get water?* [streams, rivers, ponds, lakes, puddles, and so on]

8 **RELATE** Explain that plants are living things that don't move. They live and grow in the same soil all their lives. Plants need water to come to them. Plants that are outside in the wild get water when it rains. At home or in the garden, plants also get water when people water them. Point out that plants are different from animals because they are able to make their own food. One thing plants use to make food is water. Ask, *Do you know what else plants need to make their food?* [light and air] Explain that plants soak up the light from the sun and use water and air to change it into food. Ask, *What would happen if a plant didn't get enough light and couldn't make food?* [it wouldn't be able to stay alive]

9 **DISTRIBUTE** Distribute Student Learning Page 1.A to your student. Read the directions with him or her. Have your student draw a circle around each living thing and a square around each nonliving thing. Then ask your student to choose one living thing and talk about what it needs to live.

10 **REVIEW AND EXPLAIN** Ask, *What are three things that living things need to grow?* [air, water, and food] Point out that **shelter** is something else that many living things need. Explain that shelter is a place that can protect living things from too much heat, too much cold, or too much rain. People make shelters such as houses, tents, and other buildings. People usually sleep and eat inside. We also go inside when the weather is bad. Ask, *Can you think of a time when you needed to find shelter in bad weather?* [possible answers: during a snowstorm, a rainstorm, a very cold day, a very hot day]

11 **EXPLORE** Tell your student that another reason living things need shelter is to protect themselves from other animals. Some animals build shelters to protect their babies when they are young. Some animals, such as wolves and foxes, make shelters called dens where their babies live while they are small. Other animals, such as birds and squirrels, build nests in trees where their babies can be safe and grow. Have your student name some animals that he or she knows about. Then challenge him or her to describe the type of shelter each animal builds. Talk about whether the shelter is on the ground or high up in a tree or on a cliff. Discuss how the shelter helps the animal and its

SCIENCE
LESSON 3.1

DID YOU KNOW?
Tell your student that fish are living things that don't breathe air. They use special body parts called gills to breathe underwater. Fish need to stay in water. When they are outside of the water, they can't breathe!

ENRICH THE EXPERIENCE
Show your student a picture of a tree and a bird. Ask your student to tell you how their needs are the same and how they are different. Direct your student to see that both a tree and a bird need air, water, and food, but that the bird also needs shelter.

babies grow and stay alive. Ask your student to draw a picture of one of the animals in its shelter using markers or crayons.

Some living things make shelters.

12 **DISTRIBUTE** Read the activities on Student Learning Page 1.B to your student. Have him or her decide which one he or she would like to do.

FOR FURTHER READING

Bees to Baleens: The Rhyme and the Rhythm of Living Things, by Beverly J. Hudson, Marjorie Hammons, ed., and Delise L. Hudson, photographer (NEFTA Educational Publications/Talents from God, 2001).

How Do Animals Find Food?, by Bobbie Kalman and Heather Levigne (Crabtree Publishing Company, 2001).

Living Things, by Adrienne Mason, Deborah Hodge, and Ray Boudreau (Kids Can Press, 2000).

What Is a Living Thing?, by Bobbie D. Kalman; April Fast, Lynda Hale, Kate Calder, and Heather Levigne, eds. (Crabtree Publishing Company, 1999).

Branching Out

TEACHING TIP

Visit a local nature preserve or park with your student. As you walk through the park, ask your student to point out the things he or she sees that are living and nonliving. Have your student explain why each thing belongs in each group.

CHECKING IN

To assess your student's understanding of the lesson, draw symbols, such as a cloud or a water drop, for living things, nonliving things, air, water, food, and shelter on six different index cards. Explain each symbol to your student. Lay out the cards on a table. As you name different living and nonliving things, ask your student to choose the correct living or nonliving card. If it's a living thing, have your student choose from the other cards which things the living things need. Prompt your student to explain why each living thing needs the things he or she chose. You can also ask your student to give an example of the ways that living things grow and an example of the ways that nonliving things change.

Find Living and Nonliving Things

Draw a square around the nonliving things. Draw a circle around the living things. Tell an adult about the needs of one of the living things.

Student Learning Page 1.A: Find Living and Nonliving Things **183**

What's Next? You Decide!

Teacher: Read aloud the directions and activities. Then have your student choose which activity to do next.

Now it's your turn to choose what to do next in the lesson. Read the activities and decide which one you want to do—you may want to try them both!

Watch a Plant Grow

MATERIALS

❑ 1 package plant seeds

❑ potting soil

❑ 1 clear plastic cup

STEPS

❑ Make a small hole in the bottom of the clear plastic cup.

❑ Put some potting soil in the cup.

❑ Sprinkle some seeds into the cup. Push some of the seeds against the side of the cup.

❑ Cover the seeds with a small amount of soil.

❑ Water the seeds a little every day.

❑ Watch the seeds grow. Can you see the roots through the side of the cup?

❑ Be sure your young plant gets enough light, fresh air, and water.

Make a Poster

MATERIALS

❑ several old nature magazines

❑ 1 pair scissors

❑ 1 posterboard

❑ markers or crayons

❑ glue

STEPS

❑ Look through old nature magazines to find pictures of living and nonliving things.

❑ Use the scissors to cut out the pictures.

❑ Draw a line down the middle of the posterboard.

❑ At the top of one side, draw pictures of water, food, and air.

❑ Glue the pictures of the living things onto the posterboard under your drawings.

❑ Glue the pictures of the nonliving things onto the other side.

❑ Share your poster with an adult. Talk about why each picture on your poster is a living or nonliving thing.

Finding Out About Plants

Plants give us food, medicine, fresh air, and beauty.

OBJECTIVE	BACKGROUND	MATERIALS
To teach your student where and how plants grow	Plants are able to turn the energy of the sun into food. They're the first link in all the food chains on Earth. In this lesson, your student will learn how a plant grows from a seed and the many different places in which plants live.	<ul><li>Student Learning Pages 2.A–2.B</li><li>1 apple and 1 orange</li><li>beans, lentils, nuts, or other household seeds</li><li>glue</li><li>1 plate</li><li>paper towels</li><li>1 plastic bag</li><li>1 hand lens</li><li>1 carrot with top leaves</li><li>2–3 books with pictures of plants growing in different places</li><li>1 copy Web, page 356</li></ul>

VOCABULARY

ADULT something that's fully grown

SEEDS the parts of a plant that new plants come from

SOIL a special material on Earth that plants can grow out of

ROOTS the parts of a plant that grow under the ground and bring water up to the plant

Let's Begin

1 **BEGIN** Review the idea that plants are living things that grow. Just like animals, plants begin tiny and then grow into larger **adult** plants. Take a walk with your student through an area where there are large trees. Look around the base of each tree for signs of baby trees beginning to grow. Point out the size difference between the new tree and the adult tree.

2 **RELATE** Introduce your student to or remind him or her about **seeds.** Explain that seeds make new plants. Tell him or her that there are many different sizes, shapes, and colors of seeds. Cut open an apple and an orange, taking out the seeds for your student to look at. Let the seeds dry. Look through the kitchen with your student for other kinds of seeds, such as beans, nuts, and lentils. Explain that beans, lentils, and nuts are dry plant seeds that we can eat. Have your student arrange the seeds by

ENRICH THE EXPERIENCE

Encourage your student to be in charge of watering the houseplants. He or she can water them regularly and tell you when they look like they might need a bigger pot.

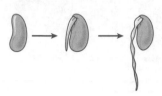

Example of a bean seed growing.

their color and size. Then encourage your student to use the seeds, paper, and glue to make a picture.

3   **GROW**   Distribute Student Learning Page 2.A. Soak a handful of small beans or lentils in water for several hours. Drain the seeds and lay them on a plate with several layers of paper towels. Cover the seeds with another paper towel and a plastic bag to keep them moist. Have your student check on the seeds each day for one week. Rinse the seeds every two days to keep them fresh. Give your student a hand lens so that he or she can see how the sprouts change in detail. Ask your student to draw what he or she sees on the first, third, and fifth day.

4   **EXPLORE**   Explain to your student that seeds need **soil** to grow. Soil gives a plant a place to attach its **roots.** As the plant grows bigger, the roots keep the plant steady and soak up water from the soil. Show your student a carrot with the leafy top attached. Point out that the part of the carrot plant we eat is the root.

5   **EXPAND**   Explain that plants grow in almost any place where there is soil, water, and light. Plants can grow high up in the mountains and at the bottom of the ocean. Some plants grow in places where the soil is dry, such as cactuses that grow in the desert. Other plants, such as ferns and mosses, grow where there is a lot of rain and the air and soil are very wet. Go to the library with your student and find books that show pictures of plants growing in several different places. Discuss each plant's shape and color and how the plant is growing.

TAKE A BREAK

Go for a walk around your neighborhood with your student. Look for examples of plants growing in unexpected places, such as in the cracks on the sidewalk, between buildings, on rooftops, and so on.

Plants live in many different places.

Branching Out

TEACHING TIP

Visit a greenhouse with your student. Ask a member of the greenhouse staff to show your student examples of plants at different stages of growth. Encourage your student to ask questions about how plants grow.

CHECKING IN

Give your student a copy of the Web found on page 356. Write "Plants" in the center. Have your student draw a picture in the outer ovals for each idea he or she learned about plants, seeds, and where plants grow. Then have your student describe the pictures to an adult.

FOR FURTHER READING

From Seed to Pumpkin, by Jan Kottke (Scholastic Library Publishing, 2000).

Oh Say Can You Seed? All About Flowering Plants, by Bonnie Worth and Aristides Ruiz, ill. (Random House, 2001).

Seeds Grow! (My First Hello Reader! Series), by Angela Shelf Medearis and Jill Dubin, ill. (Scholastic, 2000).

Draw a Seed Growing

Draw pictures of a seed growing.

Day 1

Day 5

Day 3

What's Next? You Decide!

Teacher: *Read aloud the directions and activities. Then have your student choose which activity to do next.*

Now it's your turn to choose what to do next in the lesson. Read the activities and decide which one you want to do—you may want to try them both!

Make Leaf Prints

MATERIALS

❑ 1 resealable plastic bag

❑ 1 dark-colored crayon

STEPS

Different plants have leaves with different shapes.

❑ Ask an adult to go to a park or forest preserve with you.

❑ Look at all the different kinds of plants and their leaves.

❑ Find leaves that are different shapes and sizes and put them into the plastic bag.

❑ When you get home, take your leaves out of the bag.

❑ Take the paper off a dark-colored crayon.

❑ Put two or three leaves between two sheets of paper.

❑ Rub the side of the crayon over the paper.

❑ Do you see the print of the leaves on the paper?

Grow an Avocado Plant

MATERIALS

❑ 1 ripe avocado

❑ 4 toothpicks

❑ 1 short glass jar

❑ 1 flower pot and soil

STEPS

The pit inside an avocado is a big seed!

❑ Ask an adult to cut the seed out of an avocado. Rinse the seed.

❑ Stick four toothpicks around the seed like the spokes of a wheel.

❑ Fill a short glass jar with water. Set the avocado seed into the jar with the pointy end facing up.

❑ Let the toothpicks rest on the top edge of the jar to hold the seed up.

❑ Watch for roots to begin to grow.

❑ When the jar is full of roots, plant the avocado seed in a pot with soil.

❑ Make sure your avocado plant gets enough light and water.

Understanding How Animals Grow and Live

Animals come in all shapes and sizes and live in every part of the world.

OBJECTIVE	BACKGROUND	MATERIALS
To teach your student about how animals grow and where they live	Like all living things, animals grow and live in many different places. In this lesson, your student will learn about how baby animals grow and become adults. Your student will also learn about some of the places where animals live.	■ Student Learning Pages 3.A–3.D ■ 1 copy Venn Diagram, page 355 ■ animal picture books ■ markers or crayons

Let's Begin

1 **PREVIEW AND PREDICT** Remind your student that all living things need food, water, air, and sometimes shelter. Explain that although plants and animals may look different, they both require food, water, and air to live and grow. Ask, *What do you think it means to grow?* [to get bigger or look older] Have your student look at the pictures below. Ask, *What do you think the puppy will need to grow into a big dog?* [food, water, air, and shelter] *How is the grown dog different from the puppy?* [it's bigger and stronger; it can do more things by itself]

2 **COMPARE** Explain that even though the puppy in the picture will change as it grows, it still has many of the same features as the adult dog. Ask, *How does the puppy look similar to the adult dog?* [both have four legs, fur, tails, and a similar shape] Explain that sometimes young animals don't look like their

parents. For example, a baby butterfly is a caterpillar with no wings and a baby frog is a tadpole with no legs. Give your student a copy of the Venn Diagram found on page 355. Write "Puppy" under one circle and "Dog" under the other. Have your student draw one way they're each unique. In the center, have him or her draw one way they're similar.

3 **INVESTIGATE AND DISTRIBUTE** Look through animal picture books with your student. Point out pictures that show adult animals and their young. Then distribute Student Learning Page 3.A. Explain that the pictures on the left are of baby animals and the pictures on the right are of adult animals. Ask your student to match the baby animals to what they will look like when they grow by drawing a line connecting the pictures.

4 **EXPLAIN** Explain to your student that animals live in many places. Some animals, such as sharks and whales, live in the water. Have your student name some other animals that live in the water. Then help your student name some animals that live on land, such as birds, horses, and cats. Finally, explain to your student that there are also animals that live both on land and in water, such as alligators, penguins, seals, and frogs. Ask, *If you could be any animal, which animal would you be? Why?*

5 **DISTRIBUTE** Distribute Student Learning Page 3.B. Tell your student to color the animals that live in water blue, the animals that live on land green, and the animals that live both in water and on land red.

6 **EXPAND AND DISTRIBUTE** Tell your student that some animals have body parts that protect them from harsh weather and other animals. For example, a polar bear lives in cold weather and has thick fur to keep it warm. A turtle has a hard shell that protects it from other animals. Distribute Student Learning Page 3.C. Have your student connect the dots and identify each animal. Talk about how its body covering protects it. Then read aloud the activities on Student Learning Page 3.D. Have your student decide which one to complete.

ENRICH THE EXPERIENCE

Your student can see photos of animals at www.baltimorezoo.org. Click on Kidzone to find information, activities, and pictures about animals.

FOR FURTHER READING

From Tadpole to Frog (*How Things Grow*), by Jan Kottke (Children's Press, 2000).

Where Do the Animals Live?, by Innovative Kids and Stephanie Peterson, ill. (Innovative Kids, 2001).

Branching Out

TEACHING TIP

Take a walk through your neighborhood or nearby park with your student. Look for animals. Help your student identify how each animal he or she sees grows and how its body covering helps protect it.

CHECKING IN

Take a trip to a zoo, farm, or pet shop. Ask your student to identify each animal you see as living on land, in water, or both. Have your student point out the differences between the baby and adult animals.

Match Babies and Adult Animals

Draw a line from each baby animal to the correct adult animal.

Young	Adult

1.

A.

2.

B.

3.

C.

4.

D.

Choose Land, Water, or Both

Color the land animals green. Color the water animals blue. Color the land and water animals red.

Find the Animals

Connect the dots. Name the animals.
What are their bodies covered with?

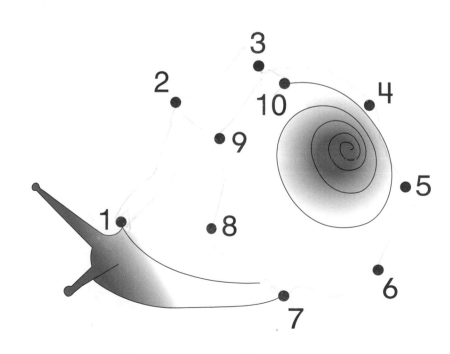

What's Next? You Decide!

Teacher: Read aloud the directions and activities. Then have your student choose which activity to do next.

Now it's your turn to choose what to do next in the lesson. Read the activities and decide which one you want to do—you may want to try them both!

Put on an Animal Play

MATERIALS

❏ household items, such as a blanket or box, to make an animal costume

STEPS

What's your favorite animal? Make a costume and put on a play.

❏ Choose an animal that you like.

❏ How does your animal grow?

❏ Where does your animal live?

❏ What type of body covering does your animal have?

❏ Make yourself an animal costume. If your animal has fur, you could use a blanket. If it has a shell, you could decorate a box to wear.

❏ Put on a play for your family.

❏ Wear your costume. Act like your animal. Make the animal's noises.

❏ Ask your family to guess what animal you are.

Create a New Animal

MATERIALS

❏ 1 posterboard

❏ finger paint

STEPS

If you could create a new animal, what would it look like? Paint it!

❏ Think about where your animal will live, such as on land, in water, or both.

❏ Then decide what kind of food it will eat to grow.

❏ Think about what kind of shelter the animal will need to survive.

❏ How will its body covering protect it from weather or other animals?

❏ Use finger paint to paint a picture of your new animal.

❏ Think of a name for your animal.

❏ Show your painting to an adult.

❏ Explain where your animal lives, its shelter, what it eats, and how its body covering protects it.

Comprehending the Human Body

Your body has many parts, but together they work as one.

OBJECTIVE	BACKGROUND	MATERIALS
To teach your student about his or her body and how it works	The human body has many parts that do many different things. In this lesson, your student will learn to identify external and internal body parts and understand their purpose. He or she will also explore similarities and differences in people.	■ Student Learning Pages 4.A–4.B ■ 1 full-length mirror ■ markers or crayons ■ 1 picture of a human skeleton ■ 1 copy Web, page 356 ■ anatomy picture books

VOCABULARY

BONES hard body parts inside the body that make up the skeleton and shape and protect the body

MUSCLES body parts that help the body move

HEART a fist-sized muscle in the chest that pumps blood through the body

BRAIN the body part inside the head that helps people think and sends messages to other body parts

ALIKE when something is similar to something else

DIFFERENT when something is not like something else

Let's Begin

1   **EXPLAIN**   Explain to your student that the human body has many parts that can do things together and separately. Have your student look in a full-length mirror. Ask, *What body parts do you have that you can see?* [feet, legs, hands, arms, head, and so on]

2   **EXPAND**   Ask your student to tell you about his or her favorite activities, games, and sports. For each activity ask, *Which body parts help you in that activity?* If your student likes to play the piano, he or she can name hands, arms, and possibly feet as body parts that allow him or her to play the piano.

3   **DISTRIBUTE AND ASK**   Distribute Student Learning Page 4.A. Ask, *What is this a picture of?* [a person's body] *Can you point to the body part that helps you pick things up?* [hands] Have your student color the hands red. Ask the same question for other body parts and have your student color them as follows:

the part that helps us reach things [arms, blue]; the part that helps us taste, see, hear, and smell [head, yellow]; the part that helps us walk, run, dance, and move [legs, orange]; the part that helps us stand and balance [feet, green].

4 **MODEL** Tell your student that his or her body can also express feelings. To illustrate this, smile at your student. Ask, *How do you think I'm feeling?* [happy] Continue this exercise by making other facial expressions for your student and having him or her guess what feeling you're trying to express. Then reverse the activity. Name several emotions, such as sadness, excitement, fear, happiness, anger, surprise, and so on. Have your student show these emotions using facial expressions.

5 **EXPAND** Explain to your student that besides facial expressions there are other ways that his or her body expresses feelings. For example, if a person is excited he or she may jump up and down or clap his or her hands. Ask, *What might someone's body do when that person is angry?* [cry, shake his or her fists, scream, stomp his or her feet, and so on] Ask the same question for other emotions. Then take turns with your student expressing different feelings using your whole body.

6 **DESCRIBE** Point out that the parts of the body that you have talked about so far are outside body parts. Explain that there are other important parts inside a person's body. Explain that **bones** are inside the body and are hard. Bones protect other body parts and give the body its shape. Show your student a picture of a human skeleton. Explain that this is what his or her bones look like. Point to the skull in the picture. Ask your student to feel his or her own skull. Do the same with the ribs, hips, and the bones in the legs and arms. Ask, *How do you think bones give your body its shape?* [bones are hard and can help hold other body parts together]

ENRICH THE EXPERIENCE

Your student may enjoy listening to heartbeats through a stethoscope. You can order an inexpensive stethoscope on the Internet at http://claflinequip.com.

7 **EXTEND** Tell your student that **muscles** are another inside part of his or her body. Explain that muscles help the body move. Ask your student to move his or her arms and legs. Explain that his or her movement is possible because he or she has muscles. Ask your student to flex his or her arm. Point out how the muscles in the upper arm get firmer and shorter. Stand up. Have your student put a hand on your calf muscle and notice how hard or soft it is. Then stand up on your toes. Ask, *Has the muscle changed?* [yes, it got harder and shorter] *Which muscle in the body helps you stand on your toes?* [the calf muscle] Then, together with your student, try to find other areas of the body that contain muscles that help the body move. Distribute a copy of the Web found on page 356 to your student. Write "Muscles" in the center. In the outer circles, ask your student to draw pictures of things that he or she can do because of his or her muscles.

8 **EXPAND** Ask your student to tell you what he or she knows about the **heart.** Explain that the heart is a very strong muscle that's about the size of a person's fist. The heart pumps blood to the different parts of the body and is always working, even during sleep. Have your student put a hand on his or her chest over the heart to feel the slight movement. Explain that the heart is inside the rib bones for protection. Help your student locate his or her pulse at his or her wrist or neck. Explain that the pulse is blood flowing from the heart through his or her body. Ask, *What happens to your heartbeat when you are exercising or playing?* [it gets faster]

9 **ASK AND EXPLAIN** Ask, *Do you know what body part you use to think with?* [my brain] *Where is your brain?* [inside my head] Explain to your student that the **brain** not only helps people think, it also sends instructions to other body parts. For example, if a person's hand touches something hot, his or her brain tells the muscles in the hand to move. Explain to your student that the brain also tells the body to do things that he or she doesn't think about, such as blinking and breathing. Ask, *Why do you think the bones around the brain are so hard and solid?* [to protect the brain]

10 **REVIEW** Talk with your student about what he or she has learned so far. Ask, *Can you name some of your outside body parts?* [arms, hands, head, legs, feet, and so on] *Can you name some inside body parts?* [bones, muscles, heart, brain, and so on] Have your student briefly describe the function of each part. Review as needed.

11 **DEFINE** Tell your student that when two or more things have something in common, they are **alike.** Explain that everyone's body is alike in some ways. For example, everyone has a heart, brain, muscles, and bones. All people have some of the same basic needs to stay alive, such as food, water, and air. Point out that people are also alike in that we all have feelings and can use our bodies to express them. Ask, *Can you name three ways that you and someone in your family are alike?*

12 **EXPLAIN** Tell your student that when two or more things have characteristics that aren't the same, they are **different.** Explain that people's bodies can be different in many ways. For instance, people may have different colored hair or skin. Some people are very tall, some are short. People may also have different interests and enjoy different things. Some people like to draw, while others may prefer to play baseball or go camping. Ask your student to name some of his or her interests and favorite things to do. Then tell him or her about some interests that you have that are different.

13 **PRACTICE** Have your student look at the drawings on the next page. Have him or her name two ways that the children are alike.

SCIENCE

LESSON 3.4

ENRICH THE EXPERIENCE

For printable activities and pictures about the body, visit www.enchantedlearning. com and click on Anatomy.

Then have your student name at least two ways that they are different. Finally, ask your student to compare himself or herself to the children in the drawings to find things that are alike and different.

14 **DISTRIBUTE** Read the activities on Student Learning Page 4.B to your student. Have him or her decide which one he or she would like to do.

Branching Out

TEACHING TIP

Use picture books to aid in your student's visual understanding of internal body parts, such as the bones, muscles, heart, and brain. Point out the relationship of these internal body parts to each other and to the external body parts. For example, the muscles and bones in our legs work together to help us walk.

CHECKING IN

To assess your student's understanding of the lesson, ask him or her to show you how external body parts can be used. Then have him or her name each internal body part he or she learned about in this lesson. Have your student point to it on his or her body and explain what it does for him or her.

FOR FURTHER READING

Human Body, by Claude Delafosse, Gallimard Jeunesse, and Pierre-Marie Valat (Scholastic, Inc., 2000).

Me and My Amazing Body, by Joan Sweeney and Annette Cable, ill. (Crown Publishing, 1999).

Decide What Each Body Part Does

Color the different body parts.

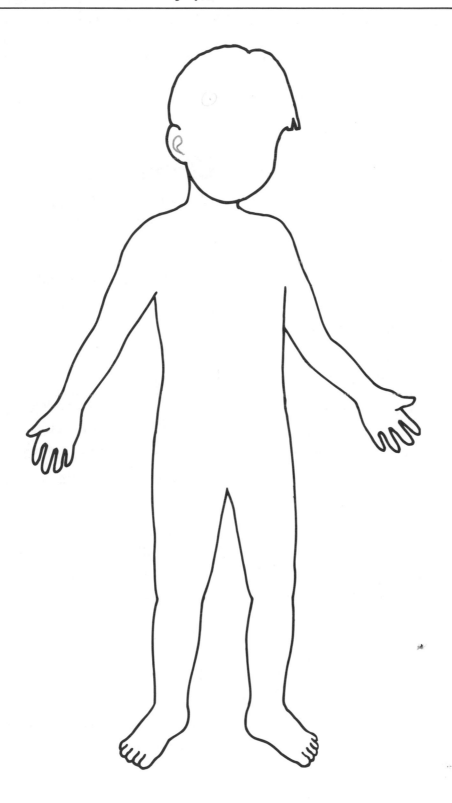

Student Learning Page 4.A: Decide What Each Body Part Does

What's Next? You Decide!

Teacher: *Read aloud the directions and activities. Then have your student choose which activity to do next.*

Now it's your turn to choose what to do next in the lesson. Read the activities and decide which one you want to do—you may want to try them both!

Paint Portraits That Are Alike and Different

MATERIALS

❑ 1 large posterboard

❑ 1 pair scissors

❑ finger paint

STEPS

A portrait is a drawing of a person.

❑ Choose a friend, sister, or brother who you would like to paint.

❑ Think of two ways that you are alike and different.

❑ Cut the large posterboard in half.

❑ On one half, paint a portrait of yourself. Show the ways you are alike and different from the other person.

❑ On the other half, paint a portrait of the other person. Show the ways that he or she is alike and different from you.

❑ Share your painting with friends and family members. Talk about how you are alike and different from the other person.

Act Out a Story with Feeling

MATERIALS

❑ various costume supplies, such as hats and scarves

❑ 1 full-length mirror

❑ 1 videocassette recorder (optional)

❑ 1 videocassette (optional)

STEPS

❑ Choose a story you like that has feeling in it. You can make one up or pick one from a book.

❑ Make a costume to wear while you tell the story.

❑ Practice telling the story in front of the full-length mirror. Use your body and face to express the feelings in the story.

❑ Use your body to move around the room as you tell the story.

❑ When you're ready, act out the story for your family.

❑ If you want, ask an adult to make a videotape of you.

Investigating Our Senses

The road to awareness begins with the senses.

OBJECTIVE	BACKGROUND	MATERIALS
To teach your student about the five senses	Our senses allow us to interact with the world and know what's going on around us. Understanding how this sensory information is gathered can help your student appreciate his or her abilities. In this lesson, your student will learn what the five senses are, how they are used, and how they work together.	■ Student Learning Pages 5.A–5.B ■ markers or crayons ■ salty, sweet, and sour foods ■ 1 scarf or bandana ■ perfume ■ 1 bar soap ■ 1 teaspoon vinegar ■ 1 pillow ■ 1 piece sandpaper ■ 1 damp towel

VOCABULARY
SENSES the abilities of sight, hearing, touch, taste, and smell

Let's Begin

1 **IDENTIFY** Ask your student to tell you what he or she knows about the **senses.** Point out that there are five senses: sight, hearing, touch, taste, and smell. Explain that we use our senses to learn about what's going on around us. Have your student suppose that he or she is at a busy restaurant. Name each sense and ask your student to identify things in the restaurant that are detected through each sense. Ask, *What things might you hear at the restaurant?* [people talking, plates and forks clattering, and so on]

2 **MODEL** Collect random objects from around the room. Present each object to your student one at a time. Have your student think about what body part and sense he or she would use to learn about each thing. For example, if your student is shown a book, the eyes and the sense of sight and the hands and the sense of touch could be used to learn about the book.

3 **DISTRIBUTE** Distribute Student Learning Page 5.A. Explain that the parts of the body shown on the page are the parts that give

us our senses. Ask your student to identify each illustration. Then ask your student to associate a color with each sense. Ask, *What color do you think the sense of _____ should be?* Have your student color the appropriate picture with the color he or she chose. Then ask your student to give an example of something that each part of the body and its sense could identify. [the nose could detect a flower, the ears could hear a car coming, and so on]

4 **EXPLORE SIGHT AND HEARING** Discuss how each sense helps your student understand the things around him or her. Explain that when people see, they become aware of different colors and shapes around them. Ask your student to name colors and shapes that he or she sees in the room. Then explain that when people use the sense of hearing, they become aware of sounds around them, such as loud or soft sounds. Take your student outside and ask him or her to look around and listen to the sounds. Then discuss the things he or she sees and hears. Ask your student to describe the colors and shapes of what he or she sees. Also ask your student to describe what he or she hears by saying whether the sounds are loud or soft.

5 **EXTEND AND ASK** The senses of sight and hearing can also keep people safe because they can see dangerous things or hear sounds that warn of danger, such as fire alarms. Ask, *What other things can you see or hear that can keep you safe?* [seeing things in your path that you might trip or slip on; hearing things such as sirens, loud noises, and safety instructions]

6 **EXPLORE TASTE** Tell your student that the sense of taste allows people to tell whether foods are sour, salty, or sweet. Discuss familiar foods with your student. Talk about what they taste like using the words *sour, salty,* and *sweet.* Then have your student taste a sour, salty, and sweet food, such as a salted pretzel, water with lemon, and a piece of candy. Ask your student to describe what he or she thinks the food tastes like. Repeat the exercise with different foods. This time, have your student close his or her eyes and focus on the sense of taste. See if your student can identify the sour, salty, and sweet food correctly.

7 **MODEL SMELL** Explain that the sense of smell allows people to distinguish between good and bad smells. Ask, *What kinds of things can you think of that smell good? That smell bad?* Tie a scarf or bandana over your student's eyes. Give your student samples of perfume, soap, and vinegar to smell. Ask your student to describe each smell as good or bad. Then see if your student can name the source of each smell. Give your student clues as necessary.

8 **MODEL TOUCH** Explain to your student that the sense of touch allows people to become aware of how things feel, such as soft, hard, rough, smooth, hot, cold, wet, or dry. Cover your student's eyes again with a scarf or bandana. Let your student feel a pillow, a piece of sandpaper, and a damp towel one at a time. Ask your student to describe what each object feels like. Challenge your student to use his or her sense of touch to determine what each object is.

9 **EXPAND** Tell your student that like sight and hearing, the senses of touch and smell can also keep people safe. Point out that the sense of touch can warn people when something is hot enough to cause a burn or when the weather is so cold that it can cause frostbite. The sense of smell can allow people to smell things such as smoke when there's a fire or gas when the stove is leaking. Discuss other examples of ways these two senses can help keep people safe.

10 **REVEAL** Explain to your student that the five senses work together at the same time. Ask your student to recall the restaurant exercise from Step 1 and consider how he or she is able to hear, smell, touch, taste, and see at the same time. Then have your student pause and notice how he or she is taking in information from each sense at the same time right now.

11 **DRAW** Reinforce your student's understanding of how the senses work together by asking him or her to draw a picture of himself or herself at a picnic. Ask him or her to draw at least one object in the picture for each sense. For example, he or she could add flowers for the sense of smell, people or trees for the sense of sight, and birds chirping for the sense of hearing. When complete, ask your student to point out each sense in his or her drawing.

12 **MODEL** Explain that the senses work together at the same time, but too much information at once can make it hard to notice what all the senses are picking up. Have your student experiment with using all his or her senses at once. Have him or her try looking at a book, listening to music, eating a cracker, smelling a flower, and touching a soft toy at the same time. Your student may only be able to do three or four of these things at the same time—that's okay. Ask, *How does the flower smell? How does the cracker taste?* and so on. Then have your student do each thing one at a time. Ask again, *How does the flower smell?* and so on. Your student may realize that he or she notices more and enjoys more when focusing on one thing at a time.

13 **EXPERIMENT** Explain that sometimes when a person is sick, his or her senses don't work well. Ask, *Have you ever had a stuffy nose? Could you smell?* When a person has a cold, he or she may not be able to smell things. He or she may not be able to taste food very well, either. Have your student plug his or her nose. Give your student a bite of a raw potato and then a bite of an apple. Ask, *Can you tell the difference?* [they will probably taste very similar] Point out that smell and taste work together.

SCIENCE
LESSON 3.5

TAKE A BREAK

Go on some field trips to highlight the senses. Plan five different trips to places where you and your student can enjoy each of your five senses. Perhaps you could go to a flower shop and perfume counter for smell, a fabric store for touch, an art museum for sight, a restaurant buffet for taste, and a children's concert for hearing.

ENRICH THE EXPERIENCE

Encourage your child to sample some foods while holding his or her nose. Can he or she taste them without smelling them?

SCIENCE

LESSON 3.5

14 **EXPAND AND CONNECT** Tell your student that some people, such as people who are blind or deaf, can't use one or more of their senses at all. A person who is blind or deaf uses his or her other senses to become informed of the surroundings. Point out that if a person can't see, he or she will rely on the senses of sound and touch to know where to walk and where things are. Remind your student of when he or she was blindfolded and had to name things using senses other than sight. Ask, *How might someone who couldn't hear communicate with other people?* [read their lips or use sign language]

15 **DISTRIBUTE** Read the activities on Student Learning Page 5.B to your student. Have him or her decide which one he or she would like to do.

Branching Out

TEACHING TIP

Conduct an empathy exercise with your student to help him or her better understand people who don't have their sense of sight or hearing. Set aside 30 minutes when you and your student can create a safe environment. During this time, have your student cover his or her eyes. Then have your student try to walk, play, eat, or perform any other activity without using the sense of sight. You can also do the exercise for hearing using earplugs.

CHECKING IN

To assess your student's understanding of the lesson, have him or her choose several objects from the room. Ask your student to describe each object using as many senses as possible. Have your student name the body part that corresponds to each sense.

FOR FURTHER READING

Five Senses, by Deirdre Englehart; Matthew Van Zomeren and Roberta Collier Morales, ills. (Instructional Fair, 1999).

My Eyes Are for Seeing (*My Five Senses*), by Jane Belk Moncure and Viki Woodworth, ill. (Child's World, 1998).

Sense-Abilities: Fun Ways to Explore the Senses, by Michelle O'Brien-Palmer (Chicago Review Press, 1998).

Match Senses and Body Parts

Color the pictures of the five senses.

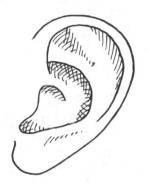

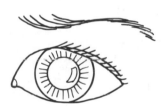

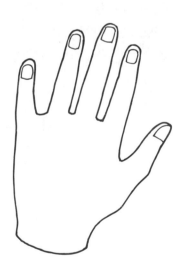

What's Next? You Decide!

Teacher: *Read aloud the directions and activities. Then have your student choose which activity to do next.*

Now it's your turn to choose what to do next in the lesson. Read the activities and decide which one you want to do—you may want to try them both!

Make Up Sense Riddles

 STEPS

Make up sense riddles for other people to guess!

Sample riddle: When I am in this place, I smell bread baking and hear a cash register and people talking. Where am I?

Answer: A bakery

❏ Think of a place you like to go.

❏ Make up a riddle about your sense of smell that will help a person guess what place you are thinking of.

❏ Think of another place or thing that you like. Make up a riddle for hearing.

❏ Think of a food and make up a riddle for the sense of taste.

❏ Make up riddles for sight and touch.

❏ Share your riddles with friends and family. See if they can guess the answers!

See a Hole in Your Hand

 MATERIALS

❏ 1 cardboard paper towel tube

 STEPS

Trick your brain into seeing something that isn't there!

❏ Hold the cardboard tube in your right hand. Put it up to your right eye. Look through it.

❏ Keep both eyes open.

❏ Hold your left hand beside the end of the tube.

❏ Slide your palm along the side of the tube toward your face. Do this slowly.

❏ Can you see a hole in your left hand?

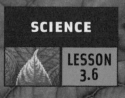

SCIENCE

LESSON 3.6

Taking Care of Your Body

Before we take care of others, we first need to take care of ourselves.

OBJECTIVE	BACKGROUND	MATERIALS
To teach your student how to care for his or her body	Taking time to care for the body helps us lead a healthy and productive life. In this lesson, your student will learn the importance of washing hands and not spreading germs as well as the benefits of exercise and proper sleep.	<ul><li>Student Learning Pages 6.A–6.B</li><li>$\frac{1}{4}$ cup flour</li><li>hand soap</li><li>1 apple</li><li>2 toothbrushes</li><li>dental floss</li></ul>

VOCABULARY

GERMS bacteria that cause illness and can spread from person to person
DENTAL FLOSS a special kind of string used to get food out from between teeth

Let's Begin

1 **PREVIEW** Tell your student that although living things need food, water, air, and sometimes shelter to live, having all of these things doesn't guarantee a healthy life. Discuss times in your student's life when he or she has been sick or tired. Talk about how your student felt. Choose a specific time when your student was sick. Ask, *Why do you think you got sick?* [caught a cold from someone else, stayed up too late at night, ate too much junk food, didn't button coat, and so on] *Why do you think it's important to take care of your body?* [so you can stay healthy and not get sick]

2 **EXPLAIN** Explain to your student that one of the best ways to stay healthy is to keep clean. Ask, *What kinds of things do you do to stay clean?* [wash hands and face, take a bath] Explain that during the day, dirt and **germs** may get on a person's skin. We can't see germs because they are very small. Point out that if germs get into your student's body he or she can get sick. Germs can cause colds, sore throats, and the flu. Ask, *What can you do to prevent germs from getting into your body?* [wash regularly]

3 **EXTEND** Tell your student that germs can spread from one person to another. Coughing or sneezing near or on someone

can spread germs and illness. Ask, *When you're sick, what kinds of things can you do to keep others from getting sick?* [cover the mouth and nose when coughing or sneezing; throw away used tissues in the wastebasket and wash hands]

4 **DISCUSS AND MODEL** Discuss ways that your student or others may get dirty over the course of a day. Tell your student that it's often very easy to get dirty because dirt and germs can be spread just by touching something that others have touched, such as money, toys, or food. Illustrate this idea by spreading a thin layer of flour over a tabletop. Have your student suppose that the flour represents germs. Then have your student place his or her hand on the table. Ask, *What happened when you touched the table?* [flour got on my hand] Have your student use the same hand to open a door. Point out that the flour is now on the doorknob. Ask, *What does this exercise show you about germs?* [germs can be spread by touching things]

5 **CONTINUE** Ask, *What would be the best way to get the flour off your hands?* [wash my hands] Have your student wash the flour off his or her hands with soap and water. Then have your student examine his or her hands. Ask, *Do you see any flour on your hands after you washed them?* [no] Explain to your student that soap and water cleans away germs and dirt just as it did the flour. Now tell your student that germs can get into the body through a person's mouth. Ask, *If germs can get into your body through your mouth, when would it be most important to wash your hands?* [before eating, drinking, or touching food]

6 **EXPLAIN** Explain to your student that teeth are another part of his or her body that need to be cared for. Ask, *What is the purpose of teeth?* [chewing] Explain to your student that besides being important for chewing food, teeth are also important because they help us talk and look nice. Ask your student to say the words *love, little,* and *long.* Have your student pay attention to how his or her tongue moves to say each word. Ask, *What did your tongue do when you said the words?* [pushed against my teeth] Explain that without teeth it would be difficult to say many words. Have your student try to repeat the same words without letting his or her tongue touch the teeth.

7 **DESCRIBE** Tell your student that different teeth have different jobs for chewing. Show your student the illustration of the teeth on the next page. Point out that the front teeth are for taking bites of food. Tell your student that the pointed teeth on each side of the biting teeth are for tearing food. Then point out the teeth in the back of the mouth and explain that these teeth are used for grinding food into small pieces before swallowing. Ask, *Why do you think each type of tooth has a different shape?* [so it can do its job better]

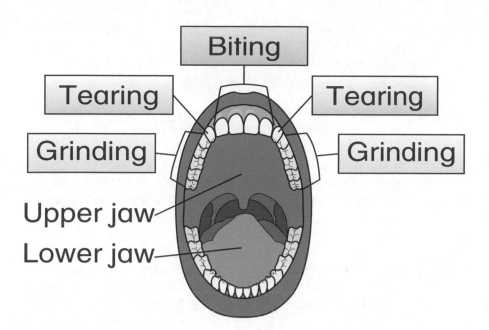

Biting

Tearing

Grinding

Upper jaw
Lower jaw

Tearing

Grinding

8 **MODEL** Give your student an apple. Have your student take a bite out of the apple and notice which teeth he or she uses. [biting] While your student is chewing the apple, have him or her continue noticing which teeth are being used. [grinding] Ask, *Which types of teeth did you use while eating the apple?* [the front biting teeth and the back grinding teeth] *Which teeth didn't you have to use?* [the pointy tearing teeth] Explain that your student didn't use his or her tearing teeth because apples are soft and can be bitten apart easily. Then discuss when your student might use his or her teeth for tearing, such as when eating meat off the bone.

9 **PRACTICE** Point out that it's important to clean your teeth. Teeth should be brushed at least two times every day, especially before bed. Model proper brushing practices for your student. Stand together in front of a mirror. Show your student how to brush up from the bottom teeth and down from the top teeth using a gentle, repeated motion. Brush the inside of the teeth and the flat surface of the teeth. Then explain that flossing is also very important for keeping teeth healthy. **Dental floss** gets food out from between teeth. Model flossing for your student. Show him or her how to take a long piece of floss and wrap it around his or her fingers. Demonstrate how to carefully move the floss back and forth between two teeth all the way to the gums. Ask, *Besides brushing and flossing, what else can you do to take care of your teeth?* [visit the dentist regularly]

10 **EXPLAIN** Explain to your student that sleep is another thing that a body needs to stay healthy. Ask, *How do you feel when you don't get enough sleep?* [tired, cranky, weak, and so on] Explain that a body without sleep is like a car without gas. A car won't run without gas and a body won't function well without sleep. Sleep is the time when we refresh our energy

---

⚠ A BRIGHT IDEA

The next time your student has a dental visit, call ahead and ask the dentist if he or she can show your student some model teeth or tooth X rays. Have your student prepare a question about his or her teeth to ask the dentist.

SCIENCE

LESSON 3.6

ENRICH THE EXPERIENCE

Illustrate for your student how the heart rate increases with exercise. Help your student find his or her pulse and calculate his or her heart rate. Then have your student participate in some form of exercise that will raise the heart rate. As soon as he or she is finished, help your student find his or her heart rate again to see how much faster the heart beats during physical activity.

FOR FURTHER READING

Exercise (*Rookie Read-About Health*), by Sharon Gordon (Children's Press, 2003).

I Know How We Fight Germs, by Kate Rowan, Jacqui Maynard, and Katherine McEwan, ill. (Candlewick Press, 1999).

Open Wide: Tooth School Inside, by Laurie Keller (Henry Holt and Company, 2000).

supply. Explain that energy allows people to move, think, and function well. Ask, *What's one thing you can do to make sure you have enough energy to learn and play during the day?* [go to bed on time and get enough sleep every night]

11 **ASK AND EXPLAIN** Tell your student that exercise is something else bodies need to be healthy. Some exercises are running, riding a bike, playing sports, and walking. Ask, *What happens to your heart when you exercise?* [it beats faster] Explain that the heart is a muscle. Just as leg muscles become stronger from repeated running, the heart gets stronger when you exercise it regularly. Point out that exercise also keeps the bones strong. Ask, *What is your favorite exercise?*

12 **DISTRIBUTE AND REVIEW** Distribute Student Learning Page 6.A. Ask your student to draw lines to match the activities. If your student needs prompting, ask, *What do you do to stay healthy before you eat?* [wash hands] *What do you do to stay healthy before you go to bed?* [brush teeth] Then have him or her draw a picture of something he or she does to keep healthy. You may wish to help your student think of some things he or she does, such as sleep, take medicine, eat good foods, exercise, and so on.

13 **DISTRIBUTE** Read the activities on Student Learning Page 6.B to your student. Have him or her decide which activity he or she would like to do.

Branching Out

TEACHING TIP

An educational video might be a good way to teach your student about taking care of teeth. A video can reinforce proper brushing and flossing techniques. A video can also provide images of what happens to teeth when they aren't cared for properly.

CHECKING IN

To assess your student's understanding of the lesson, help your student make a list of the things that he or she does to care for his or her body. Prompt your student to explain what he or she does to take care of his or her teeth, stay clean, and get enough sleep, as well as what kinds of exercises he or she does. Then together think of one thing that your student could do to be more healthy.

Stay Healthy

Draw lines to match the pictures. Then draw a picture of something you do to stay healthy.

1.

A.

2.

B.

What's Next? You Decide!

Teacher: Read aloud the directions and activities. Then have your student choose which activity to do next.

Now it's your turn to choose what to do next in the lesson. Read the activities and decide which one you want to do—you may want to try them both!

Tell a Health Story

MATERIALS

❑ drawing paper

❑ markers or crayons

STEPS

Do you like to tell stories? Tell one with a healthy, happy ending!

❑ Ask an adult to listen to you as you tell your story.

❑ Think about what you learned about caring for your body.

❑ Think of a name for the main person in your story.

❑ Begin the story by telling how the person doesn't take good care of his or her body.

❑ Explain what happens to that person and how he or she feels.

❑ You can tell the story in a funny way, a sad way, or any way you like.

❑ Then tell about how the person starts to take better care of his or her body and gets healthier.

❑ Draw a picture of the person in your story.

Become an Exercise Teacher

MATERIALS

❑ 1 music player

❑ 1 recording of a favorite song

❑ exercise clothes

STEPS

What kinds of exercises do you like to do? Put them to music!

❑ Ask an adult to help you find a recording of a song you like.

❑ Make up an exercise routine.

❑ You can use dancing and other exercises, such as jumping jacks or sit-ups. Do exercises that are fun!

❑ Put the exercises to your favorite song.

❑ Practice with the music.

❑ Teach your exercises to an adult.

❑ Do your exercise routine together with the music.

Learning About Food

A body without food is like a car without gas.

OBJECTIVE	BACKGROUND	MATERIALS
To teach your student how the body uses food and water	The human body needs energy to function. One way the body gets energy is from food and water. In this lesson, your student will learn why the body needs food and water and what kinds of food humans get from plants and animals.	■ Student Learning Pages 7.A–7.B ■ 1 drinking glass ■ 1 apple ■ 1 carrot ■ 1 egg ■ markers or crayons

VOCABULARY
ENERGY fuel from food that the body needs to work **VARIETY** all different kinds

Let's Begin

1 **PREVIEW** Remind your student that living things need certain things in order to survive. These things are food, water, air, and sometimes shelter. Ask, *What types of foods do you eat? How do those foods help your body?* [they help my body grow and give it energy] Explain to your student that his or her body works all the time, whether it's walking, talking, seeing, or just breathing. In order to do work, the body needs energy. Food is one way the body receives **energy.** Ask, *What kinds of activities do you do that require energy?* [playing, running, learning, and so on]

2 **MODEL** Fill a drinking glass almost three-quarters full with water and place it in front of your student. Ask, *How much water do you think makes up the human body?* Tell your student that more than half of a person's body is made up of water. Point out the glass and have your student imagine that it's a person and that the water in the glass represents the water in the person's body. Explain that water is very important to the body because it helps it work properly and keeps it from overheating. Our bodies are constantly using up the water they have, so we have to replace the water regularly. Ask, *How can a person tell when his or her body needs water?* [he or she gets thirsty]

3 **EXPAND** Explain that when the body is working hard, it often requires more water because more is being used. Ask, *What activities do you do that cause you to become thirsty?* [playing outside, running, working, riding a bike, and so on] *What types of drinks do you like to drink?* [water, milk, juice, soda, and so on] Explain that juice and milk are healthy things to drink because they provide nutrients that the body needs. Point out that water is the healthiest drink of all. Sodas aren't healthy because they don't provide any nutrients. Soda also contains a lot of sugar, which can cause a person to become more thirsty. Ask, *What do you think is the best thing to drink after you have been running and playing?* [water]

4 **REVEAL** Explain to your student that his or her body also needs to eat good foods to stay healthy. Point out that just as there are drinks that are healthier than others, there are also foods that are healthier than others. Ask, *Can you name some foods that are healthy?* [vegetables, fruits, lean protein, whole grains, and so on] Explain that a person should eat a **variety** of healthy foods every day. Ask, *What do you think would happen if we only ate carrots for breakfast, lunch, and dinner?* [the body wouldn't get enough variety] Point out that even though carrots are a healthy food, only eating carrots isn't healthy for the body.

5 **RELATE** Explain that there are some foods that aren't considered healthy. Sweet foods that have a lot of sugar, such as candy and cookies, and salty foods that have a lot of fat, such as french fries and potato chips, aren't very healthy. Ask, *Do you like to eat sweets or salty snack foods? What can you do to be healthy when you eat these foods?* [don't eat too much, eat them only once in a while, be sure to eat healthy foods before eating unhealthy foods when you are hungry]

6 **IDENTIFY** Have your student look at the picture below and ask, *What foods in the picture do you think would make a healthy meal?* [answers will vary but should include a variety of foods and very few sweets or fats]

It's important to eat a variety of healthy foods.

7 **EXTEND** Tell your student that different types of foods help his or her body in different ways. For example, fruits and vegetables help the body grow, while breads, pasta, and other grains give the body lots of energy. Name several foods and have your student tell you whether each one is a fruit, a vegetable, or a grain. Ask, *What foods do you eat that help your body grow?* [any fruit or vegetable] *What foods do you eat that give your body energy?* [any foods from the bread and grain group]

8 **DESCRIBE** Explain that food comes from many different places. Show your student an apple, a carrot, and an egg. Ask, *Where do you think each of these foods come from?* [the apple and carrot come from plants; the egg comes from an animal] Tell your student that fruits, such as apples and oranges, and vegetables, such as peas and carrots, come from plants. Point out that grains used to make bread and cereal also come from plants. Talk with your student about other examples of foods that come from plants and animals.

9 **EXPAND** Tell your student that foods that don't come from plants come from animals. Some foods that come from animals are milk, hamburger meat, ham, and fish. If your student eats foods that come from animals, ask, *What kind of foods that come from animals do you like to eat? What types of foods that come from animals do you not like to eat?* Then discuss with your student other foods that come from animals that he or she may be familiar with.

10 **DISTRIBUTE** Distribute Student Learning Page 7.A. Ask your student to identify the food shown in each picture. Have your student decide which foods come from plants and which foods come from animals. Your student should color the foods that come from plants green and the foods that come from animals red.

11 **EXPLAIN** Explain to your student that the foods that people buy at the store come to the store from many different places. Ask, *Can you name a place where food grows?* [farms] Explain that farmers grow plants that we use for food. They take care of the plants on the farm until the food is ready to be picked. Then they send the food to the store. Food from animals, such as beef, pork, and chicken, also comes from farms. Ask, *Besides farms, where else do you think food comes from?* [people's gardens, oceans, lakes, and so on]

ENRICH THE EXPERIENCE

Take your student to a grocery store and point out various foods as you walk through the aisles. Ask your student to tell you the name of each food and whether it comes from a plant or an animal. Look for foods that come from oceans or lakes and foods that you could grow at home in a garden.

Branching Out

TEACHING TIP

You can reinforce what your student has learned about food by asking your student to plan a healthy meal for the family. Have your student include at least one vegetable, one fruit, one food that is protein-based or comes from an animal, and a healthy drink.

CHECKING IN

To assess your student's understanding of the lesson, have him or her identify the foods in the refrigerator and cupboards. You can also have your student talk about water, why it's important to drink enough water every day, and why you should drink even more when you're active.

FOR FURTHER READING

Good Enough to Eat: A Kid's Guide to Food and Nutrition, by Lizzy Rockwell, ill. (HarperCollins Juvenile Books, 1999).

Harvest Time (*Spyglass Books*), by Jennifer Waters and Joan Stewart (Compass Point Books, 2002).

This Is the Sea That Feeds Us, by Robert F. Baldwin and Don Dyen, ill. (Dawn Publications, 1998).

Show Where Foods Come From

Color the foods that come from plants green. Color the foods that come from animals red.

What's Next? You Decide!

Teacher: *Read aloud the directions and activities. Then have your student choose which activity to do next.*

Now it's your turn to choose what to do next in the lesson. Read the activities and decide which one you want to do—you may want to try them both!

Explore Your Diet

MATERIALS

❏ 1 posterboard

❏ 3–4 old cooking or food magazines

❏ 1 pair scissors

❏ glue

❏ markers or crayons

STEPS

What are your favorite foods for each meal? Show it in a collage!

❏ Draw a line straight down the middle of the posterboard.

❏ Draw a line straight across the middle of the posterboard. You should have four squares.

❏ Look through the magazines for things you like to eat and drink for breakfast, lunch, dinner, and as a snack.

❏ Cut out the pictures.

❏ Glue the pictures of breakfast foods in the first square.

❏ Glue the pictures for lunch in the second square and dinner in the third square.

❏ Glue the pictures for snacks in the last square.

❏ Share your collage with an adult!

Plant Your Own Garden

MATERIALS

❏ 3–4 food or gardening magazines

❏ 1 pair scissors

❏ glue

❏ 5–10 craft sticks

❏ 1 shoebox

❏ potting soil

STEPS

What foods would you grow in a garden?

❏ Look through magazines.

❏ Find pictures of foods that you would plant in a garden.

❏ Cut out the pictures.

❏ Glue a craft stick to the back of each picture.

❏ Put some soil in the shoebox.

❏ Stick the craft sticks into the soil.

❏ Show an adult your garden.

❏ Name all the foods that you are growing!

Understanding the Weather

The weather is forever changing.

SCIENCE
LESSON 3.8

OBJECTIVE	BACKGROUND	MATERIALS
To teach your student about weather and the seasons	Weather is an important part of our everyday lives. It affects our lifestyle, our activities, and our community life. In this lesson, your student will learn about different kinds of daily weather, the changing of the seasons, and why weather matters so much to people.	■ Student Learning Pages 8.A–8.B

VOCABULARY
TEMPERATURE how hot or cold the air is **SEASONS** the four different periods of time in a year with different weather patterns **PREDICT** to guess what will happen in advance

Let's Begin

1   **EXPLAIN** Explain to your student that weather refers to what the air outside is like. For example, the air may be hot or cold, or it may be calm or windy. Ask, *What do you think makes the weather warm?* [the sun] Explain that **temperature** refers to how the air feels, such as hot, warm, cool, or cold. Together with your student take a trip outside to survey the weather. Ask, *What is the weather like today?* Prompt your student to use adjectives that describe temperature and air motion, such as *hot, cool, windy,* and so on.

2   **EXPAND** Point out that the weather changes all the time. It may be warm and sunny in the morning and then become cloudy and cool in the afternoon. Ask your student to talk about some examples of weather changes that he or she has experienced. Then discuss today's weather and how it might change.

3   **DESCRIBE** Tell your student that just as the weather may change during the course of a day, it also changes during the **seasons**, or the four different time periods, of the year. Ask, *What are the four seasons of the year?* [winter, spring, summer, and fall] *What season are we in right now?* Discuss the kind of weather that you usually have during the current season with your student. Then talk about what the other three seasons are typically like in your

area. Ask your student to describe some of the activities he or she enjoys doing during each of the four seasons. Then distribute Student Learning Page 8.A. Help your student complete the activity.

4   **EXPLAIN**   Explain to your student that weather can affect our plans. Being at a picnic and getting rained on can be uncomfortable. Point out that people try to predict the weather so that they can make good plans. One way to predict the weather is to look at the sky. Ask, *What might it mean if you see dark clouds forming in the sky?* [a storm is coming]

5   **EXPAND**   Point out that there are people whose job is to predict the weather. These people give weather reports on television, radio, the Internet, and in newspapers. They let us know when dangerous weather is coming. Aside from dangerous weather, weather reports can also help us decide what activities to plan and what type of clothes to wear. Ask, *If the weather report predicts rain, what might you plan on doing?* [bring an umbrella, wear a raincoat, wear rain shoes, and so on]

Weather reports warn us about severe weather.

Branching Out

TEACHING TIP

Give your student an understanding of weather reports by tuning in to a weather broadcast on the television or radio or by reading a weather report in a newspaper. Together find out the weather prediction for that day and the following day. On the next day ask your student if the weather prediction was right.

CHECKING IN

To assess your student's understanding of the lesson, take a trip outside. Have your student describe the weather conditions, making sure he or she uses adjectives describing the air.

FOR FURTHER READING

Celebrate Seasons, by Sara Jordan (Sara Jordan Publishing, 1999).

Weather, by Seymour Simon (HarperCollins Juvenile Books, 2000).

Explore Seasons

Draw a picture that shows something
special about each season in your area.

Winter	Spring
Summer	**Fall**

What's Next? You Decide!

Teacher: *Read aloud the directions and activities. Then have your student choose which activity to do next.*

Now it's your turn to choose what to do next in the lesson. Read the activities and decide which one you want to do—you may want to try them both!

Predict the Weather

 MATERIALS

❑ 1 audiocassette recorder

❑ 1 audiocassette tape

❑ 1 posterboard

❑ markers or crayons

 STEPS

Suppose you're a television weather reporter. Predict tomorrow's weather!

❑ Think about today's weather. Look at the sky.

❑ Decide what you think the weather will be like tomorrow.

❑ Think about what the temperature and wind will be like.

❑ Decide if it will be sunny or cloudy.

❑ Use an audiocassette recorder to record your weather report for tomorrow.

❑ Then draw a picture of what the day will be like.

❑ Play your weather report for an adult and show your drawing!

Play Charades

MATERIALS

❑ clothes for each season

STEPS

How could you act out each season? Try it in a game of charades!

❑ Think about how the weather is different in summer, spring, winter, and fall.

❑ Is the weather cold, hot, warm, cool, sunny, cloudy, rainy, snowy, or windy?

❑ Find different clothes that can help you act out each season.

❑ Practice acting out each season.

❑ Then ask an adult to watch you.

❑ Can he or she guess what season you are?

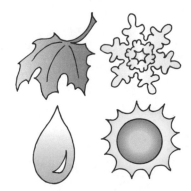

Exploring Earth's Land and Water

The first step in taking care of Earth is to understand what lies on its surface.

OBJECTIVE	BACKGROUND	MATERIALS
To teach your student about Earth's water and land formations	Understanding Earth's land and water formations and how they are created helps us appreciate the world and nature. In this lesson, your student will learn about rocks, sand, and soil, how soil is formed, and the types of land and water that can be found on Earth.	<ul><li>Student Learning Pages 9.A–9.B</li><li>1–2 geography or landscape picture books</li><li>1–2 farming or soil picture books</li></ul>

VOCABULARY

SAND small grains of rock broken into very small pieces

SOIL a mixture of rock, sand, and organic material

MOUNTAINS high land areas made of rock

PLAIN a large area of land that is relatively flat

DESERTS hot, dry lands that are often covered with sand

OCEANS very large bodies of water that cover more than half of Earth

LAKES bodies of water that are surrounded by land

RIVERS long, flowing currents of water that empty into larger bodies of water

Let's Begin

1 **EXPLAIN** Explain that much of the land on Earth is made up of rocks and **sand.** Explain that rocks can be found in many sizes, shapes, and colors. Rocks change by breaking into smaller pieces, which in turn break into even smaller pieces and become sand. Ask your student to look at the photos of rocks below and ask him or her to compare the rocks. Ask, *How are these rocks different?* [different sizes, shapes, and colors] *In what kinds of places do you think you might find sand?* [on a beach, in a desert, near water]

 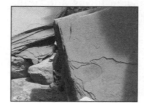  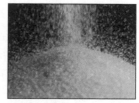

Rocks are different sizes and colors.

2 **EXPAND** Tell your student that **soil** forms when rocks, sand, and organic material get mixed together. Point out that soil is different from sand because it has a lot of plant and animal remains in it. It takes a very long time for soil to form. Soil is very important. People depend on soil for things such as growing plants on farms or in gardens for food. Take a trip outside with your student and explore the soil that's around you. Have your student search for various rocks and ask him or her to compare them. Help your student dig up a small pile of soil and examine what he or she finds in it.

3 **EXPLORE** Tell your student that the land on Earth has many shapes. Explain that some land is in the shape of **mountains.** Mountains are high areas of land that are made of rock. Another shape is a **plain.** Plains are mostly flat areas of land that are made of rocks and soil. **Deserts** can also be flat. The desert is covered with sand and is very dry. Discuss with your student other types of landforms, such as valleys and canyons. Then ask your student to decide what type of land he or she lives on or near. Show pictures of different types of landforms to your student. Then distribute Student Learning Page 9.A. Help your student with the directions.

4 **DESCRIBE** Tell your student that a large portion of Earth is covered by water. Explain that most of Earth is covered by large bodies of salty water called **oceans.** Then tell your student that **lakes** are smaller bodies of water that are usually surrounded by land. Point out that lakes are not salty. Another place where we find water is in **rivers.** Rivers are long, flowing bodies of water that empty into larger bodies of water. Ask, *Have you ever seen an ocean, a lake, or a river? Do you live near any of these bodies of water?* Then distribute Student Learning Page 9.B. Read the activities to your student and have him or her decide which one to complete.

Branching Out

TEACHING TIP

You can support the information in this lesson by connecting it with Social Studies Lessons 4.5–4.8, which are about understanding maps and globes and identifying water and land on maps.

CHECKING IN

To assess your student's understanding of the lesson, show your student pictures of different landforms and bodies of water and ask him or her to identify each one. You can also have your student talk about the land he or she lives on and how it's similar or different to mountains, plains, deserts, or valleys.

A BRIGHT IDEA

Gathering several geography or landscape picture books before beginning the lesson and sharing them with your student throughout will help your student visualize different landforms and bodies of water. You might also look for children's books about farming or soil.

DID YOU KNOW?

You and your student can learn more about soil from the U.S. Bureau of Land Management at http://www.blm.gov/nstc. Click on Just for Kids: Soil Biological Communities.

FOR FURTHER READING

Are Mountains Getting Taller?, by Melvin Berger, Gilda Berger, and Robin Carter, ill. (Scholastic, 2003).

Dirt (Jump into Science), by Steve Tomecek and Nancy Woodman, ill. (National Geographic, 2002).

Order the Pictures

How does sand form? Number the pictures from one to four in the correct order.

A. _____

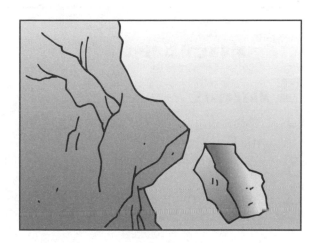

C. _____

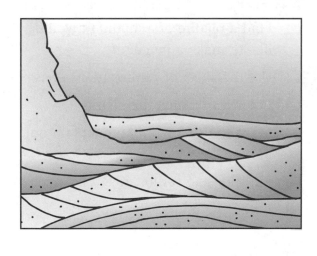

B. _____

D. _____

What's Next? You Decide!

Teacher: Read aloud the directions and activities. Then have your student choose which activity to do next.

Now it's your turn to choose what to do next in the lesson. Read the activities and decide which one you want to do—you may want to try them both!

Make a Soil Model

MATERIALS

❏ 1 clear, empty jar or other container with lid

❏ soil

❏ leaves and twigs

❏ sand

❏ small pebbles or rocks

❏ large pebbles or rocks

STEPS

Model how soil is made.

❏ Put a layer of soil in the jar.

❏ Tap the jar so that the soil is even.

❏ Put leaves and twigs on top of the soil so that they lay flat.

❏ Add a layer of sand so that the jar is half full of soil, leaves and twigs, and sand.

❏ Then put a layer of tiny rocks in the jar.

❏ Finally, add a layer of large rocks to fill the jar.

❏ Put the lid on the jar.

❏ Show your model to an adult.

❏ Explain how it shows the steps of making soil.

Make a Mountain

MATERIALS

❏ 1 picture of a mountain

❏ 1 sheet strong cardboard

❏ markers or crayons

❏ 1 package modeling clay

❏ cotton balls

❏ 1–2 sheets construction paper

❏ several small rocks, twigs, leaves, or grass

STEPS

❏ Find a picture of a mountain you'd like to make a model of.

❏ Use the sheet of cardboard as a base.

❏ Color it to match the picture.

❏ Make the shape of the mountain out of modeling clay.

❏ Put it on the cardboard.

❏ If your mountain has snow, use cotton balls to make snow.

❏ Use the twigs for trees if shown in the mountain photo.

❏ Use construction paper, small rocks, leaves, grass, or other things to make your mountain look like the picture.

❏ Show your mountain model to an adult!

Learning to Care for Earth

Our natural resources may seem plentiful, but they're too important to take for granted.

OBJECTIVE	BACKGROUND	MATERIALS
To teach your student about using natural resources wisely	Earth provides all living things with resources that allow them to survive. It's important that we learn to appreciate what we have and do all we can to make Earth's resources last. In this lesson, your student will learn about different resources, how we use them, and ways they can be conserved.	■ Student Learning Pages 10.A–10.B ■ 1 copy Web, page 356 ■ markers or crayons

VOCABULARY

RESOURCES things that are used to meet a need

CONSERVE to protect and use resources wisely

POLLUTION the dirtying or harming of natural resources

REUSING using something over again instead of throwing it away

RECYCLING making used materials into something else that's useful

Let's Begin

1 **REVIEW** Ask your student, *What do living things need in order to survive?* [food, air, water, and sometimes shelter] Explain that food, air, and water are examples of **resources,** or things that are used to meet a need. Earth provides all of these resources for us. Point out that some of the things people do can make our resources dirty or unusable. Ask, *Why do you think it's important to take care of Earth's resources?* [because living things, such as people and animals, need them to survive]

2 **EXPLORE** Ask, *Where do you think clean water comes from?* [inside Earth, rain, lakes, and rivers] Distribute a copy of the Web found on page 356 to your student. Write "Water" in the center. In the surrounding ovals, ask your student to draw pictures of ways that he or she uses water. When the Web is complete, help your student think of ways that he or she can **conserve** water in each activity pictured. For example, if one of the pictures is about brushing teeth, your student could conserve water by not letting the water run when he or she isn't using it.

3 **EXPLAIN AND EXPLORE** Explain to your student that air is another of Earth's resources that people need to take care of.

A BRIGHT IDEA

To reinforce the idea of caring for our resources and for each other, read *Children of the Earth . . . Remember* by Schim Schimmel with your student. This is a story about animals and people working together to take care of Earth.

Tell your student that **pollution** can harm natural resources. Some of the things people do cause air pollution. Ask, *How do you think the air becomes polluted?* [smoke from cars, factories, or fires, and so on] Together with your student discuss ways that people can decrease air pollution, such as by carpooling.

Cars and factories can be sources of air pollution.

ENRICH THE EXPERIENCE

To learn more about water conservation, have your student visit the U.S. Environmental Protection Agency online at http://www. epa.gov/owow. Click on Protecting Our Resources, then Watersheds for Kids.

4 **EXPAND** Tell your student that the garbage we throw away can cause harm to our resources. Point out that it's important to cut down on the amount of garbage we create and to not waste things. One way to do this is by **reusing** things. Point out that some things can be reused rather than thrown away, such as empty jars or paper. Another way is by **recycling.** Explain that recycling involves taking used things and making them into new things. We can recycle cans, paper, glass, and plastic. Point out the recycle symbol. Then distribute Student Learning Page 10.A. Have your student circle the items on the page that can be recycled.

5 **EXPLAIN** Explain that Earth Day is an annual event during which people celebrate Earth and encourage the world to care for our natural resources. Some people do special things on Earth Day, such as plant trees, recycle, or clean up litter in their area. Learn more about Earth Day and conservation at http://www. kidsdomain.com. Click on Holidays. Then distribute Student Learning Page 10.B. Read the directions and activities to your student and have him or her choose what to do next. For another activity, find out about an environmental volunteer opportunity in your area, such as litter removal, tree planting, river cleanup, or habitat restoration, that you and your student can participate in.

Branching Out

FOR FURTHER READING

Earth Day: Keeping Our Planet Clean, by Elaine Landau (Enslow Publishers, 2002).

A River Ran Wild: An Environmental History, by Lynne Cherry (Harcourt, 2002).

Waste Not: Time to Recycle, by Rebecca Weber (Compass Point Books, 2002).

TEACHING TIP

Ask your student to search around his or her home and find at least one way that he or she can conserve, reuse, and recycle.

CHECKING IN

Ask him or her to explain why Earth's resources are important to us, what pollution is, and what things we can do to conserve our resources.

Get into Recycling!

Circle the things that can be recycled.

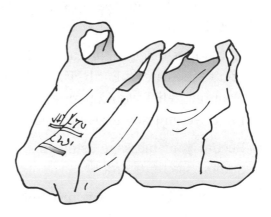

What's Next? You Decide!

SCIENCE 10.B

Teacher: Read aloud the directions and activities. Then have your student choose which activity to do next.

Now it's your turn to choose what to do next in the lesson. Read the activities and decide which one you want to do—you may want to try them both!

Record a Radio Announcement

MATERIALS

❑ 1 audiocassette recorder

❑ 1 audiocassette tape

STEPS

Become a radio announcer and record a message about conservation.

❑ Think about what you would like to tell people about conserving resources.

❑ Practice talking about the things that people can do to take care of Earth.

❑ Be sure to include ways to reuse and recycle.

❑ Talk about what might happen if we don't take care of Earth. For example, what would happen if there weren't any trees or water?

❑ Record your message using an audiocassette recorder.

❑ Play the recording for your family and friends.

Make Recycling Bins for Your Home

MATERIALS

❑ 4 medium-sized boxes

❑ 3–4 old magazines

❑ 1 pair scissors

❑ glue

STEPS

Help your family recycle by making recycling containers.

❑ Look through magazines for pictures of items that can be recycled.

❑ Cut out the pictures.

❑ Separate the pictures of paper, glass, plastic, and aluminum items.

❑ Decorate each box by gluing pictures on them.

❑ Make one box for paper, one for glass, one for plastic, and one for aluminum.

❑ Ask an adult to help you find a good place to keep the boxes.

❑ Show an adult how to recycle by placing one thing in each of the boxes.

Reuse and Recycle

Understanding Earth and Space

When exploring Earth and space, the possibilities are endless.

OBJECTIVE	BACKGROUND	MATERIALS
To teach your student about Earth and the sun, the moon, and the stars	Planetary changes can seem mysterious at first, but basic information about why things happen as they do and how planets move helps to make sense of it all. In this lesson, your student will learn what causes day and night, how Earth moves, and what happens to the sun, the moon, and the stars when we can't see them.	■ Student Learning Pages 11.A–11.B ■ 1 globe ■ tape ■ 1 flashlight ■ 1 hand mirror ■ markers or crayons ■ 1 copy T Chart, page 355

VOCABULARY

STARS large, glowing balls of gas, such as the sun, that produce light and heat

MOON the planetlike body that orbits Earth

SHADOW an area of darkness that occurs when an object blocks light

Let's Begin

1 **ASK AND EXPLAIN** Ask, *Where do you think Earth receives its light and warmth from?* [the sun] Explain that when the sun shines on Earth, it provides both light and heat. Ask your student if he or she has noticed how the sun's position in the sky changes over the course of a day. Take a trip outside and point to the east. Explain that it's where the sun rises, or appears. Then point to the west and explain that it's where the sun sets, or disappears. Point out that from Earth it looks as if the sun were moving across the sky. Explain that the sun actually doesn't move. Ask, *If the sun isn't moving, why does it seem to travel across the sky?* [because Earth is turning]

2 **EXPAND** Explain that Earth is always turning. Ask, *How long is one day?* [24 hours] Explain that this is how long it takes for Earth to make one complete turn. Demonstrate how Earth's turning makes night and day. Point out where you live on a globe and mark it with a piece of tape. Then hold a flashlight at

A BRIGHT IDEA

You may wish to have a book handy that shows photos of the sun and the moon as you go through the lesson. You can also go to http://www.weather-photography.com and click on Photo Gallery for photos.

an angle and shine it on the taped area of the globe. Slowly turn the globe. Have your student watch the place where he or she lives move away from the light until it becomes dark. Say, *This is night.* Keep turning the globe one full rotation while shining the light. Point out that the tape eventually comes around again into the light. Say, *This is the beginning of a new day.* Keep turning. As the tape moves away from the light again, ask, *What time of day is it now?* [sunset or nighttime]

3   **EXPLAIN**   Talk about the sun. Explain to your student that the heat and light from the sun keep people, plants, and animals alive. Plants need light to make their food. Animals need heat to keep warm and light to see. Animals also need healthy plants to eat. Explain that without light there would be no plants for animals to eat. Like animals, people need heat to stay warm. People also need plants and animals for food. Ask, *What would Earth be like if the sun didn't exist?* [there would be no living things]

4   **ASK AND EXPLAIN**   Ask, *What do the stars look like when you see them at night?* [bright, shiny, tiny] Tell your student that **stars** glow because they are made of burning gases that produce light and heat. Stars are much larger than they look. Point out that many stars we see at night are much bigger than Earth. They look small because they are far away. Explain that the sun is a star. It appears larger than other stars because it's closer to Earth. Though the sun is bigger than many other stars, it's also much smaller than many others. Ask, *Why do you think other stars don't look as bright as our sun?* [because they are far away]

5   **MODEL**   Tell your student that the **moon** looks bright but isn't a star. The moon doesn't shine at all. Explain that its brightness comes from the light of the sun bouncing off of its surface. Model this idea by pointing the flashlight at the globe. Then hold a hand mirror on the opposite side of the globe. Tell your student to imagine that the mirror is the moon. Now position the mirror so that the light from the flashlight reflects off the mirror toward the dark side of the globe. Make sure your student sees the reflection and understands why the moon seems to shine at night. Ask, *If the sun's light wasn't reaching the moon, would it still look bright from Earth?* [no, all the moon's light comes from the sun]

6   **DESCRIBE AND MODEL**   Point out that we can't always see the moon from where we are on Earth. Ask, *Where do you think the moon is when we can't see it?* [on the other side of Earth] Explain that the moon stays close to Earth all the time. It moves around Earth, so sometimes it's on the other side where we can't see it. Model this for your student. Go outside together and look for a large tree. Have your student stand with his or her back against the tree, looking straight ahead. Have your student suppose that the tree is Earth and you are the moon. Have your student observe while you walk in a circle around the tree. Have your student tell you when he or she has lost sight of you. Explain that you are still close to the tree, it's just that you are out of view. Then switch places with your student and create the model again.

7   **EXPLAIN AND MODEL**   Ask, *When are we best able to see the moon?* [at night] Explain that although the moon can sometimes be seen during the day, it's most clearly visible at night. Model why this is true for your student. Together take a flashlight outside in the daylight. Shine the flashlight on an object such as a flowerpot or a tree. Point out that the light is only slightly visible or not visible at all. Then go indoors to a room without a lot of windows. Shine the flashlight on an object and have your student notice that the light is more visible indoors where there's less sunlight. Ask, *Why do you think it's harder to see the moon in the daytime?* [because during the day the light from the sun is brighter than the moon]

8   **DISTRIBUTE**   Distribute Student Learning Page 11.A to your student. Point out the sun and Earth in the drawing. Ask your student to color the sun yellow. Then have your student observe the position of the sun in relationship to Earth and color the daylight half of Earth yellow. Ask your student to color the half of Earth in the picture that's nighttime black. If your student has difficulty with this, revisit the exercise from Step 2 with the globe and the flashlight. Then have your student draw the moon and stars into the picture. Ask, *In the picture, which side of Earth would we best be able to see the moon and stars from?* [the nighttime side]

9   **EXPLAIN AND MODEL**   Talk about what a **shadow** is with your student. Explain that a shadow is formed when something blocks the path of light to an object. Model this by shining the flashlight on a wall in a dark room. Have your student place his or her hand in front of the path of light. Tell your student to look at the shadow of his or her hand. Then have your student face the wall. Shine the flashlight from behind your student so that his or her full shadow is cast against the wall. Keeping the light on your student, walk to the other side of the room to simulate the Earth turning. Point out how the shape of the shadow changes when the light source changes direction.

10   **RELATE**   Explain that because Earth is always turning, the way light hits Earth changes throughout the day. This means that shadows change shape throughout the day. On the next sunny day, go outside with your student early in the morning. Choose a shadow, such as the shadow of a building or a tree. Mark the morning position of the shadow with a rock. Together observe where the sun is in the sky. Then do the same at noon and in the late afternoon. Have your student describe how the shadow changed as the sun's position in the sky changed. Ask, *Why aren't there shadows on a cloudy day?* [there isn't a bright source of light to make shadows]

DID YOU KNOW?

It takes time for light to travel from its source to an object. Because of the distance between the sun and Earth, it takes more than eight minutes for light from the sun to reach Earth.

11 **EXPAND** Ask your student if he or she has ever made shadow puppets. If not, show your student how to use his or her hands in front of a light to make animal shapes and other images. Then explain that people use shadows for other reasons. Ask your student if he or she has ever used his or her hand to block the path of light from the sun to see better on a bright day. Add that when an object blocks light, it can also block heat. Point out that another name for a shadow is shade. On a hot day, many people may sit in the shade of a tree or a building to escape the heat. Together with your student discuss other possible ways people use shadows.

12 **DISTRIBUTE** Distribute Student Learning Page 11.B. Read the activities to your student. Have your student choose which one he or she would like to complete.

ENRICH THE EXPERIENCE

For additional information and creative activities about Earth, the sun, the moon, and the stars, visit www.enchantedlearning.com and click on Astronomy.

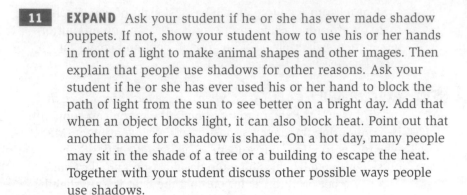

Branching Out

TEACHING TIP

Make a copy of the T Chart found on page 355. On one side have your student draw things that make their own light [sun, other stars], and on the other side have your student draw things that get their light from the sun [Earth, moon]. Be sure your student understands that the moon doesn't shine on its own. Like Earth, it gets its light from the sun. Stars, on the other hand, don't rely on other sources of light but rather produce their own.

CHECKING IN

To assess your student's understanding of the lesson, have him or her teach some of the key concepts back to you, including what causes day and night, why the moon seems to glow, and how shadows are made. Encourage your student to make use of drawings and other visual aids.

FOR FURTHER READING

Day Light, Night Light: Where Light Comes From, by Franklyn Mansfield Branley and Stacey Shuett, ill. (Scott Foresman, 1998).

Earth, Sun, and Moon (*Space*), by Robin Birch (Chelsea House Publishing, 2002).

The Sun: Our Nearest Star, by Franklyn Mansfield Branley and Edward Miller, ill. (HarperTrophy, 2002).

Color Day and Night

Color the sun yellow. Color daylight on Earth yellow. Color nighttime on Earth black. Draw the moon and stars.

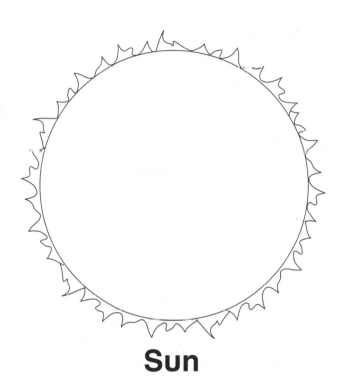

Sun

Earth

What's Next? You Decide!

Teacher: *Read aloud the directions and activities. Then have your student choose which activity to do next.*

Now it's your turn to choose what to do next in the lesson. Read the activities and decide which one you want to do—you may want to try them both!

Make a Diorama

MATERIALS

- ❑ 1 shoebox or similar sized box
- ❑ 1 pair scissors
- ❑ glue
- ❑ black construction paper
- ❑ white construction paper
- ❑ markers or crayons
- ❑ string or yarn
- ❑ tape

STEPS

- ❑ Use scissors and glue to line the bottom and sides of a shoebox with black construction paper.
- ❑ Use a white crayon to draw stars in the box.
- ❑ On the white paper, draw and color a picture of the sun. Make it small enough to fit in the box.
- ❑ Then draw and color Earth and the moon.
- ❑ Cut out the drawings of the sun, Earth, and moon.
- ❑ Tape string or yarn to the top of each cutout.
- ❑ Turn the box on its side. Use tape to hang each cutout in the box.

Perform a Puppet Show Using Shadows

MATERIALS

- ❑ 1 flashlight

STEPS

Explain day and night in a shadow puppet show!

- ❑ Think about what causes day and night.
- ❑ Think about why the stars shine.
- ❑ Think about why the moon shines.
- ❑ Point the flashlight at a light-colored wall in a dark room.
- ❑ Place your hand in front of the flashlight to make a shadow.
- ❑ Try to make your shadow look like an animal talking.
- ❑ Then have your shadow puppet talk about day and night and why the stars and the moon shine.
- ❑ Perform your puppet show for an adult.

Investigating Matter and How Things Change

No matter where we are, matter is all around us.

OBJECTIVE	BACKGROUND	MATERIALS
To teach your student about forms of matter and changes in matter	Everything we see and touch is made of matter. We are able to perceive different forms of matter through our senses. In this lesson, your student will learn about how things are alike and different, the different forms of matter, and how matter changes forms.	■ Student Learning Pages 12.A–12.B ■ 1 box crayons ■ 1 cotton ball ■ 1 piece sandpaper ■ 1 pencil ■ 1 wire hanger ■ 1 penny ■ 1 bowl of water ■ 1 balloon ■ 1 aluminum can ■ 1 rubber band ■ 1 blow dryer ■ 1 copy Sequence Chain, page 356

VOCABULARY

ALIKE when something is similar to something else

DIFFERENT when something is not like something else

MATTER anything that takes up space in the form of a solid, liquid, or gas

SOLID matter that has shape and can be seen and felt

LIQUID matter that can be poured and takes the shape of whatever holds it

GAS matter that usually can't be seen and doesn't have shape

Let's Begin

1   **ASK AND EXPLAIN** Have your student look at the box of crayons. Ask, *What sense tells you that these crayons are different colors?* [sight] Explain to your student that his or her eyes give him or her the ability to tell how things are **alike** and **different.** Then ask, *How are the crayons alike?* [they have the same size and shape]

2   **EXPLORE** Have your student explore how things are alike and different by playing a game. Name a color and ask your student to find something in the room that is that color. Then ask your

ENRICH THE EXPERIENCE

You and your student can have fun learning about differences in shape by reading *The Shape of Me and Other Stuff* by Dr. Seuss.

student to find something that's a different color. Repeat this activity by having your student find things with similar and different shapes and sizes. Point out that your student is using his or her eyes to recognize how things are alike and different. Then ask your student to find things that are similar in one way but different in another. For example, ask your student to find two things that have a similar color but a different size or shape.

3 **RELATE** Tell your student that another way to find out how things are alike or different is by how they feel to the touch. Explain that things can feel hard, soft, rough, smooth, heavy, or light. Have your student pick up a cotton ball and a piece of sandpaper. Point out that things can feel alike in some ways and different in other ways. Ask, *In what way do the cotton ball and the sandpaper feel alike?* [they are both light] *In what way do they feel different?* [the cotton ball feels soft while the sandpaper feels rough]

4 **DESCRIBE** Tell your student that everything is made of **matter.** Matter is anything that takes up space. Point out random objects in the room and explain that each object is made of matter. Also explain that although everything is made of matter, things may be made from different kinds of materials. For example, paper, wood, glass, and metal are different materials. Ask your student to find in the room something made from each of these materials.

5 **EXPLAIN AND MODEL** Explain to your student that different kinds of matter behave in different ways. For example, some kinds of matter bend while others are rigid. Show your student a pencil and a wire hanger and ask your student to predict which of the objects will bend and which won't. Then try to bend both objects, making sure to bend the pencil hard enough to snap it in half. Ask, *Why do you think the pencil broke?* [because the material it's made of doesn't bend] Next, tell your student that some kinds of matter float in water while others sink. Show your student half of the broken pencil and a penny. Ask your student to predict which one will float and which one will sink. Have your student drop the items into a bowl of water to test his or her prediction.

6 **REVEAL** Explain to your student that matter comes in three different forms. One is a **solid.** Tell your student that solids, such as a chair or a book, can be seen and have a shape of their own. Ask your student to name five other things in the room that are solids.

7 **EXPAND** Explain to your student that **liquid** is another form of matter. Water is a liquid. Like solids, liquids can be seen, but their shape changes to fit the shape of the containers they are in. Show your student the bowl of water and ask, *What shape is this liquid? Why?* [it's shaped like the bowl because the bowl is holding it] Ask your student to look around the room or the home for other examples of liquids and their shapes.

8 **RELATE** Explain to your student that the third form of matter is **gas**. Gases don't have a shape, and they usually can't be seen. Tell your student that the air we breathe is an example of a gas. Show your student a balloon without air in it. Blow up the balloon and ask, *What form of matter is inside the balloon?* [gas] *How can you tell that gas is in the balloon?* [because the gas is taking up space inside the balloon] Help your student think of other examples of matter in the form of a gas.

9 **DISTRIBUTE** Distribute Student Learning Page 12.A. Have your student identify the pictures of solids, liquids, and gases. Ask him or her to color the solids blue, the liquids green, and the gases yellow. Remind your student that liquids and gases only have shape when something is holding them. Be sure that your student determines if there is liquid or gas inside the object when deciding which form of matter each picture represents.

10 **OBSERVE** Explain that some kinds of matter can change shape. Show your student an aluminum can, a rubber band, and the bowl of water. Ask your student to observe how the shape of each kind of matter changes. First, crush the can so that the shape changes. Then stretch the rubber band, making sure your student recognizes how it expands and becomes thinner as it stretches. Finally, pour the water from the bowl into another container, such as a drinking glass. Point out that each thing changed shape but still essentially remained what it was. Ask, *Which items can be returned to their original shape and which ones can't?* [the rubber band and water can, the aluminum can can't]

11 **EXPLORE** Explain that one form of matter can change into another form of matter. For example, when water gets cold enough it will freeze and change from a liquid into a solid. Ask, *When water freezes into an ice cube, how do you know it's a solid?* [because you can see it and it has its own shape] Point out that when ice is in a warm place, it melts and changes back into a liquid. Ask, *What form of matter does an ice cube change into when it melts?* [liquid]

12 **EXPAND** Ask your student to look at the photo. Explain that just as solids can change into liquids, liquids can change into gases. Point out the steam rising from the pot and explain that when water gets very hot, it changes into a gas. If the pot were left on the stove over the heat, over a period of time all the water in the pot would change into gas and there would be no water

Water turns into a gas when it gets very hot.

,

TAKE A BREAK

Have your student experiment with solids and liquids by making ice cubes. Show him or her how to fill a tray with water. Ask, *What form is the water in?* [liquid] After the water is frozen, ask, *What form is the water in now?* [solid] Then place several ice cubes in a bowl and put them in a warm place where your student can observe the ice changing back to liquid.

left. Ask, *Based on what you just learned, what do you think happens to the water in wet clothes when you hang them to dry?* [the water in the clothes disappears because it changes into gas]

13 **DESCRIBE** Tell your student that when the gas from the pot cools down it will change back into a liquid. Ask your student if he or she has ever noticed how a mirror in a bathroom gets wet after someone has taken a hot shower. Explain that some of the hot water from the shower turns into a gas called steam. When the steam touches the cool mirror, it changes back into a liquid and sticks to the mirror in tiny drops. The next time this happens in your student's home, help him or her use a blow dryer to dry off the mirror and watch the water turn back into gas.

14 **DRAW** Distribute a copy of the Sequence Chain found on page 356. Challenge your student to draw pictures of water changing forms. For example, in the first box, he or she could draw an ice cube. In the second, he or she could draw a puddle of water. In the third box, he or she could draw steam coming from a pot of boiling water. Walk him or her through what he or she has learned in the lesson. Guide as necessary as your student shows interest.

15 **DISTRIBUTE** Distribute Student Learning Page 12.B. Read the directions and activities to your student and have him or her choose which one he or she would like to do next.

A BRIGHT IDEA

For more fun activities to do with your student, try the book *Experiments with Solids, Liquids, and Gases* by Salvatore Tocci.

Branching Out

FOR FURTHER READING

Solid, Liquid, or Gas?, by Sally Hewitt (Scholastic Library Publishing, 1998).

Solids, Liquids, Gases (*Simply Science*), by Charnan Simon (Compass Point Books, 2000).

What Is the World Made Of? All About Solids, Liquids, and Gases, by Kathleen Weidner Zoehfeld and Paul Meisel, ill. (HarperCollins Children's Books, 1999).

TEACHING TIP

Research other gases with your student so that he or she will gain a better understanding of this form of matter. For example, you could buy a balloon filled with helium so your student can see how helium causes a balloon to float, while a balloon filled with carbon dioxide doesn't float. Then have your student compare the two types of gases by asking him or her which gas is heavier.

CHECKING IN

To assess your student's understanding of the lesson, ask him or her to locate random objects around the room and identify what form of matter each item is. Once the items are collected, ask your student to compare the items by how they look and feel to find how they are alike and different.

Find the Solids, Liquids, and Gases

Color the solids blue. Color the liquids green. Color the gases yellow.

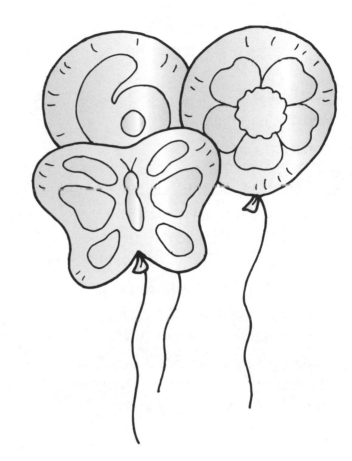

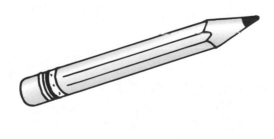

What's Next? You Decide!

Teacher: Read aloud the directions and activities. Then have your student choose which activity to do next.

Now it's your turn to choose what to do next in the lesson. Read the activities and decide which one you want to do—you may want to try them both!

Make Up a Song and Dance

MATERIALS

❑ 1 audiocassette recorder

❑ 1 audiocassette tape

STEPS

Sing a song and dance a dance about the forms of matter!

❑ Think about the different forms of matter: solid, liquid, and gas.

❑ Choose a tune from a song you know or make up your own tune.

❑ Make up a song that tells about the different forms of matter. Give examples of each form of matter in your song.

❑ Sing your song into the recorder.

❑ Play the song back and make up a dance for your song.

❑ In your dance, try to move your body to show the different forms of matter.

❑ Perform your song and dance for an adult.

Compare Objects

MATERIALS

❑ 1 sheet paper

❑ 1 sponge

❑ 1 wooden or plastic ruler

❑ 1 large bowl water

STEPS

Perform an experiment for an adult. Show how things are alike and different.

❑ Compare the color of the paper, sponge, and ruler.

❑ Compare the shape and size of each item.

❑ Compare the way each item feels when you touch it.

❑ Compare the weight of each item.

❑ Compare what each item is made from.

❑ Compare how each item acts when you try to bend it.

❑ Compare what each item does when you put it in water.

❑ Talk about what you've learned with an adult.

Comprehending How Things Move

Moving is inseparable from living.

OBJECTIVE	BACKGROUND	MATERIALS
To give your student an understanding of how and why things move	Everywhere we look we see movement, whether it's a person walking, a ball rolling down a hill, or a breeze in the air. It's important that we understand the forces that cause movement. In this lesson, your student will learn about movement, directions, pushes and pulls, and the characteristics of magnets.	■ Student Learning Pages 13.A–13.B ■ 2 magnets ■ 1 pair chopsticks ■ 2 pots, empty bottles, or empty boxes

VOCABULARY

PUSH a cause to move away from
PULL a cause to move toward
REPEL when a magnet pushes something away from it
ATTRACT when a magnet pulls something toward it

Let's Begin

1 **EXPLAIN** Tell your student that things can move in many different directions. Ask, *What are some words that describe the directions things move in?* [*left, right, up, down, above, below, over, under, straight,* and so on] Demonstrate each of these directions to your student. For example, walk up and down the stairs and ask your student to identify which direction you're moving in. Then have your student demonstrate the directions.

2 **MODEL** Tell your student that some movements are caused by a **push** and others are caused by a **pull**. Explain that a push forces an object to move away from the push. Model this idea by pushing a chair. Ask, *What direction does the chair move in when I push it?* [away] Explain that a pull is the opposite of a push. A pull causes an object to move toward the pull. Ask your student to model this idea by pulling a book, a pencil, or a toy toward him or her. Then have your student look at the photo. Ask your student to use his or her finger to show which way the shopping cart would move if it is pushed and which way it would move if it is pulled.

A BRIGHT IDEA

You can order all kinds of children's magnet games and toys online at http://www.dowling magnets.com. Click on Educational and Toy.

Things can be moved by pushing and pulling.

ENRICH THE EXPERIENCE

Combine learning about science with learning about the alphabet. Get a set of magnetized alphabet letters from a toy store. Your student can arrange and rearrange the letters on the refrigerator or on the side of a file cabinet.

FOR FURTHER READING

Find Out About Pushes and Pulls, by Terry Jennings (BBC Publications, 1999).

How Things Move (*Science*), by Don L. Curry and Gail Saunders-Smith, ed. (Pebble Books, 2000).

Magnets (*Everyday Science*), by Peter D. Riley and Rachel Cooke, ed. (Gareth Stevens, 2002).

3 **EXPAND AND DISTRIBUTE** Tell your student that pushing and pulling different things requires different amounts of effort, or force. For example, pushing a couch to a different spot requires a lot of force, while pulling a paper towel from a roll requires only a little force. Distribute Student Learning Page 13.A and help your student complete the activity.

4 **DESCRIBE** Explain that *speed* is a word used to describe the pace at which something moves. Ask, *What are some words that describe speed?* [*slow* and *fast*] Tell your student that some things can move fast, such as a car, a bicycle, or a baseball when it is thrown. Some things move slowly, such as a turtle or a snail. Point out that the speed of movement can change. Ask your student to explain what would have to happen in order for a car, a baseball, or a turtle to change its speed.

5 **REVEAL** Show your student a magnet. Explain that magnets have the ability to push and pull things that are made of certain types of metal. When magnets push something away, they **repel.** When they pull something toward them, they **attract.** Give your student a magnet. Have your student slowly move the magnet toward a metal object that it will attract, such as a metal desk or refrigerator, until he or she can feel the pull of the magnet. Then give your student a second magnet. Have your student slowly move the two magnets toward each other until he or she begins to feel them repelling each other. Now have your student touch the magnet to a book or a wooden table. Ask, *What do you notice?* [there is no push or pull] Explain that magnets don't attract or repel objects that aren't made of metal.

6 **DISTRIBUTE** Distribute Student Learning Page 13.B. Read the directions and activities to your student and have him or her choose what he or she would like to do next.

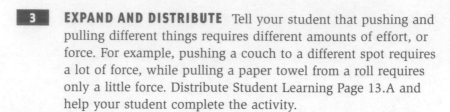

Branching Out

TEACHING TIP

Be sure to give your student enough time to fully grasp each different concept before moving on to the next. There are many opportunities in everyday life for your student to observe how things move. Encourage him or her to be on the lookout for good examples.

CHECKING IN

To assess your student's understanding of the lesson, take a walk outside with your student to observe movement. Each time your student recognizes movement, ask him or her questions that require a response using adjectives for direction or speed such as, *How fast is it moving?*

Find Big and Little Pushes and Pulls

Circle the pictures showing things that need a big push or pull. Draw a square around the pictures showing things that need only a little push or pull.

What's Next? You Decide!

Teacher: Read aloud the directions and activities. Then have your student choose which activity to do next.

Now it's your turn to choose what to do next in the lesson. Read the activities and decide which one you want to do—you may want to try them both!

Make a Push-and-Pull Poster

MATERIALS

- ❏ 1 posterboard
- ❏ several old magazines
- ❏ 1 pair scissors
- ❏ glue
- ❏ markers or crayons

STEPS

- ❏ Look through the magazines for pictures of things that can be pushed and pulled.
- ❏ Find as many pictures as you can.
- ❏ Cut out the pictures.
- ❏ Draw a line down the middle of the posterboard.
- ❏ On one side, glue all the things you think are very hard to push or pull.
- ❏ On the other side, glue all the things you think are easy to push or pull.
- ❏ Show your poster to an adult.

Measure Force

MATERIALS

- ❏ 1 small box without lid
- ❏ 1 length string
- ❏ 3 thin rubber bands
- ❏ 1 large sheet cardboard
- ❏ 15–20 marbles

STEPS

- ❏ Ask an adult to help you tie a length of string around the sides of an open box.
- ❏ Loop a thin rubber band through the string.
- ❏ Loop two rubber bands to the first to make a chain.
- ❏ Place the box on a sheet of cardboard. Put 10 marbles in the box.
- ❏ Pull on the rubber bands.
- ❏ See how far they stretch until the box moves.
- ❏ Make a mark on the cardboard to show how far the rubber bands stretched.
- ❏ Add more marbles and pull on the rubber bands again.
- ❏ Try other objects such as rocks or blocks. Guess how far the rubber bands will stretch for each one.
- ❏ Share what you learned with an adult.

In Your Community

To reinforce the skills and concepts taught in this section,
try one or more of these activities!

See Baby Animals

Locate your nearest pet shop or animal shelter for litters of puppies or kittens. Call ahead and try to arrange an appointment for you and your student to visit and observe the litter and the mother. Have your student pay attention to the size, shape, and color of the baby animals and how these characteristics compare to the mother's. Point out that if the puppies or kittens get the things they need, such as water, food, air, and shelter, each one can grow to be as big as his or her mother and father.

Discover Community Gardens

Allow your student to see how plants grow by taking him or her to a community garden. If possible arrange for your student to meet with people who are tending garden there. Have your student ask questions about what plants they are growing, what steps they are taking to care for the plants, and how each plant grows from a seed. If your student wants to, he or she can volunteer to help out in one of the gardens and learn more.

Learn About Weather Reporting

Contact a local television or radio station and try to set up an interview for your student with a member of its weather team. Before the interview, have your student think of at least two things he or she would like to learn about the seasons, the causes of different weather conditions such as snow and rain, and predicting the weather. After the interview, see if you can arrange a tour of the facilities for your student and a look at some of the tools and instruments that help the weather reporters do their job.

Visit a Water Reclamation Plant

Take your student to a water reclamation plant in your area. Try to arrange for your student to receive a tour of the facilities from a staff member. Help your student find out where the water he or she uses at home comes from, how the water is cleaned and kept safe for drinking, and any other information he or she would like to know. Perhaps your student could also see how water is tested for safety.

Take a Trip to the Zoo

Visit your local zoo or a zoo in a nearby community. Zoos are great places for your student to see and learn about a wide variety of animals. Most zoos post signs next to each animal listing facts about the animal's habitat, diet, and so on. Before you visit, find out about any new births at the zoo so your student can see firsthand young animals and the adults they will grow into. You may also wish to review Lesson 3.3 with your student before your trip.

Visit a Recycling Center

Help your student understand the recycling process by taking him or her to a recycling center in your area. Have your student collect recyclables from your home or community to bring with you. Try to arrange to meet with a center employee who can show your student what will happen to the items he or she collected and can give him or her a tour of the center. Make sure your student notes what types of materials are being recycled, where different materials are taken, and in what way they are recycled. To demonstrate the complete recycling cycle, take your student to the grocery store to look for packages and for paper and plastic products that are made from recycled materials. Point out the recycle symbol on each item.

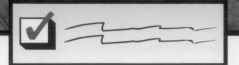

We Have Learned

Use this checklist to summarize what you and your student
have accomplished in the Science section.

❑ **Senses at Work**
❑ what the five senses do
❑ how we use the eyes, ears, nose,
tongue, and skin

❑ **Plants and Animals**
❑ living and nonliving things
❑ needs of living things: food, water,
air, shelter
❑ how a seed becomes a plant
❑ how young animals grow and
become adults
❑ where plants and animals live

❑ **Weather**
❑ the four seasons
❑ why weather matters

❑ **Earth's Land and Water**
❑ rocks, sand, soil
❑ kinds of land and bodies of water on
Earth
❑ taking care of Earth and Earth Day

❑ **Earth and Space**
❑ day and night
❑ sun, moon, stars
❑ the way Earth moves

❑ **Matter**
❑ how things look and feel
❑ matter that's alike and different
❑ what things are made of
❑ solids, liquids, gases

❑ **How Things Change**
❑ melting and freezing
❑ water and air
❑ liquid to gas and gas to liquid

❑ **How Things Move**
❑ pushes and pulls
❑ magnets

❑ **Your Body**
❑ parts of the body and how they
show feelings
❑ what the bones, muscles, heart, and
brain do
❑ how people are alike and different

❑ **Taking Care of Your Body**
❑ the importance, function, and care
of teeth
❑ staying clean and what germs do
❑ the importance of sleep
❑ different kinds of exercise
❑ food and water
❑ where food comes from

We have also learned:

_____

_____

_____

_____

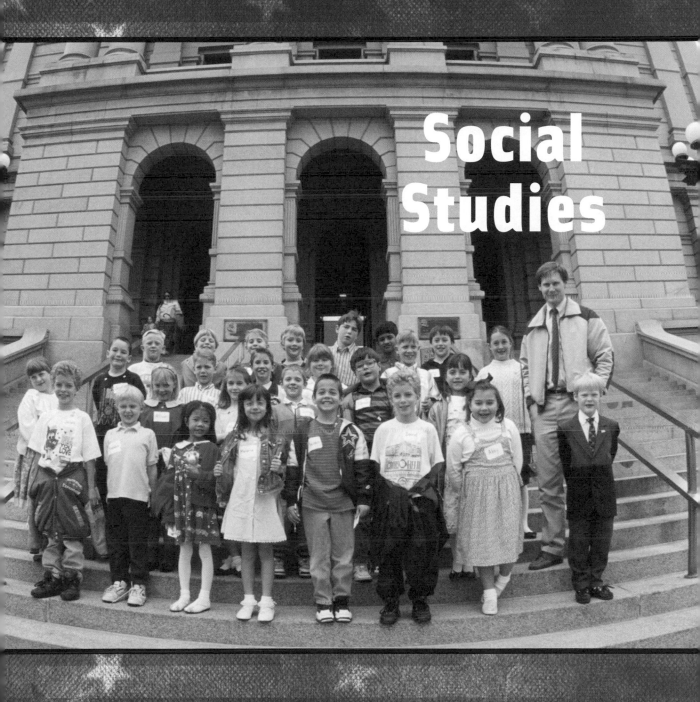

Social Studies

Social Studies

Key Topics

Understanding Who We Are

Learning about ourselves often involves looking at the people and places around us.

OBJECTIVE	BACKGROUND	MATERIALS
To help your student learn about families, homes, and cooperation	Family and home are fundamental parts of a child's life. Appreciating family and learning to live together in harmony are important skills. In this lesson, your student will learn about how families are the same and different, where families live, and how they can get along. He or she will also learn that every individual is unique.	■ Student Learning Pages 1.A–1.B ■ 1 family photo ■ markers or crayons ■ 1 copy Web, page 356 ■ 1 copy T Chart, page 355 ■ photos of your family in a city or the country (optional) ■ books or magazines with pictures of the city and the country

VOCABULARY

THE CITY a place with many large buildings where many people live close together

THE COUNTRY a place where people live, usually on or near farms, where there's a lot of open space

APARTMENTS many separate homes within a large building

COOPERATE to work together

SOLVE to find an answer or solution to a problem

Let's Begin

1 **DISCUSS** Together with your student talk about the people who make up your family. Explain to your student that families can include more than just parents and children who live in the same home. For example, a family could include grandparents, aunts, uncles, and cousins as well. Show your student a family photo. Point out each person and ask your student to identify the family member by telling his or her relationship to your family, such as mother, father, brother, sister, grandfather, grandmother, and so on.

2 **EXPLAIN AND DISTRIBUTE** Explain to your student that families are different. Some families are large and some are small, some have many children and some have just one child. In others, family members can include different relatives or close family friends. Tell your student that the differences among families make each family unique and special. Then distribute Student Learning Page 1.A. Have your student look at the picture of each family.

Discuss how families are different. Then direct your student to draw a picture of your family on the page. When completed, ask your student to identify the family members in his or her drawing.

3 EXPLORE Tell your student that, like families, people are all different, special, and unique. A person's activities, favorite foods, sports, and games, and other things, such as hair and eye color, make each person different from others. Explore with your student the things that make him or her unique. Perhaps your student plays the piano, has a strong interest in coloring or painting, or has a particular hair color or style that's special. Then have your student use a copy of the Web found on page 356 to illustrate his or her uniqueness. Have your student draw a picture of himself or herself in the center. Have your student draw pictures of the things that make him or her unique in the outer ovals.

4 COMPARE Have your student use his or her Web drawing to see how he or she is alike and different from a sibling or friend. Ask, *Can you name one way that you are both alike?* [possible answer: hair color, favorite hobby, same parents] *Can you name one way you are both different?* [possible answer: a special talent, height, favorite food] *Everybody is unique and special in their own ways. What are other things that make you special?*

5 DESCRIBE Tell your student that different families live in different places. Two different places are **the city** and **the country.** Ask your student to tell you what he or she knows about the city and the country. Explain that a lot of people live in a city and that there are many buildings, cars, and trains. A city can also be noisy. Explain that in the country there is more space, fewer people, fewer buildings, and lots of trees. Families tend to live farther apart, and many people have farms or live in small towns. Ask, *How might living in the country be different from living in the city?* [in the country there is less noise, it's less crowded, there are not a lot of buildings, and there is more open space]

6 DISTRIBUTE AND COMPARE Distribute a copy of the T Chart found on page 355 to your student. Label the left side of the T Chart "City" and the right side "Country." Then review with your student the characteristics of both. Ask your student to draw a picture of a characteristic under each heading. For example, under City your student could draw a picture of a tall building. Encourage your student to try to write as well by asking him or her to write the first letter of each characteristic, such as writing the letter *b* next to the picture of a building.

7 EXPLAIN Explain to your student that just as cities and the country have different features, so do the homes that people live in. In the country, most families have their own house and the houses are usually far apart. In the city, many people live in houses, but the houses are closer together. Some houses in the city are divided in half, with one family living on each side.

Some people in the city live in apartment homes. **Apartments** are many separate homes inside a large building. Apartment buildings usually have many levels and a lot of people and families living there. Ask, *What is your home like?* Have your student describe his or her home in relation to the country, the city, a house, or an apartment. Then have your student draw a picture of where he or she lives.

8 **REVEAL** Explain to your student that in order for families to get along, they must **cooperate** and work together. Sharing and helping each other are important ways of working together. Ask, *How do you share and help in your family?* [possible answers: picking up toys, washing windows]

9 **TELL A STORY** Have your student tell a story about a time when he or she helped or shared with someone in his or her family. Prompt your student to think of a specific event to tell about. Let your student tell the story creatively and at his or her own pace. When your student is finished, follow up with specific questions about how it worked out, what would have happened if he or she didn't share or help, and so on.

10 **RELATE** Tell your student that sometimes getting along with someone requires solving a problem. Explain that **solve** means "to find an answer to a problem." Problems that can occur between two people include wanting to use the same toy at the same time and wanting to listen to different music while they draw. Tell your student that there are many ways to solve problems. Sharing is one important way. Taking turns is another very good way. Have your student look at the illustration below. Explain that the two children have a problem. Both children would like to swing, but there's only one swing. Ask, *If you were one of the children in the picture, how would you solve the problem?* [take turns swinging and give up the swing nicely when the turn is over] *How would your solution help the children get along?* [both children would get a chance to swing]

SOCIAL STUDIES

LESSON 4.1

11 **EXPLORE AND DRAW** Tell your student about a time when you faced a problem getting along with someone in your family. Explain what your solution was, how it helped you get along with the person, and what would have happened if you hadn't solved the problem. Then ask your student to think of a problem he or she has faced in getting along with the family. Have your student describe the problem in detail and talk about what happened. Ask, *Did you find a good solution? What was it?* If not, ask, *Can you think of a solution that would have helped you get along?*

12 **DISTRIBUTE** Read the activities on Student Learning Page 1.B to your student. Have him or her decide which one he or she would like to do.

Branching Out

TEACHING TIP

Ask your student to tell you the stories of Suzie from the city and Kevin from the country. Have your student tell you what their houses look like, what their neighborhood sounds like, where they like to play, and so on.

CHECKING IN

To assess your student's understanding of the lesson, select several photos or pictures from magazines that show city and country characteristics, such as population, buildings or farms, apartments, and so on. Show each one to your student and ask him or her to point out if the picture shows a city or the country and why. Then present your student with a simple problem about two people who aren't getting along and ask him or her to offer a solution.

FOR FURTHER READING

Apt. 3 (Puffin Picture Books), by Ezra Jack Keats (Penguin Putnam Books, 1999).

Families, by Ann Morris (HarperCollins Juvenile Books, 2000).

The Treasure Tree: Helping Kids Get Along and Enjoy Each Other, by John T. Trent (Thomas Nelson, 1998).

Look at Different Families

Look at the people in these families.
Draw a picture of your family.

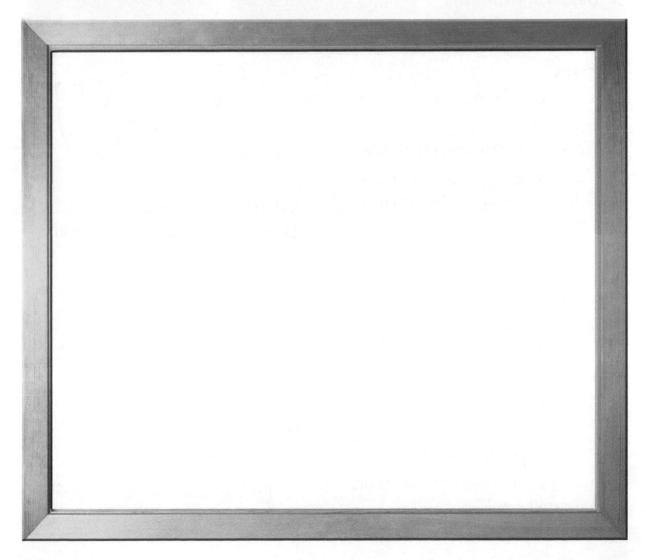

What's Next? You Decide!

Teacher: Read aloud the directions and activities. Then have your student choose which activity to do next.

Now it's your turn to choose what to do next in the lesson. Read the activities and decide which one you want to do—you may want to try them both!

Create a Collage

★ MATERIALS

- ❑ 1 sheet paper as large as you
- ❑ 3–4 old magazines
- ❑ 1 pair scissors
- ❑ crayons or paint
- ❑ glue

★ STEPS

Make a collage that shows what you like to do!

- ❑ Think about what makes you unique.
- ❑ Look through the magazines. Find pictures of things you like and things you like to do.
- ❑ Cut out the pictures.
- ❑ Then lie down on the big sheet of paper. Ask an adult to draw the outline of your body on the paper.
- ❑ Decorate your paper "body" with crayons or paint.
- ❑ Glue the pictures onto your paper body.
- ❑ Cut out your body collage.
- ❑ Ask an adult to help you hang your collage on a wall.

Make Helping Hands

★ MATERIALS

- ❑ newspaper
- ❑ 1 paper plate
- ❑ finger paint
- ❑ 5 sheets paper
- ❑ 1 pair scissors

★ STEPS

- ❑ Spread out newspaper over your work space.
- ❑ Pour paint onto the plate.
- ❑ Lay your hand into the paint.
- ❑ Make five handprints on paper.
- ❑ Let your handprints dry. Cut them out.
- ❑ Ask an adult to help you choose a place on the wall to hang your "helping hands."
- ❑ For one week, each time you help, hang a hand on the wall.

Learning About Family Activities

All families are different, but every family is a group of people living together.

OBJECTIVE	BACKGROUND	MATERIALS
To help your student learn about special family routines and customs	People in families create daily routines and customs that help the family live and have fun together. In this lesson, your student will learn about everyday routines, special foods, celebrations, similarities and differences, and how families change over time.	■ Student Learning Pages 2.A–2.B ■ 1 copy Sequence Chain, page 356 ■ 1 orange ■ 1 banana

VOCABULARY

ROUTINE things that a person does on a regular basis

CELEBRATE to do something special to honor a person or an event

COMPARE to find similarities and differences between two or more things

ALIKE when something is similar to something else

DIFFERENT when something is not like something else

Let's Begin

1 **DISCUSS AND DISTRIBUTE** Talk about **routine** with your student. Explain that a person's or a family's routine is made up of the things they do on a regular basis, such as every day or every week. For example, part of a person's morning routine could be getting dressed, eating breakfast, brushing his or her teeth, and starting lesson work. Then distribute a copy of the Sequence Chain found on page 356. Ask your student to complete the Sequence Chain by drawing pictures of things that he or she does that are part of his or her everyday routine. Have your student draw the pictures in the order they are done during the course of the day.

2 **DESCRIBE** Tell your student that some routines involve the family doing things together, such as eating dinner. Explain that different families have special foods they eat. For example, one special food that many American families eat is turkey on Thanksgiving. A popular food that many Mexican American families eat are tamales. Ask, *What are some special foods that our family enjoys?*

3 **EXPLORE** Tell your student that another thing a family does together is **celebrate,** which is doing something special to honor a person or an event. Families often celebrate birthdays, weddings, and graduations. On a birthday, families do special things such as sing a song or have a cake or piñata. Ask, *What are some of the special things your family does to celebrate?*

4 **RELATE AND EXPLAIN** Mention that families also go places together. The places might be close to home, such as the library, grocery store, or playground. Families may also travel to faraway places, such as another state, or to visit relatives. Ask your student to tell a story of a time when his or her family went somewhere fun or new. Explain that many families also play games together. Ask, *What games do you like to play with your family?* If your student's family doesn't have a game, help your student think of a fun game he or she can suggest.

5 **DEFINE** Tell your student that when you **compare** things you are trying to find what is **alike** or what is **different.** Things that are the same are alike. Things that aren't the same are different. Have your student look at an orange and a banana. Ask, *How are an orange and a banana different?* [shape and color] *How are they the same?* [they're both fruits, they both taste sweet]

6 **EXPLAIN AND DISTRIBUTE** Explain to your student that things have changed since his or her parents were children. Cars, telephones, and clothes look different. Have your student talk with a grandparent or older family member about how things are different now than they used to be. Distribute Student Learning Page 2.A and explain that the pictures represent the way three things have changed. Ask your student to draw a line connecting each "then" picture to its "now" picture. Then read aloud the activities on Student Learning Page 2.B. Have your student decide which one he or she would like to do.

Branching Out

FOR FURTHER READING

All Families Are Different, by Sol Gordon and Vivien Cohen, ill. (Prometheus Books, 2000).

Then and Now, by Richard Thompson and Barbara Hartmann (Fitzhenry and Whiteside, 1999).

TEACHING TIP

Ask your student to compare things as often as possible. You could find pictures of families in magazines and ask your student to compare the families or to compare his or her family to those in the pictures.

CHECKING IN

To assess your student's understanding of the lesson, ask your student to tell you about his or her morning routine, family foods and celebrations, and how things have changed from how they used to be.

Connect Then with Now

Draw lines to match the pictures.

Then	**Now**
1. 	A. 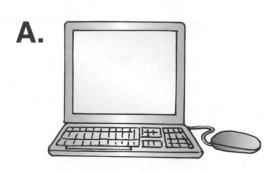
2. 	B. 
3. 	C. 
4. 	D. 

What's Next? You Decide!

Teacher: *Read aloud the directions and activities. Then have your student choose which activity to do next.*

Now it's your turn to choose what to do next in the lesson. Read the activities and decide which one you want to do—you may want to try them both!

Make a Family Recording

MATERIALS

❑ 1 audiocassette recorder

❑ 1 audiocassette tape

STEPS

❑ Choose an upcoming family celebration or get-together.

❑ Use a tape recorder to record the sounds of the celebration.

❑ Ask each family member to talk into the recorder about what your family does at celebrations.

❑ Have older family members talk about what celebrations were like before. What is now the same? What is now different?

❑ Be sure to record yourself talking about the celebration.

❑ At the end of the day, play the recording for your family!

Put on a Puppet Show

MATERIALS

❑ 2 or more old socks

❑ markers, yarn, and buttons

❑ 1 pair scissors

❑ glue

❑ 1 large sheet paper

STEPS

❑ Make a sock puppet for each member of your family. Use yarn, markers, and buttons to make the puppets look like the people in your family.

❑ Draw a backdrop that looks like your home on the large sheet of paper.

❑ Ask an adult to help you hang your backdrop on the wall.

❑ Put on a puppet show for your family. Show your family during their morning or nighttime routine.

❑ Put on another puppet show that shows your family at a celebration.

❑ Have your family members join in the puppet show with you. Put on a show together.

❑ Have fun!

Exploring Communities

Strong communities are the foundation of a healthy society.

OBJECTIVE	BACKGROUND	MATERIALS
To teach your student about communities	All communities share basic features. In this lesson, your student will learn about the people, places, and things that are found in communities and how people within communities live and work together.	■ Student Learning Pages 3.A–3.B ■ 1 copy Web, page 356 ■ pictures of road signs ■ markers or crayons ■ construction paper ■ photographs of your student's family

VOCABULARY

NEIGHBORHOOD the buildings, streets, and other things near where a person lives

COMMUNITY a group of people who live, work, and play together

RULES guides for how to act when you are in a group

LAWS the rules of a community that are made and enforced to keep people safe and to help people live together

HOLIDAY a day on which people celebrate to remember or honor people or events

Let's Begin

1 **EXPLAIN** Explain to your student that he or she lives in a **neighborhood.** Discuss some of the features of a neighborhood, including buildings, parks, and streets. Describe the types of buildings that your student might see near the place where he or she lives, such as houses, apartment buildings, stores, office buildings, schools, libraries, churches, and so on. Ask, *Who lives in your neighborhood?* [possible answer: my family and my friends] Ask, *What things are in your neighborhood?* [possible answer: houses, a school, a store, a park]

2 **DISTRIBUTE** Distribute a copy of the Web from page 356 to your student. Have your student draw a picture of his or her home in the center of the Web. Have him or her draw pictures of things that are found in his or her neighborhood in the outer ovals.

3 **EXPAND** Tell your student that he or she also lives in a **community.** A community is a group of people who live, work, and play together. Discuss the ways people in communities depend on each other. Point out that mail carriers, firefighters,

A BRIGHT IDEA

Before you get to Step 7, look through newspapers and magazines and cut out pictures of road signs. You might also visit the secretary of state's office or Web site to get a booklet that shows road signs, their shapes, and their colors.

librarians, store owners, neighbors, parents, and children are all members of your student's community. Ask, *What is the name of the town or city you live in?* [student should correctly name the place in which he or she lives]

4 **INTRODUCE** Introduce your student to specific places in his or her community and talk about the people who work at those places. For example, tell your student that doctors work at hospitals to help care for people who are ill. Police officers work at police stations as well as out in the community to keep people safe. Bus drivers drive buses to help people get from one place to another. Ask, *Who is another person who helps in your community? What does he or she do?* [possible answer: the librarian helps me find books]

5 **DISCOVER** As your student shows interest, arrange to have a tour of your post office, fire station, or police station. Many towns even offer celebrations or events at police and fire stations, often coinciding with community events. Prepare in advance and help your student think of one or two questions he or she would like to ask a postal carrier, firefighter, or police officer on the tour.

6 **EXPLORE** Explain to your student that people in communities make **rules** and **laws** to help everyone live and work together safely. Tell your student that, like communities, families also make rules. Discuss the rules that your student must follow in his or her family. Ask, *In our family, who makes sure that you follow certain rules?* [possible answer: parents] Mention that people must follow rules, such as taking turns, in order to work together. Ask, *When you play a game with the family, do you take turns?* [yes] *What might happen if you didn't take turns with each other?* [everyone would be confused, someone might not get a turn, someone could get angry or sad]

7 **RELATE** Explain that besides keeping everyone safe, rules and laws help people respect one another's property and make good choices. Laws can make it easier for people in a community to share and work together comfortably. Name some laws that your student might be familiar with. For example, there is a law against littering or dumping garbage in the street. This law helps keep the community clean and healthy. It's also against the law to take things that don't belong to you. This law helps people protect the things they work hard to have. Discuss other laws and the reasons why these laws are important. Ask, *What might happen if we didn't have these laws?* [people might argue or get in fights, it would be harder to live together]

8 **DISCUSS AND EXPLAIN** Discuss the importance of road signs and traffic lights. Explain to your student that many road signs are there to help keep people safe while they travel. Stop signs or traffic lights at intersections help keep people safe by organizing traffic to prevent accidents. Explain the meanings of the colors on a traffic light to your student. Ask, *What does each color on a traffic light mean?* [green means go; yellow means slow down, the light is changing; red means stop] Have your student draw a traffic light using construction paper and markers or crayons.

9 **EXPAND** Tell your student that other types of signs tell people what is or isn't allowed in certain areas. A picture with an X drawn through it means that something is not allowed. For example, at a park you might see a sign showing a picture of a dog with an X drawn through it. Explain that this sign means that dogs aren't allowed. Other signs help people identify locations. For example, street signs tell people the names of streets and help us find our way. A sign showing a picture of a telephone helps people find a public telephone. Ask, *What is another sign that helps people find a place?* [the sign for a public restroom, the sign for the entrance to a shopping center, and so on]

10 **DISTRIBUTE** Distribute Student Learning Page 3.A. Have your student identify the community member in each picture. Then read each instruction aloud and guide your student to draw each picture on a separate sheet of paper.

11 **INTRODUCE** Tell your student about communities that are located in the city and in the country. Discuss the differences between the city and the country. You can refer to Lesson 4.1 for information about the differences between the country and the city. Together think about places that he or she has been to that are in the country or in the city. Ask him or her how those places were different and alike.

+

ENRICH THE EXPERIENCE

Gather photographs of your student's family celebrations to share with him or her before beginning Step 12.

12 **DEFINE AND ASK** Point out that people in communities celebrate different holidays. Explain that a **holiday** is a special day on which a person or an event is honored or remembered. Ask, *What are some holidays that our family celebrates?* [New Year's Day, Thanksgiving, and so on]

People sometimes celebrate holidays with a parade.

Exploring Communities   **263**

SOCIAL STUDIES

LESSON 4.3

13 **EXPLAIN** Tell your student that people in the United States celebrate some specific national holidays, such as Presidents' Day, Thanksgiving, and Independence Day. Independence Day is celebrated every year on July 4. Explain that Americans celebrate this holiday to remember the birthday of the United States, July 4, 1776. Ask, *Why do people celebrate holidays?* [to remember and honor people and events] Have your student tell you about his or her favorite holiday. Ask him or her what makes this day special and what he or she does on this day.

ENRICH THE EXPERIENCE

Discover if specific ethnic groups hold any festivals in your town or in a nearby town. Find out about a holiday and take your student to see how the people celebrate.

14 **EXPLORE** Tell your student that people from other countries may celebrate different holidays than those he or she celebrates. For example, Cinco de Mayo, which means "the Fifth of May," is a Mexican holiday. Cinco de Mayo is celebrated every year in May to remember the day in 1862 when the Mexican army defeated the French army, which was trying to take over Mexico. Together with your student find out more about Cinco de Mayo or another ethnic holiday, including how it's celebrated.

15 **EXPAND** Tell your student that people often celebrate holidays with parades, parties, picnics, food, decorations, costumes, and gifts. Point out that celebrating holidays helps us remember important things that have happened in the past. Ask, *How do people in your community celebrate Independence Day?* [a parade, fireworks, picnics, and so on] *What do you think this helps us remember?* [that we are happy to live in the United States]

16 **DISTRIBUTE** Distribute Student Learning Page 3.B to your student. Read the directions out loud to your student and have him or her choose and complete one of the activities on the page.

FOR FURTHER READING

Grandpa's Corner Store, by DyAnne DiSalvo-Ryan, ill. (HarperCollins Juvenile Books, 2000).

My Neighborhood: Places and Faces, by Lisa Bullard and Omarr Wesley, ill. (Picture Window Books, 2002).

On the Town: A Community Adventure, by Judith Caseley (HarperCollins Publishers, 2002).

Branching Out

TEACHING TIP

Extend the lesson by taking your student on a walking tour of his or her community. On your tour, point out important places such as the library, police station, or city hall. Talk with your student about what the people who work there do and why people in the community need their help. Point out street signs, traffic signs, and other types of signs. Talk about what they mean and why they should be followed. Identify places where parades or other events often take place.

CHECKING IN

To assess your student's understanding of the lesson, have your student draw a picture of his or her neighborhood or community. Ask your student to point out the things in the picture that he or she learned about in the lesson.

Draw Community Pictures

1. Draw the thing that I drive and use to put out fires.

2. Draw the building where I help people get well.

Student Learning Page 3.A: Draw Community Pictures **265**

What's Next? You Decide!

Teacher: Read aloud the directions and activities. Then have your student choose which activity to do next.

Now it's your turn to choose what to do next in the lesson. Read the activities and decide which one you want to do—you may want to try them both!

Learn the Signs in Your Community

MATERIALS

❏ 1 disposable or instant camera

STEPS

What do the road signs in your community mean? Find out!

❏ Ask an adult to help you use the camera.

❏ Go on a walk together in your neighborhood.

❏ Take photographs of the important signs, such as the street signs, stop signs, and caution signs.

❏ Get close to the signs when you take the pictures so they will be easy to see.

❏ When you're in a car with an adult, bring the camera. Look for other signs and photograph them.

❏ Have your pictures developed.

❏ Use your photographs to help you learn what each sign means.

Make a Holiday Card

MATERIALS

❏ 1 sheet construction paper

❏ markers or crayons

❏ several old magazines (optional)

❏ 1 pair scissors

❏ glue

STEPS

Make a card to celebrate your favorite holiday.

❏ Fold the sheet of construction paper in half.

❏ Think about what your favorite holiday means. Why is it celebrated?

❏ Look in magazines to find pictures about your holiday, or use construction paper to make your own.

❏ Cut the pictures out. Glue the pictures to your card.

❏ Use crayons and markers to decorate the cover and inside.

❏ Sign your name.

❏ Share the celebration! On the day of the holiday, give the card to a friend.

Examining Jobs, Work, and Money

The jobs we do help support our families and communities.

OBJECTIVE	BACKGROUND	MATERIALS
To teach your student about jobs, money, needs, and wants	There are many kinds of jobs that people do to earn money and support their families. It's important to use money wisely and make sure your basic needs are met. In this lesson, your student will learn to identify different kinds of jobs and understand how individuals and families make choices when using money.	■ Student Learning Pages 4.A–4.B ■ red and blue crayons or markers

VOCABULARY

JOB what a person does to contribute to his or her community

BASIC NEEDS things that are necessary for survival, such as food, clothing, and shelter

WANTS things that are nice to have but are not necessary for survival

GOODS the things that people buy with money

SERVICES the things that people do for other people

Let's Begin

1   **EXPLAIN** Explain to your student that a **job** is what a person does to contribute to his or her community. Discuss with your student the jobs he or she may have to do around the home, such as cleaning his or her room or feeding a pet. Explain that these jobs are important because they help his or her family in some way. Ask, *What would happen if no one did the jobs that you do at home?* [possible answer: the pet wouldn't get fed, my room would be messy]

2   **EXPAND** Explain that people can earn money by doing certain jobs. For example, firefighters, police officers, teachers, and chefs all get paid money to do their jobs. Ask, *Can you name other kinds of jobs?*

3   **DISCUSS** Tell your student that when people earn money, it's important that they use the money wisely. Money can be used to buy the things that people and families need or want. Explain that **basic needs** are the things that people need for survival,

such as food, clothing, and shelter. Tell your student that clothes, a home, and food are examples of needs. Explain that **wants** are the things that are nice to have and that we enjoy very much, but that aren't necessary for survival. Ask, *Can you name some things that you want but don't need to survive?* [a new toy, candy, and so on]

4 EXPLAIN Explain that people use money to buy things that they need and want. These things are called **goods.** Food, clothes, toys, and furniture are all goods. Another thing that people use money for is **services.** Services are things that people do for other people. When a plumber fixes the sink or a dentist cleans a person's teeth, he or she is doing a service. Ask your student to name some things he or she needs and wants. Ask, *Is that a good or a service?*

5 DISTRIBUTE AND IDENTIFY Distribute Student Learning Page 4.A. Have your student use a red crayon to circle the pictures that show goods and a blue crayon to circle the pictures that show services. Then talk about whether each picture shows something that is a basic need or a want.

6 EXPLORE Mention that as time passes, jobs can change. For example, firefighters today have fire trucks that can carry a lot of equipment and can arrive at a fire very quickly. In the past, firefighters rode in horse-drawn wagons that were much slower. Have your student choose other jobs that he or she is interested in. Together use library books or the Internet to find out how each job has changed over time. Read the activities on Student Learning Page 4.B to your student. Have him or her decide which one he or she would like to do.

?

DID YOU KNOW?

Farmers used to have to plant and harvest their crops by hand or with the help of a donkey or an ox. Today farmers use powerful machines to plant and harvest their crops. There are also special machines that help farmers water the plants in places where there's less rain.

Branching Out

TEACHING TIP

Help your student understand that some very important jobs don't earn money. Talk about the things your student and his or her family members do at home, such as cooking, cleaning, taking care of each other, and cutting the grass. Ask, *How do people get paid for these jobs in other ways?* [people feel loved and cared for, they have a nice home to live in]

CHECKING IN

Have your student explore his or her home. Ask your student to identify objects that represent needs and objects that represent wants.

FOR FURTHER READING

Career Day, by Anne F. Rockwell (HarperCollins Juvenile Books, 2000).

Jobs People Do, by Christopher Maynard (DK Publishing, 2001).

What Will I Be?, by James Levin (Cartwheel Books, 2001).

Find the Goods and Services

Draw a red circle around the goods.
Draw a blue circle around the services.

What's Next? You Decide!

Teacher: Read aloud the directions and activities. Then have your student choose which activity to do next.

Now it's your turn to choose what to do next in the lesson. Read the activities and decide which one you want to do—you may want to try them both!

Make a Needs and Wants Collage

MATERIALS

- ❑ several old magazines
- ❑ 1 pair scissors
- ❑ 1 posterboard
- ❑ markers or crayons
- ❑ glue

STEPS

Review the difference between basic needs and wants.

- ❑ Look through old magazines.
- ❑ Cut out pictures of things that are needs and things that are wants.
- ❑ Draw a line across the middle of a posterboard to divide the top and bottom.
- ❑ Glue the pictures of the needs onto the bottom half.
- ❑ Glue the pictures of the wants onto the top half.
- ❑ Show your poster to an adult.
- ❑ Talk about what might happen if you spent money to get the things you want before buying the things you need.

Create a Job

STEPS

Create a job that you could do to make money!

- ❑ Would you like to sell goods? You could set up a lemonade stand in front of your house.
- ❑ Would you like to do a service job? You might ask a neighbor if you could pull weeds in his or her garden.
- ❑ Decide on a job that you would like to try.
- ❑ Ask an adult to help you plan your job and get the materials you will need.
- ❑ Decide how you would like to spend the money you earn.

LEMONADE FOR SALE

Comprehending Maps

Maps help us find where we are and get to the places we want to go.

OBJECTIVE	BACKGROUND	MATERIALS
To teach your student about maps	Maps are made to help people locate specific areas and objects. In this lesson, your student will learn about maps, overhead views, and map keys and symbols.	■ Student Learning Pages 5.A–5.B ■ small objects to make a miniature town (building blocks, toy cars, cotton balls, and so on) ■ different colored sheets construction paper ■ 1 map of your town ■ 1 posterboard ■ 1 ruler ■ markers or crayons

VOCABULARY

MAP a drawing that represents a specific area or place

SYMBOLS something used to represent something else

MAP KEY the part of a map that shows what the symbols on the map stand for

Let's Begin

1 **REVIEW** Review direction and location words such as *above, below, up, down, top, bottom, near,* and *far* with your student. Have your student practice using the words. For example, have your student sit on a chair. Ask, *Are you above or below the chair?* [above] Then have your student stand next to the chair. Ask, *Which is nearer to you, the chair or the door?* [the chair]

2 **EXPLORE** Build a model neighborhood with your student to help him or her learn about maps. You can use gray construction paper for roads, building blocks for houses, toy cars, cotton balls for trees, and any other small household items that work. Build the model where it won't be disturbed, such as on a tabletop or desktop. Demonstrate how different views make certain places easier to see. Ask your student to observe the model from a side view, as if he or she were actually walking down the street. Then have your student observe the model from above. Ask, *Which view makes it easier to see everything in your neighborhood?* [the view from above]

3 **DISTRIBUTE** Distribute Student Learning Page 5.A. Have your student match the side view and top view for each object by drawing a line between them. If your student has a difficult time picturing the objects from above, find small items, such as toys, that are similarly shaped and have your student look at these objects from the side and above while he or she is matching the objects on the page.

4 **EXPLAIN** Tell your student that a **map** is a drawing that shows a place, such as a town, park, or country, from above. Explain to your student that the items on maps are smaller in size than the actual places they show. Show your student a map of your town. You should be able to find a map of the area where your student lives in a local telephone book. Point out that there is a big difference in the size of the town and the size of the map. Ask, *Why do you think maps are smaller than the areas they show?* [a map that's the same size as the actual area would be too large to use]

5 **EXPAND** Show your student the neighborhood park illustration and the neighborhood park map. Ask, *What view does the illustration of the neighborhood park show?* [the view from above]

6 **EXPLAIN** Have your student look at the illustration and the map of the park again. Tell your student that both the illustration and the map show the same view of the park, but that the map uses **symbols** to show certain objects and areas. For example, a circle might indicate a tree, a square might be used to show a house or another building, and a line might indicate a path, road, or river.

Point out the **map key** on the map of the park. Explain that a map key explains the symbols used on the map. Have your student look at the tree in the upper-left-hand corner of the illustration of the park. Then have your student find the object that is in the same area on the map. Ask, *What is the symbol that's used to show a tree on the map of the park?* [a circle]

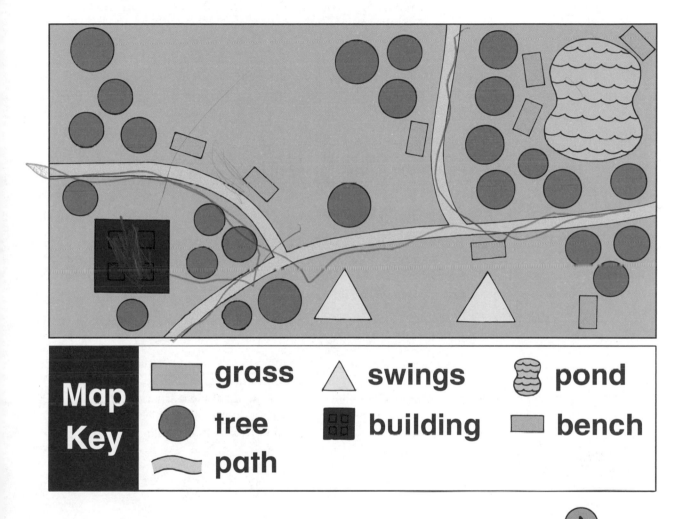

Map Key

▭ **grass**   △ **swings**   ⧆ **pond**

● **tree**   ⊞ **building**   ▭ **bench**

〰 **path**

---

7 **RELATE** Review the symbols for grass, swings, pond, tree, building, bench, and path on the map key with your student. Point out that colors can also be used as symbols, such as green representing grass. Show your student the map of your town again. Find the map key together. Talk about the symbols on the map key and what they mean.

8 **EXPAND AND DIRECT** Help your student see that the roads, buildings, and other places on maps are drawn in the same positions as they are in reality. Have your student locate a specific object on the drawing of the park. Then have him or her choose three other surrounding objects. Next, have your student locate the same objects or areas on the map of the park. Ask, *What do you notice about where the objects are in the picture compared to the map?* [they're in the same place]

ENRICH THE EXPERIENCE

To see an overhead view of your neighborhood, visit the U.S. Geological Survey Web site at http://mapping.usgs.gov. Click on View Maps and Aerial Photos, then TerraFly. Enter your street address and see your neighborhood from above!

SOCIAL STUDIES

LESSON 4.5

9 DRAW Together with your student look at the model neighborhood he or she built in Step 2. Have your student use a ruler and markers or crayons to draw a map of the neighborhood on posterboard. Before he or she begins, help your student decide what objects will appear on the map and what symbols to use for each one. Then help your student draw the map key. Remind your student to follow the colors and shapes from the map key to draw his or her neighborhood map.

10 DISTRIBUTE Distribute Student Learning Page 5.B to your student. Read the directions out loud to your student and have him or her choose and complete one of the activities on the page.

Branching Out

TEACHING TIP

Take your student to a tall building or another high viewing area in his or her town. Bring a map of the town with you. Help your student identify the place he or she sees from the view and match them to the objects shown on the map.

CHECKING IN

To assess your student's understanding of the lesson, have him or her use the illustration and map of the neighborhood park to reteach the lesson. Your student should go over the main ideas from the lesson: how objects on maps are shown in relation to other objects, how a map shows a view from above, and how to read a map key and understand map symbols.

FOR FURTHER READING

Muck's Map, by Kim Ostrow and Mike Giles, ill. (Simon Spotlight, 2002).

My Map Book, by Sarah Fanelli (HarperCollins Juvenile Books, 2001).

Where's That Bone?, by Lucille Recht Penner and Lynn Adams, ill. (Kane Press, 2000).

Match the Views

Draw a line to match the side and top views of each object.

1.

A.

2.

B.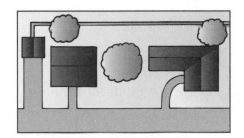

3.

C.

4.

D.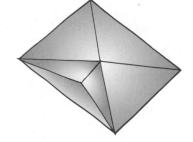

What's Next? You Decide!

Teacher: Read aloud the directions and activities. Then have your student choose which activity to do next.

Now it's your turn to choose what to do next in the lesson. Read the activities and decide which one you want to do—you may want to try them both!

Dance with Symbols

★ MATERIALS

- ❏ 4 different colored sheets construction paper
- ❏ 1 pair scissors
- ❏ 1 radio or stereo

★ STEPS

- ❏ Draw a symbol for a house, a street, a park, and a pond on construction paper. Use different colors and shapes for each symbol. Make the symbols large enough for you to stand on.
- ❏ Cut out the symbols.
- ❏ Lay out the symbols on the floor.
- ❏ Put on some music that you like to dance to. Start dancing around your symbols.
- ❏ Ask an adult to call out different symbols for you to dance on. *Dance in the street! Now dance in the house! Dance in the park!*
- ❏ Dance with your feet on the symbols that are called out.
- ❏ Have fun dancing!

Map Your Room

★ MATERIALS

- ❏ several different-colored sheets construction paper
- ❏ 1 pair scissors
- ❏ glue

★ STEPS

What does your room look like from above? Make a map.

- ❏ Choose a sheet of construction paper to be the floor of your room.
- ❏ On different colors of construction paper, draw symbols for all the things that are in your room.
- ❏ Draw the bed, the dresser, the door, and so on.
- ❏ Cut out the symbols.
- ❏ Glue the symbols to the paper that shows the floor. Try to put each thing in the same place it is in your room.
- ❏ Share your map with your family!

Reading a U.S. Map

Maps help us see a bigger picture of what's around us.

OBJECTIVE	BACKGROUND	MATERIALS
To help your student understand a U.S. map	Maps provide information that is useful in understanding where we are and what's around us. In this lesson, your student will learn to identify borders, water, and land on a U.S. map and to recognize the symbols that represent them.	■ Student Learning Pages 6.A–6.C ■ 1 North American map ■ markers or crayons

VOCABULARY
COUNTRY an area of land with specific borders and a specific government **STATES** smaller areas inside a country **BORDER** the line at the edge of an area of land that marks where an area ends

Let's Begin

1 **INTRODUCE** Tell your student that he or she lives in the **country** of the United States of America. Explain that a country is a large area of land. Point out that the United States is made up of individual **states** inside the country. Show your student the map of North America. Remind your student that maps are drawn using the view of a place from above. The view from above is what you would see if you were in a plane very high in the air. Point out the United States on the map. Trace the outline of the United States with your finger. Then have your student do the same. Explain that the United States is made up of 50 states. Ask, *What state do you live in?*

2 **DISTRIBUTE AND IDENTIFY** Distribute Student Learning Page 6.A. Together with your student find the state that he or she lives in. Then ask your student to color that state red. Make sure your student colors inside the boundary lines of his or her state. Explain that the lines show the state's **border.** Crossing the border means crossing into another state. Illustrate this by pointing out the states that surround the state your student lives in. Ask your student to trace around each state you name with his or her finger to become more aware of borders and what they represent.

3 **EXPLAIN** Explain that maps often show where landforms and bodies of water are. Maps use symbols, which are colors, shapes,

ENRICH THE EXPERIENCE

The next time you take a driving trip with your student, provide your student with a road map and highlight the route you'll be taking. Have him or her draw pictures on the map of sights he or she sees along the way.

or pictures that represent something, to show where things are (see Lesson 4.5). For example, maps often use a small circle or dot as a symbol for the location of a city. Ask your student to look at the map on Student Learning Page 6.A. Ask, *What is the symbol on the map for the state you live in?* [the color red]

ENRICH THE EXPERIENCE

Find more maps of the United States by going to http://www. enchantedlearning.com and clicking on United States. This site contains different U.S. maps as well as fun map activities for each state.

4 **RELATE** Show your student the map of North America again. Point out the Great Lakes and the Atlantic and Pacific Oceans. Point out Hawaii and Alaska. Explain that these states are part of the United States but that they don't touch the other states. Mention that since these states are far away, they are often shown in boxes on a map so they can fit on the page. Lay the map on Student Learning Page 6.A next to the map of North America. Ask your student to add color symbols for land and water to the map on Student Learning Page 6.A. Have your student color the water blue. Then ask your student to use the color green to fill in all the areas of the map that are bodies of land.

5 **DISTRIBUTE AND CONNECT** Distribute Student Learning Page 6.B. Point out both maps of the United States. Explain that maps show a much smaller version of the place they represent. Also explain that different maps can be different sizes and still show the same things. Help your student find the state of California on the larger map. Have your student color California green. Then do the same with the smaller map. Ask your student to compare the size of California on both maps. Ask, *What is the same?* [the shape and position] *What is different?* [the size] Have your student repeat the process for each state using different colors until both maps are fully colored. The same state should have the same color on both maps. Ask, *What two states are not shown on these maps?* [Alaska and Hawaii]

6 **DISTRIBUTE** Read the activities on Student Learning Page 6.C to your student. Have him or her decide which one he or she would like to do.

Branching Out

FOR FURTHER READING

Mapping Our World, by Janine Scott (Compass Point Books, 2002).

My Map Book, by Sara Fanelli (HarperCollins Juvenile Books, 2001).

We Need Directions, by Sara De Capua (Children's Press, 2002).

TEACHING TIP

Ask your student, *After looking at a map of the United States, what can you tell me about the country?* Prompt your student to talk about the country having land and water, that there are oceans on some of the borders, and that there are many states. Ask, *How many states are there?* If your student doesn't remember that there are 50 states, have him or her count the states on the map on Student Learning Page 6.A.

CHECKING IN

Ask your student to identify the borders of the United States on the map of North America. Then have your student point out land and water features and find his or her state.

Put Symbols on a U.S. Map

Color the state you live in red. Color the water blue and the land green.

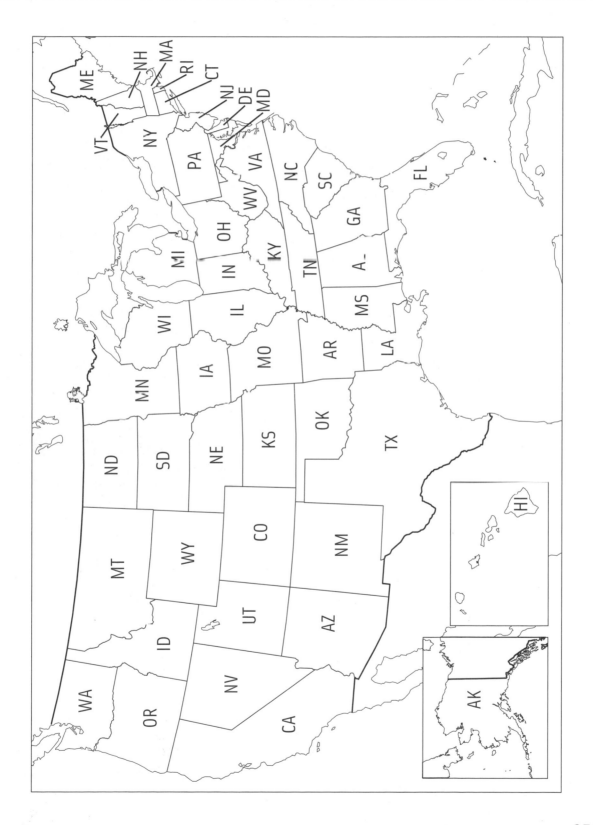

Compare Different Maps

Color California green on both maps.
Color the other states different colors.

What's Next? You Decide!

SOCIAL STUDIES 6.C

Teacher: *Read aloud the directions and activities. Then have your student choose which activity to do next.*

Now it's your turn to choose what to do next in the lesson. Read the activities and decide which one you want to do—you may want to try them all!

Make a Map Puzzle

MATERIALS

- ❏ 1 large copy Student Learning Page 6.A
- ❏ markers or crayons
- ❏ 1 small posterboard
- ❏ glue
- ❏ 1 pair scissors

STEPS

- ❏ Ask an adult to make a large copy of the map of the United States on Student Learning Page 6.A.
- ❏ Color all the water on the map the same color.
- ❏ Color all the states different colors.
- ❏ Glue your map onto the posterboard.
- ❏ Cut out the map along the edges of the country's border.
- ❏ Then cut the map in 5 to 10 different pieces.
- ❏ Be sure to cut along the borders of the states.
- ❏ Practice putting your U.S. map puzzle together!

Explore Land and Water

MATERIALS

- ❏ 1 copy Student Learning Page 6.A
- ❏ markers or crayons

STEPS

Find out which states in the United States touch bodies of water!

- ❏ Ask an adult to make a copy of the map on Student Learning Page 6.A.
- ❏ Color the oceans on the map dark blue.
- ❏ Find the states on the map that touch the oceans.
- ❏ Color those states green.
- ❏ Color the Great Lakes on the map light blue.
- ❏ Find the states that touch the Great Lakes.
- ❏ Color those states yellow.
- ❏ Share your map with an adult.

(CONTINUED) ▶

Make a Treasure Map

MATERIALS

- ❑ 1 old pillowcase or piece of bedsheet
- ❑ several old newspapers
- ❑ markers or paint
- ❑ 1 short piece string or yarn

STEPS

Suppose you've hidden a treasure in your home. Draw a treasure map to help someone find it!

- ❑ Spread the newspapers on a clean, hard part of the floor.
- ❑ Lay the pillowcase on top of the newspapers. (This will prevent you from accidentally coloring on the floor.)
- ❑ Suppose the pillowcase is your home. Draw a map showing where you've hidden a secret treasure.
- ❑ Use different colored markers or paints to show different things, such as doorways, rooms, or furniture.
- ❑ Remember to wear a smock if you're using paint and to ask an adult's permission first.
- ❑ When you're done, roll up the pillowcase and tie it with string or yarn.
- ❑ Give your treasure map to a family member or friend. See if he or she can find the treasure!

Draw a Travel Poster

MATERIALS

- ❑ 1 posterboard
- ❑ markers or crayons

STEPS

- ❑ Think of the places you've learned about in the lesson or places you've heard about.
- ❑ Choose one of those places—it can be a city, a state, or a country.
- ❑ Draw a travel poster for the place you chose!
- ❑ Think of what you know about this place. Is it hot? Is it cold? Does it snow? Can you go swimming there? Can you go skiing there?
- ❑ Now draw pictures on the posterboard of this place.
- ❑ Remember that you're trying to get people to visit.
- ❑ Share your poster with your family.

Exploring World Maps

Maps help us understand the shape of our world.

OBJECTIVE	BACKGROUND	MATERIALS
To show your student how the world looks on a map	In this lesson, your student will look at various world maps and find different land formations and bodies of water.	■ Student Learning Pages 7.A–7.B ■ blue and green markers or crayons

VOCABULARY
WORLD all the countries and other places on Earth **CONTINENTS** very large areas of land surrounded by water

Let's Begin

1   **EXPLAIN**   Show your student the photograph of Earth. The photograph was taken from above Earth and shows the **world** as a flat image. Point out that the photograph is really many photographs put together. Tell your student that a map of the world shows the same view of Earth as the photograph. Ask, *Why do you think the photographs needed to be taken separately?* [because Earth is round]

This photograph of Earth shows different landforms and bodies of water.

2   **RELATE**   Have your student look at the world map. Explain that the blue areas on the map represent water and the green areas represent land. Have your student point to the areas that show water and the areas that show land. Ask, *Do you see more land or more water on the world map?* [more water]

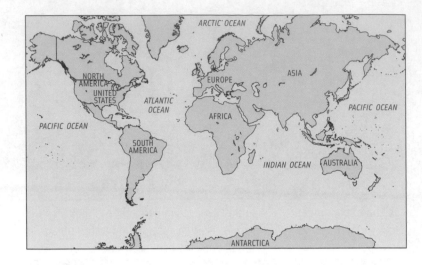

3 **EXPAND** Point out the different landmasses on the world map to your student. Explain that the oceans on Earth separate the land into **continents.** Tell your student that there are seven different continents in the world: North America, South America, Africa, Europe, Asia, Australia, and Antarctica. Show your student the different continents on the map. Have your student point to each continent and say its name. Then explain that there are four major oceans: the Pacific Ocean, Atlantic Ocean, Indian Ocean, and Arctic Ocean. Have your student point to each ocean on the map and say its name.

4 **EXPAND** Point to North America on the world map and tell your student that this is the continent where he or she lives. Ask, *What country do you live in?* [the United States] Have your student point to the United States on the world map.

5 **DISTRIBUTE** Distribute Student Learning Page 7.A and help your student with the directions. Then distribute Student Learning Page 7.B and read the directions out loud.

Branching Out

TEACHING TIP

Help your student look through a newspaper or watch the news and record the names of countries that are mentioned. Then help your student locate the countries on a world map.

CHECKING IN

Take your student to the local library and investigate the different types of world maps that are available. Help your student point out the seven continents and four oceans on different world maps. The goal is not for your student to memorize the name of each one, but for him or her to be aware of them.

Color the World

Color the water blue and the land green. Then circle the United States.

SOCIAL STUDIES 7.A

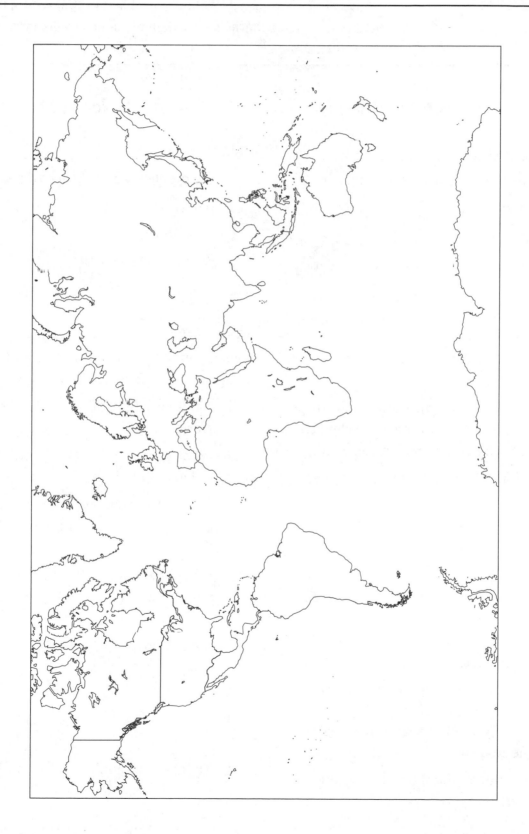

What's Next? You Decide!

Teacher: *Read aloud the directions and activities. Then have your student choose which activity to do next.*

Now it's your turn to choose what to do next in the lesson. Read the activities and decide which one you want to do—you may want to try them both!

Link the World

MATERIALS

❑ several sheets construction paper

❑ 1 ruler

❑ 1 pair scissors

❑ glue

❑ crayons or markers

STEPS

Make a paper chain showing good things in the world.

❑ Cut the construction paper into strips that are about two inches wide. (The strips can be as long as you want.)

❑ Ask an adult to help you measure.

❑ On each strip of paper, draw or write something good in the world, such as birds, sunshine, your family, books, and you!

❑ Then make a large ring with the first strip of paper and glue the ends together so that your picture shows on the outside.

❑ Take another strip of paper and make a ring looping the paper strip through the first ring of paper. Then glue this strip together in a ring.

❑ Continue making the rest of your chain.

Make a World Flag

MATERIALS

❑ 1 old pillowcase or piece of bedsheet

❑ paint

❑ 1 paintbrush

❑ several newspapers

❑ 1 painting smock

STEPS

Each country in the world has its own flag. Design a flag for the entire world!

❑ Think of what you learned about the world today.

❑ What would you want a world flag to look like?

❑ Think of the shapes, designs, and colors you would want your world flag to have.

❑ Place newspapers down on a clean, flat part of a floor.

❑ Then place the pillowcase on top of the newspapers.

❑ Put on your smock and paint your flag on the pillowcase.

❑ When you're done, allow enough time to dry.

❑ Then ask an adult to help you hang it for others to see.

Investigating a Globe

*Globes show us something that a flat map can't—
how our spherical world really looks.*

OBJECTIVE	BACKGROUND	MATERIALS
To teach your student about globes and what they represent	A globe is a small model of Earth and shows true-to-scale sizes and positions of the continents and oceans. In this lesson, your student will learn how globes are representations of Earth, how to interpret globe symbols such as those for land and water, and the viewpoint a globe provides.	■ Student Learning Pages 8.A–8.B ■ 1 globe ■ 1 world map ■ 1 photo Earth ■ markers or crayons ■ basketball or beach ball

VOCABULARY
GLOBE a small model of Earth that shows land, water, and other features **SYMBOLS** something used to represent something else

Let's Begin

1 **ASK AND EXPLAIN** Ask, *Do you know what shape Earth is?* [round] Explain to your student that one way to understand the shape of Earth is to look at a **globe.** Tell your student that a globe is a model of Earth that shows where land, water, countries, and other important things are. A globe is different from a map. A map is flat, while a globe is round like Earth. Show your student this picture of a globe. Point out the United States and the Atlantic and Pacific Oceans. If you have a globe on hand, show it to him or her. Then show him or her a world map. Point out the United States and its surrounding oceans. Ask, *How is the globe different from and similar to the map?* [they both show land and water, but one is round and one is flat]

2 **EXPAND** Tell your student that, like maps, globes use **symbols** to represent land and water. Explain that symbols are things that represent something else. Sometimes colors are used as symbols. Colors are used on globes as symbols for water and land. Point out areas of land on the globe and ask, *What color is used as a symbol for land?* [answers will vary depending on the globe] Then point out areas of water on the globe and ask, *What color is used as a symbol for water?* [most likely blue] Ask your student to locate and point out other examples of land and water on the globe.

A BRIGHT IDEA

Before you get to Step 4, check out http://www. spacepix.net/earth/ for photographs of Earth.

3 **DISTRIBUTE** Distribute Student Learning Page 8.A. Point out the two illustrations of the globe. Have your student compare the drawings to an actual globe. Ask your student to find on the globe the views shown in the drawings. Then have your student color the land areas green and the water areas blue in each illustration.

4 **EXPLAIN** Ask your student to look at a photo of Earth. Explain that it's a picture of Earth taken from far out in space. Explain that this is similar to the kind of view we get when looking at a globe, except that a globe doesn't show clouds. A globe gives us a bird's-eye view of Earth. It shows what Earth would look like if we could see it from high above and far away. Show your student a basketball or a beach ball. Have your student put his or her cheek against the ball. Point out that this is similar to what we see when we stand on Earth. Ask, *How much of the ball can you see right now?* [just a small part] *Can you describe what it looks like?* [it looks flat] Then have your student hold the ball at arm's length and look at it. Ask, *How much of the ball can you see now?* [all of one side] *How does it look?* [it looks round]

5 **REVEAL** Point out that the water and landforms on a globe appear as they would to a person looking at them from far away. Explain that Earth is too big for us to see it all from where we stand on the ground, so people make proportional models of it to show what it looks like from above. Ask, *Why do we need to make a model of Earth to get a good idea of what it looks like?* [because Earth is round and very big]

6 **DECIDE** Read the activity choices on Student Learning Page 8.B to your student. Have your student decide which one he or she would like to do.

DID YOU KNOW?

Make sure your student understands that globes are much smaller than Earth. While many globes are about the size of a basketball, Earth is almost 25,000 miles in circumference at the equator.

Branching Out

TEACHING TIP

Give your student a better understanding of globes as small versions of Earth by making analogies using other kinds of models. For example, a doll is a small model of a person and a stuffed animal is a small model of an animal.

CHECKING IN

To assess your student's understanding of the lesson, review the concepts covered. Ask, *What are the symbols for land and water on a globe?* [answers will vary; blue is usually water] *A globe helps us see what Earth would look like from where?* [above] *How are maps and globes alike and different?* [they both show water and land; one is flat and one is round]

FOR FURTHER READING

Looking at Maps and Globes (*Rookie Read-About Geography*), by Carmen Bredeson (Children's Press, 2001).

Maps, Globes, and Graphs, by Henry Billings (Raintree/ Steck-Vaughn, 2000).

Use Symbols on a Globe

Color the land areas green. Color the water areas blue.

What's Next? You Decide!

Teacher: Read aloud the directions and activities. Then have your student choose which activity to do next.

Now it's your turn to choose what to do next in the lesson. Read the activities and decide which one you want to do—you may want to try them both!

Create Night and Day

⬟ MATERIALS

❏ 1 globe

❏ 1 large flashlight

⬟ STEPS

Model night and day on a globe.

❏ Do this exercise at night or in a room with no windows.

❏ Place the globe on the floor or on a table.

❏ Shine the large flashlight onto the globe.

❏ Ask an adult to turn off the lights in the room.

❏ Notice that half of the globe is lit up by the flashlight. Notice that the other half is dark.

❏ Find the United States on the globe. Shine the light on it.

❏ Keep holding the flashlight. Ask an adult to turn the globe slowly.

❏ Watch how the United States goes from the dark to the light to the dark—from day to night!

Tell the Story of Earth

⬟ MATERIALS

❏ 1 globe

⬟ STEPS

Tell your own story about how Earth got to be the way it is.

❏ Look at the globe to get ideas for your story.

❏ Think about why Earth is round.

❏ Think about how the land and water on Earth got to be where they are.

❏ Now make up a story.

❏ Practice telling the story about Earth to yourself or someone else.

❏ Then tell your story to your family.

❏ Be sure to talk about the shape of Earth and its size.

❏ Don't forget to mention the land and water on Earth.

Recognizing U.S. Symbols

*Understanding your country's symbols will allow
you to understand your country.*

OBJECTIVE	BACKGROUND	MATERIALS
To teach your student about U.S. symbols and what they represent	National symbols are important because they represent the values of a country, honor specific events or individuals, help unite people, and encourage national pride. In this lesson, your student will learn about various symbols of the United States and their importance.	▪ Student Learning Pages 9.A–9.B ▪ 1 photo of the current U.S. president ▪ 1 copy Pledge of Allegiance ▪ markers or crayons ▪ several U.S. coins with national symbols (or 1 picture book showing national symbols)

VOCABULARY

SYMBOLS something used to represent something else
PRESIDENT the highest elected leader of the United States

Let's Begin

1 **INTRODUCE** Tell your student that **symbols** are things that represent something else, such as a person, place, event, or belief. Share a symbol of your state with your student, the state flag. Show him or her a photo of it and explain that this symbol helps describe the ideas, history, and personality of your state. Ask, *Can you name any symbols of the United States?* [the Statue of Liberty, bald eagle, Mt. Rushmore, and so on]

2 **EXPLAIN** Explain to your student that the U.S. flag is an important symbol of the country. Ask, *What colors are on the U.S. flag?* [red, white, and blue] Show your student the flag. Explain that there's a reason why the stars and stripes are on the flag. The 50 stars stand for the 50 states that now make up the United States. The 13 stripes represent how many colonies there were when the country declared its independence from England. Tell your student that the U.S. flag is often hung at government buildings, such as the post office and state capitol buildings, as well as at community centers. Together, name some other places where you and your student have seen the U.S. flag.

The U.S. flag has 13 stripes and 50 stars.

3 **DESCRIBE** Ask, *What is the leader of the United States called?* [the president] Explain that citizens of the United States vote to elect the **president.** The president is responsible for leading the country. Show your student a photograph of the current president. Say, *This is our president.* Then ask, *Have you seen his or her picture before? Do you know the name of our president?* If not, help your student learn the president's name and recognize his or her picture.

4 **EXPAND** Tell your student that the Pledge of Allegiance is another important national symbol. Explain that the Pledge of Allegiance is something that U.S. citizens say to promise to be loyal to the flag, the country, and what it stands for. Recite the Pledge of Allegiance to your student. Make sure your student notes the mention of the U.S. flag to strengthen his or her understanding of the importance placed on the flag. Ask, *Does your family have a symbol or thing that's very special or important to all of you?* [special photos, heirlooms, and so on] Talk with your student about why these things are special to his or her family and how they make the family feel.

5 **DISTRIBUTE** Distribute Student Learning Page 9.A. Have your student draw the U.S. flag. When the drawing is complete, ask your student to talk about what the stars and stripes mean.

6 **SING** Sing aloud one of your favorite songs about the United States, such as "America," "You're a Grand Old Flag," or "America the Beautiful." Sing it a few times and encourage your student to sing along with you. If you'd like, make up hand movements to the words.

7 **DISCUSS AND DISTRIBUTE** Have your student think about the other symbols of the United States besides the flag that he or she has learned about in this lesson. Distribute Student Learning Page 9.B. Read the activities to your student and have him or her decide which one he or she would like to do.

Branching Out

TEACHING TIP

For more information about U.S. symbols, such as the flag, visit http://www.enchantedlearning.com. Click on U.S. States or World Flags for useful activities and printouts that will help your student understand national and state symbols and their meanings.

CHECKING IN

To assess your student's understanding of the lesson, use a picture book of U.S. symbols or use U.S. coins that display various national symbols. Show your student each symbol and ask him or her to identify it. Then discuss with him or her its meaning and importance.

?

DID YOU KNOW?

The U.S. flag has changed many times over the course of U.S. history. The first U.S. flag had 13 stars and 13 stripes. As more states entered into the union, more stars were added. Aside from the 1795 flag, which had 15 stripes, the number of stripes has stayed at 13 to represent the number of original colonies.

FOR FURTHER READING

American Eagle: The Symbol of America, by Jon Wilson (Child's World, Inc., 1998).

The Pledge of Allegiance, by Lola Schaefer (Heinemann Library, 2002).

Red, White, and Blue: The Story of the American Flag, by John Herman and Robin Roraback, ill. (Grosset and Dunlap, 1998).

Draw the Flag of the United States

What's Next? You Decide!

Teacher: Read aloud the directions and activities. Then have your student choose which activity to do next.

Now it's your turn to choose what to do next in the lesson. Read the activities and decide which one you want to do—you may want to try them both!

Learn the Pledge of Allegiance

MATERIALS

❑ 1 audiocassette recorder

❑ 1 audiocassette tape

STEPS

❑ Ask an adult to say the Pledge of Allegiance while you make a recording of his or her voice.

❑ Listen to the cassette.

❑ Try to remember the words.

❑ Practice saying the pledge by yourself.

❑ Play the cassette over and over until you can remember all the words.

❑ Make another recording, this time of you saying the Pledge of Allegiance.

❑ Look at your drawing of the U.S. flag while you say the pledge.

❑ Play your recording for an adult.

❑ Explain what the Pledge of Allegiance means to you and how it makes you feel.

Build a National Monument

MATERIALS

❑ 1 picture book with national symbols and monuments

❑ 1 package modeling clay

STEPS

Build a model of a national monument, which is something that has been built to honor the United States.

❑ Look through a picture book for symbols that are important in the United States.

❑ Check out the Liberty Bell, the Statue of Liberty, the Washington Monument, and the Capitol.

❑ Choose one of the monuments and make a model of it with the clay.

❑ When your model is done, ask an adult to help you find out more about the monument you chose.

❑ Find out when it was built, what it's a symbol of, and why it's important to the United States.

❑ Share your model with a friend.

❑ Tell your friend what you have learned.

Exploring Our Origins

Learning about who we are often requires examining who we once were.

OBJECTIVE	BACKGROUND	MATERIALS
To teach your student about the origins of the United States and how the nation has changed over time	Important people and events have shaped our country and society. Remembering historical changes can help us make better decisions concerning our future. In this lesson, your student will learn about the first Americans, the early American explorers, the first American celebrations, and how things such as travel and cities have changed over time.	■ Student Learning Pages 10.A–10.B ■ 1 world map ■ 1 copy Web, page 356 ■ markers or crayons

VOCABULARY

EXPLORERS people who travel to unknown lands
SETTLEMENTS camps or small communities

Let's Begin

1 **ASK AND PREVIEW** Ask, *Do you know who the first Americans were?* [Native Americans] Tell your student that before **explorers** from Europe came to America, Native American people were living all over North America. Explain that Native Americans lived differently than we do today. They hunted, gathered, or grew their own food. They made their own clothes and homes out of the things around them, the land, trees, and animals. Ask, *How do most people today get their food, clothing, and shelter?* [they buy them at a store, they buy houses]

2 **EXPLORE** Together with your student, research a Native American group that has origins in the area where you live. Find out where they were located and how they used their environment for food, clothing, and shelter. For example, the Native American Sioux tribes lived on the Great Plains. They hunted various types of animals but were especially dependent on the buffalo. The buffalo not only provided a source of food, but their hides were used for clothing and to make shelter. Buffalo bones were used for weapons and tools. After you discuss the Native American tribe in your area, ask your student to name at least three ways his or her life is different from theirs.

A BRIGHT IDEA

For resource links and information about Native American history, visit the Smithsonian Web site at http://www. si.edu/resource/faq and click on Native American History and Culture. Or go to http://www.si. edu/history_and_culture and click on Native Americans.

3 **EXPLAIN** Explain to your student that Christopher Columbus was one of the first explorers from Europe to travel to America. Point out Europe and North America on a world map. Explain that Columbus sailed from Spain with three ships, the *Niña*, the *Pinta*, and the *Santa María*. Point out Spain and the Bahamas to your student and have him or her trace a line on the map from one to the other to represent the Columbus voyage. Then point out the Indies, the area of India, China, and Japan. Explain that this was where Columbus was trying to go. When Columbus landed, he thought he had reached the Indies. That's why he called the people he met there Indians. Ask, *What stopped Columbus from sailing around the world to the Indies?* [North America]

4 **RELATE AND ASK** Tell your student that even though his discovery of a new land was accidental, Columbus made an important historical discovery. This is why, on the second Monday of every October, we celebrate a holiday called Columbus Day. Ask, *Why do you think we have a holiday named after Columbus?* [to remember Columbus and his discovery]

5 **EXPLAIN AND ASK** Explain to your student that one of the first **settlements** founded by people from Europe in America was called Plymouth. We call the people who lived there the Pilgrims. The Pilgrims had a very hard time surviving in their new home, but they were helped by a Native American tribe called the Wampanoag. The Wampanoag taught the Pilgrims how to hunt, fish, and grow corn so they would have food. To thank the Wampanoag, the Pilgrims held a feast where they ate foods made with pumpkins, corn, fish, turkey, and deer. Point out that Americans remember this special celebration feast each year. Ask, *What is the name of the holiday that honors the Pilgrim and Wampanoag feast?* [Thanksgiving]

6 **DISTRIBUTE AND COMPARE** Ask your student to describe how your family celebrates Thanksgiving. Have him or her describe the kinds of food he or she eats, who is involved in the celebration, and what he or she is thankful for. Then distribute a copy of the Web found on page 356 to your student. Write "Thanksgiving" in the center. In the surrounding ovals, ask your student to draw pictures of things related to Thanksgiving, such as a turkey, people saying grace or being with family, and so on. Then have him or her look at the illustration on the next page of the First Thanksgiving. Ask your student to compare his or her Thanksgiving to the one in the illustration. Have your student talk about how the celebrations are alike and how they're different.

A BRIGHT IDEA

For more information on Christopher Columbus, visit http://www.enchantedlearning.com and click on Explorers. This site contains a brief history of Columbus and many other explorers, as well as many interesting activities for your student to participate in, such as Columbus Day crafts.

The First Thanksgiving honors the special Pilgrim and Wampanoag feast.

7 **EXPAND** Tell your student that we celebrate other holidays to honor the history of the United States. On Independence Day, we celebrate our country's independence from England. Ask, *What do you do to celebrate Independence Day?* [wear red, white, and blue; watch fireworks; have a picnic; and so on] *Why do you think Independence Day is an important holiday?* [because it celebrates our freedom] Discuss other national holidays and their importance, such as Presidents' Day, Martin Luther King Jr. Day, and Veterans Day.

8 **CREATE AND DO** For loads of ideas on holidays, crafts, and activities, go to http://www.activitiesforkids.com with your student. Don't wait for the next holiday to have your student learn about why people celebrate certain days.

9 **EXPLAIN** Explain to your student that many things in the United States have changed since the country was founded. Ask, *How do people today travel from one place to another?* [cars, trains, airplanes, and so on] Then have your student imagine what it would be like if we didn't have such things as cars, trains, or airplanes. Ask, *How do you think people traveled before they had these things?* [walked or rode horses] Explain that as time has passed, the way people have traveled from one place to another has changed. For example, Christopher Columbus and the Pilgrims traveled to America on a sailing ship powered by the wind. Today boats are safer and have powerful engines that make the boats go much faster. Ask, *How do you think airplanes today are different from the first planes?* [planes today are faster and safer]

10 **DISTRIBUTE** Distribute Student Learning Page 10.A and tell your student that the illustration shows a group of people traveling to a new home a long time ago. Ask your student to draw a picture in the space provided of how these people might travel today. Then ask your student to compare the way people are traving in each picture.

DID YOU KNOW?

Many of the first European settlers in the western United States traveled from the east on wagon trains. The settlers lined up their wagons and horses one behind the other like a train. There weren't any roads, and it often took months to get out west. Today we can fly from the East Coast to the West Coast in a matter of hours.

11 **EXPLORE** Tell your student that cities also change and grow. A long time ago cities were much smaller than they are today and less people lived there. Today more people live in cities and there are more buildings, including skyscrapers. Ask your student to look at the two photos of New York City. Explain that one is a photo from a long time ago and one is a recent photo. Ask your student to explain how New York City has changed over time.

New York City: Yesterday

New York City: Today

12 **DISTRIBUTE** Distribute Student Learning Page 10.B. Read the directions and activities to your student. Have him or her choose which activity he or she would like to do next.

Branching Out

FOR FURTHER READING

Christopher Columbus (*Rookie Biographies*), by Mary Dodson Wade (Children's Press, 2003).

Native Americans (*First Discovery Book*), by Gallimard Jeunesse; Ute Fuhr and Raoul Sautai, eds. (Scholastic Trade, 1998).

Steam, Smoke, and Steel: Back in Time with Trains, Patrick O'Brien, ill. (Charlesbridge Publishing, 2000).

The Very First Thanksgiving, by Rhonda Gowler Greene and Susan Gaber (Atheneum, 2002).

TEACHING TIPS

❏ You can further develop your student's understanding of the growth of cities by researching the history of your own city or town to find out how it has changed or grown over the years. Try to find historical photos that show how your city or town used to look and have your student compare them to your city or town today.

❏ Before the next holiday, help your student find a holiday song to sing. It can be one that's regularly sung on that day or an original one of your student's creation. Have your student teach it to other family members and then sing it on the holiday. Suggest that he or she dress in a costume and create hand movements to go with the words.

CHECKING IN

To assess your student's understanding of the lesson, ask him or her to talk about the meaning of Columbus Day and of Thanksgiving. Challenge your student to tell you why we celebrate these two holidays. Be sure your student talks about Christopher Columbus and his voyage, the Plymouth settlement, the Pilgrims and the Native Americans, and the First Thanksgiving.

See How Travel Has Changed

SOCIAL
STUDIES

10.A

Draw a picture of how people travel today.

Early Travel

Travel Today

What's Next? You Decide!

Teacher: *Read aloud the directions and activities. Then have your student choose which activity to do next.*

Now it's your turn to choose what to do next in the lesson. Read the activities and decide which one you want to do—you may want to try them both!

Make a Transportation Mobile

★ MATERIALS

- ❏ several sheets construction paper
- ❏ markers or crayons
- ❏ 1 hole puncher
- ❏ 1 pair scissors
- ❏ 1 hanger
- ❏ string or yarn

★ STEPS

Make a mobile to show how travel has changed.

- ❏ Draw pictures on construction paper of two ways that people used to travel.
- ❏ Draw pictures on construction paper of two ways people travel today.
- ❏ Cut out the drawings.
- ❏ Punch a hole at the top of each drawing.
- ❏ Use string or yarn to hang one new-travel drawing from one old-travel drawing.
- ❏ Do the same for the other two drawings.
- ❏ Then tie the top drawings to the hanger.
- ❏ Have an adult help you hang your mobile.

Describe the First Thanksgiving

★ MATERIALS

- ❏ 1 posterboard
- ❏ markers or crayons

★ STEPS

Imagine you attended the First Thanksgiving. How would you describe it?

- ❏ Think about what you learned about the First Thanksgiving.
- ❏ Draw a picture of the First Thanksgiving.
- ❏ Then think about how you would describe it in a story.
- ❏ What did the Pilgrims and the Native Americans do?
- ❏ What did they eat?
- ❏ What were they thankful for?
- ❏ Tell a story about the First Thanksgiving to an adult.
- ❏ Use the picture you drew to help you describe it.

In Your Community

To reinforce the skills and concepts taught in this section,
try one or more of these activities!

Explore Signs, Symbols, and Logos

Take a walk with your student through his or her neighborhood and look for road and community signs and symbols. Explain to your student that the signs are there to make your community safe. Point out that you can usually tell what a sign means by its shape. As you walk, explain each sign's significance and the consequences of not paying attention to what it says. When your walk is done, together with your student try to remember all the signs that you saw. Make a drawing of each sign and have your student talk about what each one means.

Use Map Skills in Your Town

Show your student a map of his or her town. Find your student's home on the map. Together think of a few places that your student visits frequently, such as the library, grocery store, or park, and locate them on the map. Discuss with your student where each location is in relation to his or her home. Talk about whether each place seems close or far, which place is closest, and which place is farthest away. Ask your student to predict how long it will take to get from his or her home to each place. Then take a trip to each place to test the predictions.

Visit Historical Sites

Just as the United States has an important history, so does your student's own town. Visit your local library with your student and research the beginnings of your town. Also visit the local historical society and find out about historical sites that still stand, such as the oldest building or the first train station. Read about the history of each site and talk about it with your student. Then visit each place and experience it firsthand.

Become a Community Volunteer

Remind your student that getting along with the members of his or her family requires helping each other. The same is true for the greater community. One way to help in the community is by volunteering. Find out about different volunteer opportunities in your community, such as litter cleanup days, food drives, delivering meals to disabled community members, or spending time with people in a retirement center. Make a list of possible options and have your student choose which one he or she would like to explore. Before volunteering, be sure to prepare your student for the types of things that he or she might see or experience. Point out that different people have different lifestyles and different challenges and that we all need to help each other get along.

Conduct Family History Interviews

Have your student compare his or her family history with the history of other families in the community. Set up two interviews for your student: one with an older member of his or her family and another with an older member of another family in your community, perhaps a neighbor or friend. Ask your student to prepare at least five questions to ask about what celebrations, food, daily life, and recreation were like in the past and how things have changed. If he or she wants, your student can ask for permission to record the interviews. Then discuss how things have changed over time.

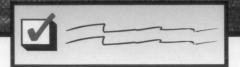

We Have Learned

Use this checklist to summarize what you and your student have accomplished in the Social Studies section.

❏ **Home and Family**
❏ how people are alike and different
❏ family members: parents, grandparents, guardians, and so on
❏ different types of homes
❏ getting along with others and solving problems

❏ **Communities**
❏ neighborhoods
❏ the city and the country

❏ **Rules**
❏ common road signs and community symbols
❏ why we need rules and laws
❏ taking turns and consequences

❏ **Community Helpers**
❏ people and places in the community
❏ community needs and community workers

❏ **Celebrations**
❏ the purpose of celebrations and holidays
❏ celebrations in other places and cultures

❏ **Jobs and Work**
❏ jobs we do at home
❏ different kinds of jobs
❏ jobs then and now

❏ earning money and how people use money
❏ wants versus basic needs of food, clothing, and shelter

❏ **Maps**
❏ locating and reading symbols and features of a map
❏ overhead view and position of objects
❏ identifying symbols and states on a U.S. map
❏ water and land symbols on a world map and a globe

❏ **Our Country**
❏ national symbols: flag, Pledge of Allegiance, the president
❏ American explorers, first Americans, Thanksgiving
❏ American celebrations
❏ changes in travel, city growth

❏ **Family Stories**
❏ differences then and now
❏ everyday routines
❏ family celebrations, special foods and games
❏ places families go together

We have also learned:

_____

_____

Teacher: Read aloud the directions. Then read each question followed by the answer choices. Have your student answer the questions.

> **Read each question and the answer choices that follow. Circle the letter of the correct answer.**

1. Which word has the short *a* sound?

A car

B pat

C rain

D date

2. The word *bead* rhymes with—

A red.

B need.

C mail.

D hold.

3. Which word begins with the *f* sound?

A go

B food

C seal

D dark

4. Which word has the short *e* sound?

A get

B eat

C feet

D deal

5. The word *slow* rhymes with—

A row.

B held.

C sun.

D lie.

Use for 6–7.

The Pond

Freddy the frog lived at the pond. He liked swimming around and hunting for flies. His best friend was Tom the turtle. One day they sat on a log talking. Just then a large bear walked up to the water's edge. Freddy and Tom got scared and swam away.

6. This story takes place at a—

A field.

B forest.

C pond.

D farm.

7. Why did Freddy and Tom get scared?

A They saw a fly.

B They heard a snake.

C They heard a man.

D They saw a large bear.

8. Which word begins with the *j* sound?

A hat

B fall

C jump

D kite

9. Which word has the short *i* sound?

A light

B sit

C ray

D peel

10. Which word begins with the *w* sound?

A set

B wet

C net

D get

11. Which word has the short *u* sound?

A flute

B dune

C host

D nut

12. Which letter comes after *l*?

A *i*

B *k*

C *m*

D *f*

13. Which word ends with the *ks* sound?

    A sack

    B six

    C rash

    D hut

14. Which word has the short *o* sound?

    A sock

    B down

    C story

    D tool

15. Which word begins with the *z* sound?

    A quit

    B pen

    C help

    D zone

16. Which letter comes after *t?*

    A *q*

    B *s*

    C *u*

    D *r*

17. Which word begins with the *g* sound?

    A jump

    B go

    C bike

    D sat

18. Which word ends with the *t* sound?

    A map

    B box

    C sit

    D fun

19. Write the letters of the alphabet in order. Use lowercase letters.

Draw a line from the word on the left to its opposite on the right.

20. big   light

21. heavy   tall

22. short   small

Circle the word that shows how each person feels.

23.    sad   mad   glad

24.    sad   mad   glad

Use for 25–27.

Animal Friends

Once there was a moose,
Who made friends with a goose.
While playing near a road,
They met a funny toad.
They all began to laugh,
When they saw a green giraffe.

25. Circle the word that rhymes with *moose*.

toad   goose   they

26. Circle the animal that they saw last.

giraffe   goose   toad

27. Circle the word that rhymes with *laugh*.

near   funny   giraffe

28. Circle the word that begins with the *n* sound.

ring   hand   nine   gone

29. Circle the word that has the short *a* sound.

bait   take   steak   tack

30. Circle the word that ends with the *s* sound.

box   miss   fish   pack

31. Circle the word that begins with the *v* sound.

oval   star   vase   give

32. Circle the word that has the short *i* sound.

feel   pit   far   night

Circle the word that completes each sentence.

33. I _____ the  .

with   see   some

34. He _____ a  .

has   with   at

35. She is _____ her .

to   with   has

36. I _____ in the  .

the   it   go

37. Write your name.

Circle the word that describes each object.

38.

round

flat

square

39.

dark

tall

hairy

40.

shiny

wet

broken

Teacher: *Read aloud the directions. Then read each question followed by the answer choices. Have your student answer the questions.*

> **Read each question and the answer choices that follow. Circle the letter of the correct answer.**

1. This is a—

   A square.

   B circle.

   C triangle.

   D rectangle.

2. How many footballs are there?

   A 2

   B 3

   C 4

   D 5

3. How many faces are there?

   A 6

   B 7

   C 8

   D 9

4. Which animal is fourth in line?

   A snake

   B duck

   C pig

   D turtle

5. How many are left?

5 – 2 = _____

A 5

B 3

C 2

D 1

6. What time is it?

A 6:00

B 8:00

C 10:00

D 12:00

7. How much money is there?

A 1 cent

B 3 cents

C 5 cents

D 10 cents

8. How many triangles are there?

$4 + 2 =$ _____

A 8

B 6

C 4

D 2

$4 \quad + \quad 2 \quad = \quad$ _____

9. How many ants are there?

A 13

B 14

C 15

D 16

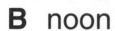

10. What time of day is it?

A morning

B noon

C afternoon

D evening

Circle the one that weighs more.

11.

12.

13.

Draw the shape that comes next.

14.   _____

15.   _____

16. 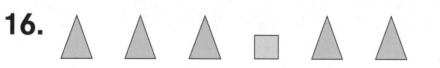   _____

17.    _____

Making the Grade: Everything Your Kindergartner Needs to Know

Circle the one that is different.

18.

19.

20.

Write the missing numbers.

21. 1, 2, _____, 4, 5, 6, 7, 8, _____, _____

22. 11, 12, _____, 14, _____

23. 16, 17, 18, _____, 20

24. Write your age. _____

25. Write the numbers 15–20.

_____

_____

_____

_____

_____

Add or subtract.

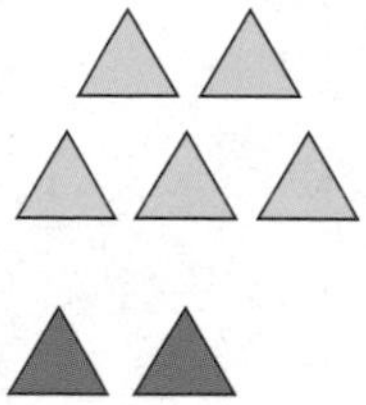

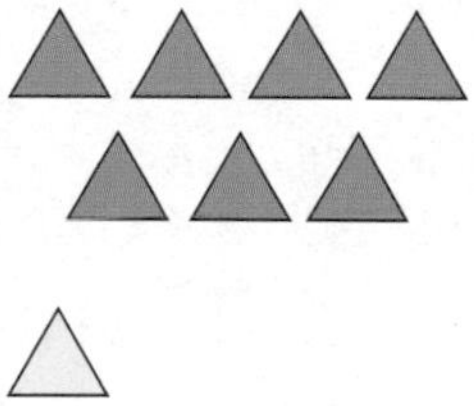

26.

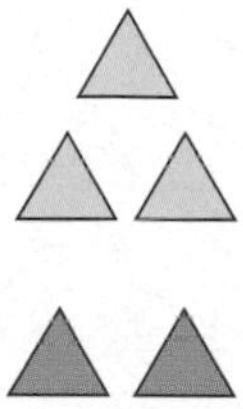

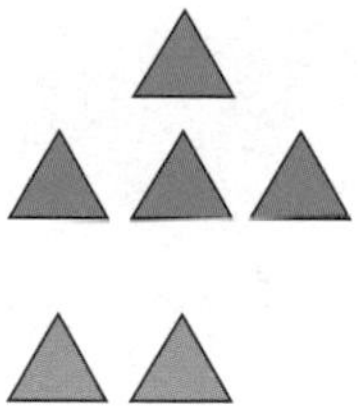

3 △△△

+ 2 △△

_____

_ _ _

27.

5 △△△△△

+ 2 △△

_____

_ _ _

28.

7 △△△△△△△

− 1 △

_____

_ _ _

29.

4 △△△△

− 2 △△

_____

_ _ _

Color one half of each shape.

30.

31.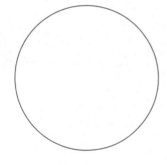

32. Draw shapes to make a pattern.

Teacher: Read aloud the directions. Then read each question followed by the answer choices. Have your student answer the questions.

> **Read each question and the answer choices that follow. Circle the letter of the correct answer.**

1. This person is—

A angry.

B sad.

C happy.

D confused.

2. All living things need air, food, water, and—

A plants.

B shelter.

C animal.

D weather.

3. Which has salty water?

A rivers

B oceans

C lakes

D ponds

4. We use this body part to—

A taste.

B hear.

C see.

D feel.

5. Which helps make your teeth healthy?

A cavities

B flossing

C eating

D biting

6. Which pushes blood to other parts of your body?

A bones

B muscles

C skeleton

D heart

7. The tadpole will grow into a—

A lizard.

B fish.

C frog.

D turtle.

8. Which is inside a basketball?

A gas

B solid

C weather

D liquid

9. Which helps make your body strong?

    A germs

    B exercise

    C washing

    D reading

10. Cows give us—

    A milk.

    B eggs.

    C plants.

    D water.

11. Which comes from a farm?

    A cake

    B corn

    C pizza

    D tacos

12. Our sun is a—

A moon.

B planet.

C star.

D space.

13. Which season is it?

A winter

B spring

C summer

D fall

14. Which is living?

A rock

B fish

C mountain

D light

15. What do you do with your nose?

A taste

B touch

C smell

D hear

Draw a line from the plant part to the word that names it.

16.

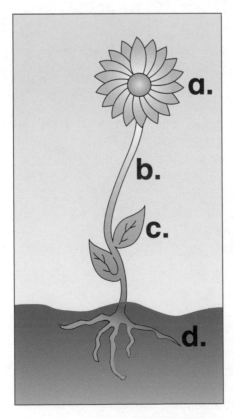

a.   stem

b.   flower

c.   root

d.   leaf

Circle the living thing.

17.

 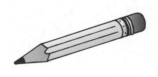  

18.

Circle "solid," "liquid," or "gas."

19.  solid
liquid
gas

20.  solid
liquid
gas

Circle the one that is different.

21.

22.

Circle "left," "right," "above," or "below" to tell where the ball is.

23.  left   right   above   below

24.  left   right   above   below

25.  left   right   above   below

26.  left   right   above   below

Draw a line from the part of Earth to the word that names it.

27.

mountain

28.

ocean

29.

desert

> # Draw a line from the young animal to its parent.

30.

31.

32.

Teacher: Read aloud the directions. Then read each question followed by the answer choices. Have your student answer the questions.

> **Read each question and the answer choices that follow. Circle the letter of the correct answer.**

1. This sign tells you to—

   A go.

   B stop.

   C pass.

   D be careful.

2. All people need—

   A toys.

   B food.

   C telephones.

   D cars.

3. Which is a symbol of our country?

   A flag

   B dog

   C state

   D president of the United States

4. He earns money by—

   A putting out fires.

   B building houses.

   C helping sick people.

   D cooking food.

5. Who sailed to America?

   A Native Americans

   B explorers

   C Abe Lincoln

   D president of the United States

6. Which has many tall buildings and many people?

A city

B forests

C country

D farms

7. Globes are—

A flat.

B round.

C square.

D tiny.

8. Which continent do you live on?

A Africa

B Asia

C North America

D South America

9. Which helps keep your community safe?

   A police officer

   B doctor

   C farmer

   D artist

10. This picture shows—

   A a townhouse.

   B the country.

   C the city.

   D an apartment.

11. Which keep us safe?

   A goods and services

   B wants and needs

   C toys and games

   D rules and laws

12. These children are—

    A arguing.

    B taking turns.

    C fighting.

    D breaking the rules.

13. Which are the colors of our nation's flag?

    A red, white, and green

    B green, white, and blue

    C red, white, and blue

    D blue, white, and orange

14. How many states are there?

    A 10

    B 13

    C 50

    D 100

15. How many people are in your family?

_____

- -

_____

16. Draw two different families.

Use for 17–19.

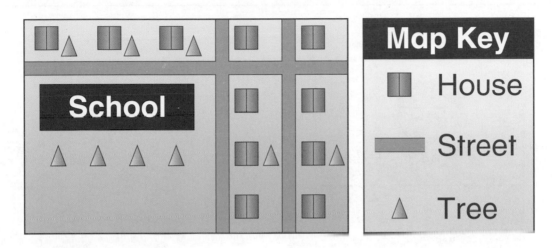

17. What shape does the map use to show trees?

18. How many trees are behind the school?

_____

- - - - - - - - - - - - - - - - - - - -

_____

19. How many houses have trees next to them?

_____

- - - - - - - - - - - - - - - - - - - -

_____

Draw a line from the problem to the solution.

20.

21.

22.

Draw a line from the old way of doing things to the way we do them today.

23.

24.

25.

Circle the pictures that show people helping others.

26.

Assessment Answers

PROMOTING LITERACY

1.	B	10.	B
2.	B	11.	D
3.	B	12.	C
4.	A	13.	B
5.	A	14.	A
6.	C	15.	D
7.	D	16.	C
8.	C	17.	B
9.	B	18.	C

Scoring Rubric for Question 19:

4 POINTS
The letters of the alphabet are written in the correct order. All letters are included. All letters are written in lowercase.

3 POINTS
The letters of the alphabet are written in the correct order. All letters are included. Most of the letters are written in lowercase.

2 POINTS
Most of the letters of the alphabet are written in the correct order. Several letters are missing or out of order. Several letters are written in uppercase.

1 POINT
Many of the letters of the alphabet are written out of order or are not included. There are more letters written in uppercase than lowercase.

0 POINTS
Few of the letters of the alphabet are written in the correct order, or only a handful of the letters are included.

20.	small	31.	vase
21.	light	32.	pit
22.	tall	33.	see
23.	glad	34.	has
24.	sad	35.	with
25.	goose	36.	go
26.	giraffe	37.	Answers will vary.
27.	giraffe	38.	round
28.	nine	39.	tall
29.	tack	40.	shiny
30.	miss		

MATH

1.	D	13.	couch
2.	C	14.	triangle
3.	B	15.	rectangle
4.	C	16.	square
5.	B	17.	triangle
6.	B	18.	square
7.	C	19.	circle
8.	B	20.	triangle
9.	A	21.	3, 9, 10
10.	D	22.	13, 15
11.	horse	23.	19
12.	computer	24.	Answers will vary.

Scoring Rubric for Question 25:

4 POINTS
All six numbers are written correctly and in the correct order.

3 POINTS
Five of the six numbers are written correctly and in the correct order.

2 POINTS
Most of the numbers are written correctly and in the correct order. Some numbers are missing or are out of order.

1 POINT
Most of the numbers are written incorrectly or are out of order or are not included.

0 POINTS
None of the numbers are written correctly and there is little understanding of their order.

26. 5
27. 7
28. 6
29. 2
30. One half of the rectangle should be colored.
31. One half of the circle should be colored.
32. Answers will vary. Possible answer:

Assessment Answers

SCIENCE

1.	C	9.	B
2.	B	10.	A
3.	B	11.	B
4.	B	12.	C
5.	B	13.	D
6.	D	14.	B
7.	C	15.	C
8.	A		

16. **a.** flower, **b.** stem, **c.** leaf, **d.** root

17.	flower	25.	right
18.	ant	26.	above
19.	liquid	27.	desert
20.	solid	28.	mountain
21.	hat	29.	ocean
22.	adult face	30.	deer
23.	below	31.	bull
24.	left	32.	chicken

SOCIAL STUDIES

1.	B	8.	C
2.	B	9.	A
3.	A	10.	B
4.	D	11.	D
5.	B	12.	B
6.	A	13.	C
7.	B	14.	C

15. Answers will vary.

Scoring Rubric for Question 16:

4 POINTS
Drawings demonstrate a full understanding of the fact that there are a wide variety of families. Drawings may include grandparents and other adults, may show very small or very large families, and may show a variety of people of different ages. Example: One family is a single-parent family with one child. The other family is a traditional nuclear family with three children.

3 POINTS
Drawings demonstrate a solid understanding of the fact that there are a wide variety of families. Drawings show two families that are clearly different. Example: One is a large extended family and the other is a small nuclear family.

2 POINTS
Drawings demonstrate a partial understanding of the fact that there are a wide variety of families. Drawings show two different families, but the differences between them are small. Example: Both are nuclear families but have different numbers of children and no older family members, such as grandparents.

1 POINT
Drawings demonstrate a weak understanding of the fact that there are a wide variety of families. Drawings show two very similar families. Example: Both are nuclear families with the same number of children, but the genders of the children are different.

0 POINTS
Drawings don't demonstrate an understanding of the fact that there are a wide variety of families. Drawings show two identical families, or don't show any family structure or organization at all.

17. A triangle should be drawn.
18. 4
19. 5
20. boy cleaning up milk
21. girl reading book
22. girl gluing toy back together
23. woman driving car of today
24. man putting food in microwave oven
25. man typing on computer
26. boy and girl folding blanket, boy holding dustpan as girl sweeps

Answers

Lesson 1.1

Student Learning Page 1.A

1. b e k
2. A F J
3. d h m

Student Learning Page 1.B

The correct lines and curves to write each uppercase and lowercase letter should be used.

Student Learning Page 1.C

The *G, m, i,* and *H* in the pictures should be colored correctly.

Lesson 1.2

Student Learning Page 2.A

1. s
2. O
3. f
4. X

Student Learning Page 2.B

The correct lines and curves to write uppercase and lowercase letters should be used.

Student Learning Page 2.C

Letters in big building: Q, R, Y, B, F, G

Letters in small building: b, g, r, q

The uppercase and lowercase letters should be correctly matched by coloring the windows for each pair the same color.

Lesson 1.3   Student Learning Page 3.A

1. The <u>b</u>ird sees a <u>t</u>oad.
2. A <u>m</u>an can go to the <u>m</u>oon.
3. I can <u>r</u>un.
4. The <u>d</u>uck sees a <u>f</u>ish.
5. The <u>b</u>oy has <u>s</u>ocks.

Lesson 1.4   Student Learning Page 4.A

The following pictures should be colored: the cup, girl, hat, lamp, noodles, pot, and window. The following sight words should be circled: *The, can, see,* and *some.*

Lesson 1.5   Student Learning Page 5.A

The following letters should be circled: *X, j, k,* and *z.*

Lesson 1.6   Student Learning Page 6.A

Lines connecting the following pictures should be drawn: cat and hat, mop and pot, bug and cup, and pig and six.

Lesson 1.7   Student Learning Page 7.A

su<u>n</u>, fo<u>x</u>, we<u>b</u>, do<u>g</u>

Lesson 1.8

Student Learning Page 8.A

Answers will vary. The student's name should include all letters in the correct order.

Student Learning Page 8.B

Answers will vary. The words that complete each sentence starter should make sense.

Student Learning Page 8.C

Top row: hat, book, girl

Middle row: boy, ball, bike

Bottom row: dog, cup, cat

Lesson 1.9   Student Learning Page 9.A

The following pictures should be colored: the jar of jam (first row, second box); the apple (second row, fourth box); the ant (third row, third box); and the bat (fourth row; first box).

Lesson 1.10   Student Learning Page 10.A

The following boxes should be shaded: *pet, bed, men, ten,* and *hen.*

Lesson 1.11   Student Learning Page 11.A

A line should be drawn from each picture to the word that correctly describes it.

Lesson 1.12   Student Learning Page 12.A

A box should be drawn around the pictures of the fox, the pot, the hot boy, the box, and the rock.

Lesson 1.13   Student Learning Page 13.A

The bubbles with the following words should be colored: *nut, gum, up, cup, sun, rug, fun,* and *tub.*

Answers

Lesson 1.14 *Student Learning Page 14.B*

1. bug
2. jug
3. Pug
4. hugs

The picture should accurately depict one of the sentences.

Lesson 1.15 *Student Learning Page 15.A*

Lines connecting the following pictures should be drawn: short tree to tall tree, smiling person to crying person, nighttime to daytime, and person sleeping to person exercising.

Lesson 1.16 *Student Learning Page 16.A*

Answers will vary. The words *glad, sad, mad,* and *excited* should be written on the lines and that the faces reflect the emotions.

Lesson 1.17 *Student Learning Page 17.B*

1. Pat's hat went flying.
2. Pat's friends went to get the hat.
3. Pat's hat was flat.

The pictures should reflect the events.

Lesson 2.1 *Student Learning Page 1.A*

The cars should be colored blue and the bears should be colored red. The small toys should each have an X drawn on them and the larger toys should be circled.

Lesson 2.2

Student Learning Page 2.A

1. green circle
2. flower
3. large house

Student Learning Page 2.B

Row 4: tree; Row 5: triangle, circle; Row 6: triangle; Row 7: triangle, circle, star, tree

Student Learning Page 2.C

The pattern of the path through the maze is yellow, purple, yellow, purple, and so on.

Lesson 2.3

Student Learning Page 3.A

Each shape in the box should be traced, and the house should include all the shapes from the box.

Student Learning Page 3.B

1. D
2. A
3. B
4. C

Student Learning Page 3.C

The shapes should be colored correctly.

Lesson 2.4 *Student Learning Page 4.A*

A group of items should be drawn for each number, and the correct number should be written for each group on the right.

1. E
2. C
3. F
4. B
5. A
6. D

Lesson 2.5 *Student Learning Page 5.A*

The numbers should be correct and the jars should be in the correct order.

Lesson 2.6 *Student Learning Page 6.A*

The numbers 3, 6, 10, 13, 17, and 18 should be written in order on the blank rocks. The rocks numbered 2, 4, 6, 8, 10, 12, 14, 16, 18, and 20 should be colored blue. The rocks numbered 5, 10, 15, and 20 should be colored yellow. The rocks 10 and 20 should be colored twice.

Lesson 2.7

Student Learning Page 7.A

1. Three circles should be drawn and the number 3 written.
2. Five squares should be drawn and the number 5 written.
3. Six triangles should be drawn and the number 6 written.

Student Learning Page 7.B

1. 2, 1, 3
2. 4, 2, 6
3. 1, 1, 2
4. 2, 3, 5

Student Learning Page 7.C

1. 2, 2, 4
2. 5, 1, 6
3. 4, 1, 5
4. 3, 2, 5

Answers

Lesson 2.8

Student Learning Page 8.A

1. Two circles should be drawn, one circle should be crossed out, and the number 1 should be written.
2. Five squares should be drawn, three squares should be crossed out, and the number 2 should be written.
3. Three triangles should be drawn, two triangles should be crossed out, and the number 1 should be written.

Student Learning Page 8.B

1. 3, 1, 2
2. 5, 4, 1
3. 2, 2, 0
4. 6, 3, 3

Student Learning Page 8.C

1. 5, 3, 2
2. 3, 3, 0
3. 4, 1, 3
4. 6, 5, 1

Lesson 2.9   Student Learning Page 9.A

A circle should be drawn around the nickel and the group of five pennies, a square should be drawn around the group of eight pennies and the group of one nickel and three pennies, and a triangle should be drawn around the dime and the group of one nickel and five pennies.

Lesson 2.10   Student Learning Page 10.A

The times should be correctly connected.

Lesson 2.11   Student Learning Page 11.A

1. The giraffe, the horse, and the fox should be circled.
2. The mouse and the bird should be circled.
3. The penguin should be circled.

SCIENCE

Lesson 3.1   Student Learning Page 1.A

The cup and the shoe should have a square drawn around them. The fish, giraffe, flowering plant, and frog should be circled.

Lesson 3.2   Student Learning Page 2.A

Three drawings of a seed at different stages of sprouting should be drawn.

Lesson 3.3

Student Learning Page 3.A

1. B
2. C
3. A
4. D

Student Learning Page 3.B

The fish and whale should be colored blue, the dog and squirrel green, and the alligator and penguin red.

Student Learning Page 3.C

The connect-the-dot pictures of the rabbit and snail should be completed. They're covered in fur and a shell, respectively.

Lesson 3.4   Student Learning Page 4.A

The body outline should be colored in as follows: red hands, blue arms, yellow head, green feet, and orange legs.

Lesson 3.5   Student Learning Page 5.A

Each figure should be colored.

Lesson 3.6   Student Learning Page 6.A

1. B
2. A

Drawing should show student doing something healthy.

Lesson 3.7   Student Learning Page 7.A

The carrots, banana, and bread should be colored green. The eggs, milk, and chicken leg should be colored red.

Lesson 3.8   Student Learning Page 8.A

The chart should be completed with four drawings relating to the four seasons.

Lesson 3.9   Student Learning Page 9.A

A. 2
B. 4
C. 1
D. 3

Lesson 3.10   Student Learning Page 10.A

All the pictures on the page should be circled.

Answers

Lesson 3.11 *Student Learning Page 11.A*

The sun and the half of Earth facing the sun should be colored yellow. The half of Earth facing away from the sun should be colored black. The moon and stars should be drawn into the picture.

Lesson 3.12 *Student Learning Page 12.A*

The telephone and pencil should be colored blue, the water green, and the balloons yellow.

Lesson 3.13 *Student Learning Page 13.A*

The pictures of the desk and the box and ramp should be circled. The pictures of the ball and the cup should have squares drawn around them.

SOCIAL STUDIES

Lesson 4.1 *Student Learning Page 1.A*

A drawing of the student's own family should be completed.

Lesson 4.2 *Student Learning Page 2.A*

1. C
2. A
3. B
4. D

Lesson 4.3 *Student Learning Page 3.A*

1. A drawing of a fire engine should be completed on a separate sheet of paper.
2. A drawing of a hospital should be completed on a separate sheet of paper.

Lesson 4.4 *Student Learning Page 4.A*

1. blue
2. red
3. red
4. blue

Lesson 4.5 *Student Learning Page 5.A*

1. C
2. D
3. B
4. A

Lesson 4.6

Student Learning Page 6.A

Student's home state should be colored red, bodies of water should be colored blue, and bodies of land should be colored green.

Student Learning Page 6.B

California should be colored green on both maps. The other states should be colored in. The color of each state on the large and small maps should match.

Lesson 4.7 *Student Learning Page 7.A*

The water should be colored blue and the land green. The United States should be circled.

Lesson 4.8 *Student Learning Page 8.A*

Land areas on both globes should be colored green. Water areas should be colored blue.

Lesson 4.9 *Student Learning Page 9.A*

A drawing of the U.S. flag should be accurately completed.

Lesson 4.10 *Student Learning Page 10.A*

A drawing of people traveling by car, truck, airplane, or another modern method should be completed.

GLOSSARY

Like any other specialty area, teaching and homeschooling have their own unique vocabulary. We've included some terms we thought might be helpful.

accelerated learning

when a student completes a certain set of lessons faster than most students; this can happen due to a student's natural motivation or in a more structured manner, such as continuing lessons throughout the year versus taking the summer off

assessment

a review of a student's learning progress and comprehension; traditionally done through tests or grades; assessments in progressive learning environments such as homeschooling take on many different forms, including summary discussions, demonstrative projects, and oral questions and answers; formalized assessment is included in this book, beginning on page 303

auditory learner

an individual who absorbs new information most effectively by listening; an auditory learner will remember information that is spoken or related through sound such as musical lyrics, reading aloud, or audiocassettes

child-centered learning

a type of learning in which the teaching style places the child at the center of his or her learning, meaning that a child begins and proceeds with new subjects, such as reading, as he or she is ready; this style of teaching requires intimate awareness of the student by the teacher

correlated to state standards

a phrase that means that something meets or exceeds a particular state's mandatory educational requirements for the intended grade level

critical thinking skill

the ability to assess information, make independent judgments, and draw conclusions; this skill is independent of and goes beyond the memorized information that a student has learned

curriculum

an ordered list of specific topics of study that is used as a teaching map

distance learning

a type of instruction in which classes are completed at a different physical location than at the school that offers them; formerly known as correspondence classes, this term now includes video and Internet classes

graphic organizer

a way to visually organize information for the purpose of learning enhancement; usually referring to charts and graphs, these can be useful for visual learners; several graphic organizers are included in this book: Venn Diagram, T Chart, Web, and Sequence Chain

inclusive

a homeschool group that is inclusive and welcomes anyone who homeschools regardless of religious or educational beliefs or practices; as homeschooling becomes more popular, more inclusive groups have been formed; in the traditional classroom setting, an inclusive school is focused on reaching out to the increasingly diverse student populations to provide a supportive and quality education to all students regardless of economic status, gender, race, or disability

kinesthetic learner

an individual who absorbs new information most effectively through experience; a kinesthetic learner will understand information by completing hands-on exercises, doing, and moving

learning style

the singular manner and rate that each child naturally pursues his or her education; educators have identified three primary ways of describing learning styles: auditory, kinesthetic, and visual

lesson plan

a detailed description of the part of the curriculum one is planning to teach on a certain day

multicultural

adapted to relate to diverse cultures; many teachers incorporate multicultural learning materials into their lessons to encourage exposure to different traditions

real books

books you get at the library or the bookstore that aren't textbooks; some homeschoolers work almost exclusively from real books and don't use textbooks at all; this book provides a curriculum that's based on reading and research with real books

scoring rubric

a measurement tool used to assess student work that includes a system of scoring levels of performance; scoring rubrics are used with some lessons in this book and with the formalized assessment section in the back of this book

self-directed learner

an individual who is free to pursue education by his or her own means and guidance versus through traditional classes or schools; a term often used in homeschool literature

self-teaching

when an individual naturally learns about a topic of particular interest on his or her own, without formal instruction and usually as a result of natural attraction to or talent in the subject matter

standardized test

a test is considered standardized when it is given in the same manner, with the same directions to children of the same grade level across a school district, state, or country; the test shows how your student is doing compared to other students; the assessment section beginning on page 303 offers examples of standardized test questions

teaching strategy

a creative way to motivate and inspire students, such as using a visual aid, entertaining or humorous delivery, interactive activity, or theme-based lessons; if your student is bored, he or she might benefit from a change in teaching strategies

unschooling

a teaching philosophy first identified by educator John Holt that's based on the idea that the child directs his or her own learning based on his or her own interests; works under the assertion that textbook-type teaching can dull a child's natural zest for learning and the belief that a student will learn more when he or she is engaged, uninterrupted, and enjoying

visual learner

an individual who absorbs new information most effectively through the sense of sight; a visual learner will comprehend information by reading, watching a video, using a visual computer program, and looking at pictures in books

Waldorf

a method of education that was developed by Rudolph Steiner and attempts to teach the whole child: physical, emotional, and academic; Waldorf schools are located throughout the country, and there is also a network of Waldorf homeschoolers

Venn Diagram

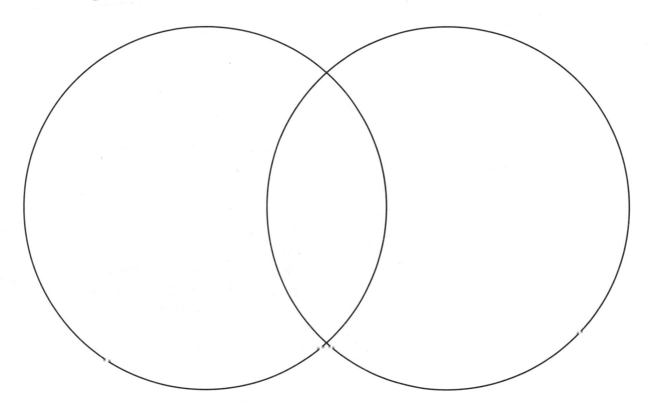

T Chart

Web

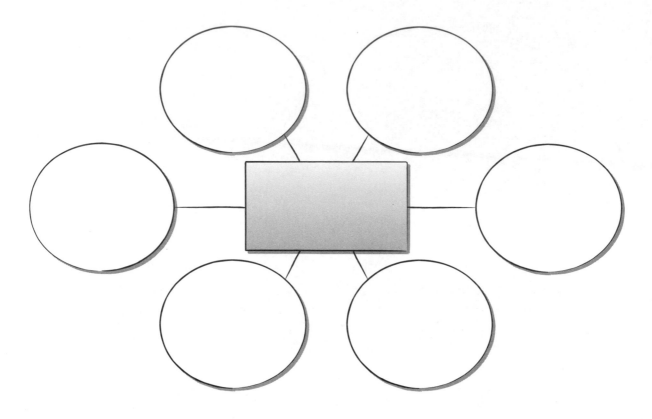

Sequence Chain

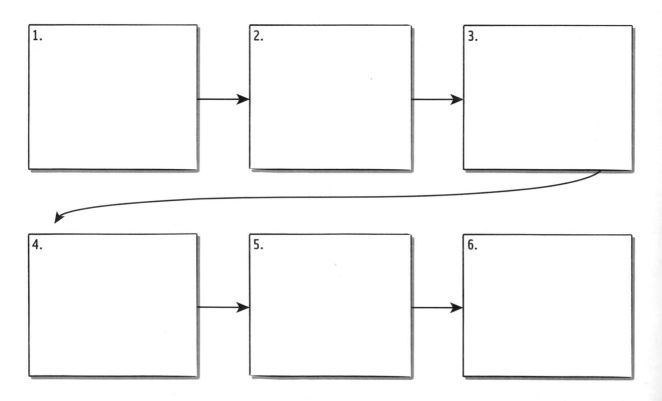

Note: Page numbers in bold indicate the definition of a term.

Index

Note: Page numbers in bold indicate the definition of a term.

F

Families
 concepts and analysis, 251–254
 drawing exercise, 255
 military, homeschooling, xi–xii
 optional activities, 174, 256
Family activities
 concepts and analysis, 257–258
 matching exercise, 259
 optional activities, 260
Feelings. *See* Emotion(s)
Fewer, **123,** 124
Fiction
 concepts and analysis, 83–84
 optional activities, 90
 reading selection, 85–88
Flags
 drawing exercise, 293
 optional activities, 20, 114, 286
 U.S., concepts, 291, 292
Food
 concepts and analysis, 213–216
 living things and, 181
 optional activities, 54, 218
 sources exercise, 217
Force. *See* Movement
Fourth of July, 297
Front position, 100–101

G

Games
 consonant hopscotch, 26
 counting, 134
 number matching, 134
 seasons charades, 222
 using addition, 150
 using coins, 162
 using middle sounds, 36
 using short *o,* 62
 using subtraction, 158
Garden activity, 218
Gases, **237,** 239, 240. *See also* Matter
Geography
 map concepts (*See* Maps)
 resources (*See* Natural resources)
Germs, **207**–208
Gifted students, xv–xvi
Globe, **287.** *See also* Maps
 concepts and analysis, 287–288
 optional activities, 290
 symbol exercise, 289
Glossary, 353
Goods, **268,** 269

Greater numbers
 concepts and analysis, 135–140
 optional activities, 142
 practice exercise, 141
Groups, sorting, 103–104
Groups of numbers
 0 to 5, 124–125
 0 to 10, 130–131
 adding, 143–144, 147
 equal, 124
 optional activities, 128
 subtracting, 151–152, 155
Grow, **180**
Growth, 180
 of animals, 189–191
 of living things, 188
 of patterns, 109–110, 112
 of plants, 184–188

H

Halves, **117**–118, 121
Hand(s)
 family poster activity, 174
 helping hands print activity, 256
 hole in your hand activity, 206
 washing, 208
Hat art activity, 90
Health
 concepts and analysis, 207–210
 matching exercise, 211
 optional activities, 212
Hearing, 202, 205
Heart, **197**
Height chart, 174
Helping hands print activity, 256
Hole in your hand activity, 206
Holiday card activity, 266
Holidays, **263**
 Earth Day, 228
 national, 264, 296–297
 optional activities, 266, 300
Homeschooling, xi
 military families, xi–xii
 regulations, xi
 resources, xii–xiv
Hopscotch with consonants, 26
Human body
 body parts exercises, 32, 199, 205
 concepts and analysis, 195–198, 201–202
 food and, 213–218
 health, 207–212
 optional activities, 200, 206, 212, 218, 256
 senses, 201–206
Hundreds chart, 139–140

I

Independence Day, 297
Inside position, 102–103

J

Jobs, **267,** 268, 270. *See also* Economics
Journal exercise, 44

K

Kindergartners, xvii–xx
Kite activity, 158

L

Lakes, **224**
Land
 concepts and analysis, 223–224
 map concepts, 277, 278
 map exercises, 279–280, 285, 289
 optional activities, 226, 281
 sand formation exercise, 225
Laundry sorting activity, 106
Laws, **262**–263
Leaf print activity, 188
Length, **169**
 concepts and analysis, 169–170
 ordering exercise, 173
Less *versus* more time, 164
Letters of alphabet, **3**
 a–m, 3–8
 concepts and analysis, 3–4, 9–10
 n–z, 9–14
 optional activities, 8, 14
 practice exercises, 5–7, 11–13
 uppercase and lowercase, 4, 6, 7
Liquids, **237,** 238, 240. *See also* Matter
Literacy skills
 alphabet, *a–m,* 3–8
 alphabet, *n–z,* 9–14
 assessment, 303–316
 assessment answers, 347
 descriptive words, 79–82
 ending sounds, 37–40
 initial consonants *b, d, f, m, r, s,* and *t,* 15–20
 initial consonants *c, g, h, l, n, p,* and *w,* 21–26
 initial consonants *j, k, q, v, x, y,* and *z,* 27–32
 middle sounds, 33–36

opposites, 75–78
poetry, 67–74
rhyming words, 67–74
short *a,* 47–50
short *e,* 51–54
short *i,* 55–58
short *o,* 59–62
short *u,* 63–66
writing and print, 41–46
Literature
 fiction, 67–74, 83–90
 poetry, 91–94
Living things, **179**
 concepts and analysis, 179–182
 identification exercise, 183
 optional activities, 184
Lowercase letters, **3**
 concepts and analysis, 4
 optional activities, 8, 14
 practice exercises, 6, 7, 12–13

M

Magnets, 244
Map key, **273**
Maps, **272**
 concepts and analysis, 271–274, 277–278, 283–284, 287–288
 exercises, 275, 279–280, 285, 289
 globes, 287–290
 optional activities, 276, 281–282, 286, 290
 symbols, 272–273, 276, 277–278, 287, 289
 U.S., 277–282
 views and keys, 271–276
 world, 283–286
Mask activity, 82
Matching exercises
 animals, 191
 body parts and senses, 205
 clock times, 167
 coins and monetary amounts, 161
 middle sounds, 35
 numbers, 134
 opposites, 77
 shapes, 120
 short *i* words and pictures, 57
 then and now activities, 259
Mathematics
 addition concepts, 143–150
 assessment, 317–326
 assessment answers, 347
 counting money, 159–162
 greater numbers, 135–142

Index

Note: Page numbers in bold indicate the definition of a term.

Credits

Art & Photo Credits

Promoting Literacy
Background/Icon: © PhotoDisc
Opener (page 1): © PhotoDisc
Page 5: Precision Graphics; **6, 7:** PP/FA, Inc., **Inset:** Carol Stutz Illustration; **8, 11:** Precision Graphics; **12:** PP/FA, Inc., **Inset:** Carol Stutz Illustration; **13, 14:** Precision Graphics; **16:** © PhotoDisc; **19 (2a, 4, 5a):** Carol Stutz Illustration; **19 (1, 2b, 3, 5b), 20:** Precision Graphics; **22:** © EyeWire; **25:** Carol Stutz Illustration; **26, 28, 29:** Precision Graphics; **31:** PP/FA, Inc., **Insets:** Carol Stutz Illustration; **34:** Precision Graphics; **35, 36:** Carol Stutz Illustration; **38:** Precision Graphics; **39:** PP/FA, Inc., **Insets:** Carol Stutz Illustration; **40, 43, 44:** Precision Graphics; **45:** PP/FA, Inc., **Insets:** Carol Stutz Illustration; **46, 48:** Precision Graphics; **49, 50:** Carol Stutz Illustration; **52:** Precision Graphics; **53, 54:** Carol Stutz Illustration; **56:** Precision Graphics; **57, 61:** Carol Stutz Illustration; **64:** Precision Graphics; **65:** Carol Stutz Illustration; **68:** Precision Graphics; **69, 71, 73:** Carol Stutz Illustration; **75, 76:** Precision Graphics; **77, 78, 79:** Carol Stutz Illustration; **81:** PP/FA, Inc., **Insets:** Carol Stutz Illustration; **85, 87, 88, 93:** Carol Stutz Illustration

Math
Background/Icon: © PhotoDisc
Opener (page 97): © Steve Cole/Getty Images
Page 100, 101 (top): Carol Stutz Illustration; **101 (bottom):** © Photodisc Collection/Getty Images; **105:** Carol Stutz Illustration; **109, 111, 112, 113, 116, 119, 120, 121, 125 (top):** Precision Graphics; **125 (bottom):** PP/FA, Inc.; **127, 128:** Precision Graphics; **130:** PP/FA, Inc.; **131, 133:** Precision Graphics; **136:** PP/FA, Inc.; **139:** Precision Graphics; **141, 142:** Carol Stutz Illustration; **144, 148, 149, 151, 153, 156, 157, 158:** Precision Graphics; **161 (top):** Carol Stutz Illustration; **161 (bottom), 162, 164, 165:** Precision Graphics; **167:** PP/FA, Inc.; **168, 170:** Carol Stutz Illustration; **171:** Precision Graphics; **173:** Carol Stutz Illustration

Science
Background/Icon: © CORBIS
Opener (page 177): © PhotoDisc
Page 180: Precision Graphics; **182, 183 (top left, middle, bottom):** Carol Stutz Illustration; **183 (top right), 186 (left):** Precision Graphics; **186 (middle):** © Photodisc Collection/Getty Images; **186 (right):** © Royalty-free/CORBIS; **187:** PP/FA, Inc.; **189:** © EyeWire; **191, 192:** Carol Stutz Illustration; **193:** Precision Graphics; **198, 199, 205, 206:** Carol Stutz Illustration; **209:** Precision Graphics; **211 (bottom):** PP/FA, Inc.; **211 (top, middle), 214, 217:** Carol Stutz Illustration; **220:** © PhotoDisc; **221:** Precision Graphics; **222:** Carol Stutz Illustration; **223 (left):** © C Squared Studios/Getty Images; **223 (middle left):** © Ken Samuelson/Getty Images; **223 (middle right):** © Siede Preis/Getty Images; **223 (right):** © Don Farrall/Getty Images; **225:** Carol Stutz Illustration; **228 (middle, right):** © Photodisc Collection/Getty Images; **228 (left), 229:** Carol Stutz Illustration; **230, 235:** Precision Graphics; **239:** © Andy Sotiriou/Getty Images; **241:** Carol Stutz Illustration; **243:** © Milton Montenegro/Getty Images; **244, 245 (top left):** Precision Graphics; **245 (top right, bottom):** Carol Stutz Illustration

Social Studies
Background/Icon: © PhotoDisc
Opener (page 249): © PhotoDisc
Page 253: Carol Stutz Illustration; **255 (left):** © Ryan McVay/Getty Images; **255 (middle):** © Getty Images; **255 (right):** © Photodisc Collection/Getty Images; **255 (bottom):** © PhotoDisc; **256, 259, 260:** Carol Stutz Illustration; **263:** © Ariel Skelley/CORBIS; **265:** Carol Stutz Illustration; **266:** Precision Graphics; **269:** Carol Stutz Illustration; **270:** Precision Graphics; **272, 273, 275:** Carol Stutz Illustration; **279, 280:** Mapping Specialists; **283:** © StockTrek/Getty Images; **284, 285, 287:** Mapping Specialists; **289:** Precision Graphics; **291:** © Paul Wootton Associates; **293:** Carol Stutz Illustration; **297:** © Bettmann/CORBIS; **298 (left):** © William England/Getty Images; **298 (right):** © PictureNet/CORBIS; **299 (top):** Library of Congress, Prints & Photographs Division, LC-USZ62-5073; **299 (bottom):** PP/FA, Inc.

311, 314 (top, middle bottom): Carol Stutz Illustration; **314 (middle top, bottom):** Precision Graphics; **316 (top):** PP/FA, Inc.; **316 (middle, bottom):** Carol Stutz Illustration; **317 (top):** PP/FA, Inc.; **317 (bottom), 318 (top):** Precision Graphics; **318 (bottom), 319 (top):** Carol Stutz Illustration; **319 (middle, bottom), 320 (top):** Precision Graphics; **320 (middle, bottom), 321:** Carol Stutz Illustration; **322, 323, 325:** Precision Graphics; **326:** PP/FA, Inc.; **327, 328:** Carol Stutz Illustration; **329:** Precision Graphics; **330, 331:** Carol Stutz Illustration; **332:** Precision Graphics; **333 (top, middle top):** Carol Stutz Illustration; **333 (middle bottom, bottom):** Precision Graphics; **334, 335, 336:** Carol Stutz Illustration; **337:** Precision Graphics; **338:** Carol Stutz Illustration; **339:** Mapping Specialists; **340, 341:** Carol Stutz Illustration; **343:** Precision Graphics; **344, 345, 346:** Carol Stutz Illustration; **347:** Precision Graphics; **355, 356:** PP/FA, Inc.

Literature Credits

69–72, From *The Bug Club* by Kelli C. Foster and Gina C. Erickson. Copyright © 1991 by Kelli C. Foster, Gina C. Erickson, and Kerri Gifford. Reprinted by arrangement with Barron's Educational Series, Inc., Hauppauge, NY.

85–88, From WHAT A DAY FOR FLYING! by Kelli C. Foster and Gina C. Erickson. Copyright © 1993 by Kelli C. Foster, Gina C. Erickson, and Kerri Gifford. Reprint by arrangement with Barron's Educational Series, Inc., Hauppauge, NY.

93, I'M SMALL AND OTHER VERSES Text © 2001 by Lilian Moore. Illustrations © 2001 by Jill McElmurry. Reproduced by permission of the publisher, Candlewick Press, Inc., Cambridge, MA.